PLAYDATE *with* Salt Lake City

and Utah's Wasatch Front

200 CREATIVE ADVENTURES FOR UNFORGETTABLE FAMILY FUN

Provo to Ogden, Park City to Daybreak & Everything in Between

Emily Smith Robbins & Meilani Smith Kongaika

Playdate with Salt Lake City & Utah's Wasatch Front

by Emily Smith Robbins and Meilani Smith Kongaika

Playdate Publishing

Playdate Publishing is an imprint of Sharp End Publishing LLC

Published and distributed by
Sharp End Publishing, LLC
PO Box 1613
Boulder, CO 80306
t. 303.444.2698 www.playdatepublishing.com

ISBN: 978-1-892540-87-4
Library of Congress Control Number: 2013910499

Cover Design: Russ Gray
Book Original Design: Sarah Durkee

Front Cover photo credits, clockwise from upper left corner:

BYU Museum of Paleontology, photo courtesy of Emily Smith Robbins / Heber Valley Railroad, photo courtesy of Rachel Clarke / Dolly and Me Dress-Up Tea, photo courtesy of Georgelle Doll Shop / Pineview Reservoir, photo courtesy of Jacob Kongaika / Legacy Park, photo courtesy of Corie Balls / photo courtesy of This is the Place Heritage Park / Accessible Playground at Veteran's Memorial Park, photo courtesy of Meilani Smith Kongaika / Max Zipline Canopy Tour, photo courtesy of Emily Smith Robbins.

Back Cover photo credits:

Orem Mall Treehouse Court, photo courtesy of University Mall / Utah State Botanical Center, photo courtesy of Corie Balls / Discovery Park, photo courtesy Emily Smith Robbins / This is the Place, photo courtesy of This is the Place Heritage Park

Opening page photo credit:

Courtesy of Red Butte Garden

Photo credits are found in Appendix 11. All unlabeled photos taken by Emily Smith Robbins or Meilani Smith Kongaika or are a part of the Robbins or Kongaika collection.

Acknowledgements

Meilani:

I would like to thank Joel for believing in me and for supporting me 200%. I love you and couldn't have done this without you! To my children, thank you for making so many wonderful memories with me as I worked on this project. Anna, we never saw the donut at Donut Falls, but I loved spending the day with you. Eryn, we didn't see any birds on the Birdsong Trail either, but our time together was so special. Joseph, I should have known laser tag would be your favorite! Lily, you have inspired me along this journey. You can do so many things!

Emily:

To my sweet Andy, the best part of every adventure was coming home to you. This book means nothing without you.

Dedicated to my four adventurers: Gabe, Noah, Eve, and Esther. There is no one I'd rather be with. My favorite memories of the book include: Gabe laughing to tears at Comedy Sportz, Noah's "ho hum" face as he zip-lined, Eve being so excited to fish at the trout farm and then dropping her pole into the pond when she got startled by all the swarming fish, Esther collecting rocks at every location and clutching them in her chubby hands all the way home, and Andy patiently mentioning each month that I had once again exceeded my data plan on my phone; which brings me to my last acknowledgement. To the 4G Network and the Around Me app on my phone, I would have been dead in the water without you.

The Sisters:

Thank you to our parents for their support, for raising us with the confidence to accomplish big crazy projects, and for taking us on "Saturday Outings" all over the North Shore of Oahu while growing up.

Also, our gratitude goes to our wonderful friends and family who supported us through hours of babysitting our kids so we could write. Thank you for sharing your ideas and opinions, enduring our endless conversations about the book, and encouraging us along the way. We will never be able to repay your many kindnesses. To our sister, Becca, thank you for the grueling hours you spent editing with us.

Foreword

by Jeanette Herbert

I was raised in the little town of Springville, Utah. My family spent a lot of time in the summers visiting sites throughout Utah. We loved to camp and hike through the national parks, fish at Fish Lake, and visit Dinosaur National Monument, as well as other sites and museums.

My dad always made sure we read the roadside markers wherever we traveled so we could appreciate the state's history and the sacrifices many of its founders made. I treasure those memories with my family.

I also want my children to be able to have great memories of their childhood. Our family enjoys many traditional activities that keep us close and we love spending time together. Now as a grandmother, I enjoy planning outings and activities with my grandchildren.

Strong families are the cornerstone of strong communities and key to maintaining Utah's exceptional quality of life. Studies show that when children have a sense of belonging and enjoy close relationships with other family members, they are less likely to become involved in drugs, alcohol, and other anti-social behaviors. Time spent with parents is fundamental to a child's overall well-being, including his or her sense of security, safety, love, and support.

Creating family traditions is important in building meaningful family relationships. It is the glue that keeps us together. Family traditions last far beyond the moment when so much in our lives these days is temporary. Traditions build trust and family unity. Traditions give us a sense of identity.

Utah is a great place for families. We have wonderful parents who are involved in their children's lives. But building strong families does take some work and planning. A guide to activities and places of interest throughout the state can assist you in planning and discovering your own family memory-making traditions and adventures.

Parents may use these adventures not only as entertainment, but also as education. Reading a book about the place you are going will bring greater enjoyment to the activity, as well as build a love for reading. Throughout the state, there are places that teach Utah history and foster a greater appreciation for the great state in which we live.

Meilani Kongaika and Emily Robbins are like many Utah moms who want to spend quality time with their children, while exposing them to new experiences. After hundreds of hours researching and experiencing each location with their children, they have compiled their discoveries and recommendations into one place. What a tremendous resource this book is for parents!

Jeanette Hebert *Photo by Amanda Peterson Photography*

Chapters at a Glance

1 Museums & More....17
2 Animal Attractions....45
3 Historic Sites....51
4 Gardens & The Outdoors....63
5 Playgrounds & Parks....81
6 Hikes & Nature Walks....91
7 Performing Arts....111
8 Indoor Play Spaces....117
9 Hands-On Experiences....131
10 Amusement Parks & Fun Centers..139
11 Splash Pads & Fountains....159
12 Indoor Swimming....179
13 Outdoor Swimming....195
14 StoryTime & Libraries....213
15 Tours!....223
16 Unique Adventures....239
17 Ski Areas & Resorts....255
18 Sporting Events....265
19 Park City....273
20 Heber City....287
21 Appendices & Index....295

1 Museums & More 17

BYU Museum of Art - Site 1 18
BYU Museum of Paleontology - Site 2 19
BYU Museum of Peoples and Cultures - Site 3 20
Clark Planetarium - Site 4 21
Discovery Gateway: The Children's Museum of Utah - Site 5 22
The Gale Center of History and Culture - Site 6 24
Hill Aerospace Museum - Site 7 25
John Hutchings Museum of Natural History - Site 8 26
LDS Church History Museum- Site 9 27
Monte L. Bean Life Science Museum - Site 10 28
Museum of Ancient Life at Thanksgiving Point - Site 11 30
Natural History Museum of Utah - Site 12 32
Ogden Dinosaur Park and Museum - Site 13 34
Ogden Union Station - Site 14 36
Ott Planetarium - Site 15 37
Royden G. Derrek Planetarium - Site 16 38
The Leonardo - Site 17 39
Treehouse Children's Museum - Site 18 40
Utah Museum of Contemporary Art - Site 19 42
Utah Museum of Fine Arts - Site 20 43
Utah Pioneer Museum - Site 21 44

2 Animal Attractions 45

Farm Country at Thanksgiving Point - Site 22 46
Tracy Aviary - Site 23 47
Utah's Hogle Zoo - Site 24 48
Local Pet Stores 50
The Loveland Living Planet Aquarium 50

3 Historic Sites 51

Cathedral of the Madeleine - Site 25 52
Fort Buenaventura - Site 26 53
Fort Douglas Military Museum - Site 27 54
Gardner Village - Site 28 55
Temple Square - Site 29 56
This is the Place Heritage Park - Site 30 58
Utah State Capitol - Site 31 60
Wheeler Historic Farm - Site 32 62

4 Gardens & The Outdoors 63

Antelope Island - Site 33 64
Children's Discovery Garden at Thanksgiving Point - Site 34 66
Cold Springs Trout Farm - Site 35 67
Gilgal Sculpture Garden - Site 36 68
The Great Salt Lake Shorelands Preserve - Site 37 69
International Peace Gardens - Site 38 70
Ogden Nature Center - Site 39 72
Red Butte Garden - Site 40 74
Robert N. Hasenyager Great Salt Lake Nature Center - Site 41 76
Thanksgiving Point Gardens - Site 42 78
(West Jordan) Conservation Garden Park - Site 43 80

5 Playgrounds & Parks 81

Accessible Playground at Veteran's Memorial Park - **Site 44** 82
Castle Heights Playground at Nicholls Park - **Site 45** 83
Legacy Electric Park - **Site 46** 84
Liberty Park - **Site 47** 85
Memory Grove Park - **Site 48** 86
Neptune Park - **Site 49** 88
Novell Children's Discovery Park - **Site 50** 89
Wild West Jordan Playground at Veteran's Memorial Park - **Site 51** 90

6 Hikes & Nature Walks 91

Battle Creek Falls Hike - Site 52 92
Birdsong Trail - Site 53 93
Bridal Veil Falls - Site 54 94
Cascade Springs Nature Trail - Site 55 95
Cecret Lake Hike - Site 56 96
Donut Falls - Site 57 97
Ensign Peak Hike - Site 58 98
Hidden Falls - Site 59 99
Lisa Falls - Site 60 100
Ogden River Parkway - Site 61 101
Provo River Parkway - Site 62 102
Silver Lake Trail - Site 63 104
Stewart Falls - Site 64 105
Temple Quarry Nature Trail - Site 65 106
Timpanogos Caves - Site 66 107
Timpanogos Falls - Site 67 108
Y Mountain Hike - Site 68 110

7 Performing Arts 111

Ballet West - Site 69 112
The Children's Theatre - Site 70 113
Mormon Tabernacle Choir - Site 71 114
Utah Symphony/Utah Opera Family Concerts - Site 72 116

8 Indoor Play Spaces 117

Airborne - Site 73 118
City Creek Dinosaur Play Area - Site 74 119
Edutainment Play Center - Site 75 120
Get Air Sportsplex - Site 76 121
Hang Time Extreme Trampolines - Site 77 122
Jake's Archery - Site 78 123
Jump Around Utah - Site 79 124
Jump 'N Bounce - Site 80 125
Jump On It! - Site 81 126
Kangaroo Zoo - Site 82 127
Lowes Xtreme Air Sports - Site 83 128
Provo Towne Centre Play Area - Site 84 129
Tree House Court - Site 85 130

9 Hands-On Experiences 131

Color Me Mine - Site 86 132
Creativity Art Studio - Site 87 133
Harmons Cooking School - Site 88 134
Lakeshore Learning - Site 89 136
Lowes Build and Grow Clinics - Site 90 137
The Home Depot Kids Workshops - Site 91 138

10 Amusement Parks & Fun Centers 139

Boondocks Food & Fun - Site 92 140
Classic Fun Center - Site 93 142
Fastkart Speedway - Site 94 144
FatCats - Site 95 146
Hollywood Connection - Site 96 147
Jack and Jill Lanes - Site 97 148
Jungle Jim's Playland - Site 98 149
Lagoon - Site 99 150
Nickel City Fun Center - Site 100 152
Provo Beach - Site 101 154
Seven Peaks Fun Center - Site 102 156
Toad's Fun Zone - Site 103 158

11 Splash Pads & Fountains 159

Creekside Park - Site 104 160
Engage Fountain at City Creek - Site 105 161
The Gateway - Site 106 162
Harrisville City Park - Site 107 163
Heritage Park - Site 108 164
Highland Town Center Splash Pad - Site 109 165
Legacy Park - Site 110 166
Mountview Park - Site 111 167
Nature Park (South Ogden Nature Park) - Site 112 168
Nolan Park - Site 113 169
Old Farm Splash Park - Site 114 170
Pioneer Park - Site 115 171
Riverdale Park - Site 116 172
Rosecrest Park - Site 117 173
Shops at Riverwoods - Site 118 174
Umbria Splash Park - Site 119 175
Valley Fair Mall - Site 120 176
Western Springs Park - Site 121 177
Willow Pond Park - Site 122 178

12 Indoor Swimming 179

Clearfield Aquatic Center (also outdoor) - Site 123 180
Dimple Dell Recreation Center Pool - Site 124 181
Fairmont Aquatic Center - Site 125 182
Gene Fullmer Recreation Center - Site 126 183
Holladay Lions Fitness and Recreation Center - Site 127 184
J.L. Sorenson Recreation Center (also outdoor) - Site 128 185
Lehi Legacy Recreation Center (also outdoor) - Site 129 186
Northwest Recreation Center - Site 130 188
The Park Center - Site 131 189
Provo Recreation Center - Site 132 190
South Davis Recreation Center (also outdoor) - Site 133 192
South Jordan Recreation Center - Site 134 193
West Valley Family Fitness Center - Site 135 194

13 Outdoor Swimming 195

American Fork Fitness Center Leisure Pool - Site 136 196
Blackridge Reservoir - Site137 197
Centennial Pool - Site 138 198
Cherry Hill - Site 139 199
Cottonwood Heights Recreation Center - Site 140 200
Kearns Oquirrh Park Fitness Center - Site 141 201
Kennecott-Magna Aquatics Complex - Site 142 202
Layton Surf 'N Swim (also indoor) - Site 143 203
Lindon Aquatic Center - Site 144 204
Manila Creek Pond - Site 145 205
Murray Aquatics Center - Site 146 206
Pineview Reservoir - Site 147 207
Roy City Aquatic Center - Site 148 208
Scera Pool - Site 149 209
Seven Peaks - Site 150 210
Taylorsville Community Swimming Pool - Site 151 212

14 Story Time & Libraries 213

Public Libraries - Site 152 214
Barnes & Noble Story Time - Site 153 216
Children's Library at the Provo City Library - Site 154 217
Salt Lake City Public Library - Site 155 218
The King's English Story Time - Site 156 220
Three Little Monkeys - Site 157 221
Other story time Hours in this Book 222

15 Tours! 223

BYU Broadcasting - Site 158 224
Great Harvest Bread Co. - Site 159 225
Hale Centre Theatre Backstage Tour - Site 160 226
Holdman Studios - Site 161 227
Krispy Kreme - Site 162 228
LDS Conference Center Tour - Site 163 229
Later-day Saint Humanitarian Center - Site 164 230
Mrs. Cavanaugh's Chocolate Factory - Site 165 231
Peery's Egyptian Theater - Site 166 232
Sweet Candy Factory - Site 167 234
Taffy Town - Site 168 235
Utah Truffles - Site 169 236
V Chocolates - Site 170 237
Welfare Square - Site 171 238

16 Unique Adventures 239

Cabela's - Site 172 240
CLAS Ropes Course - Site 173 242
Coleman's Motor-VU Drive-In - Site 174 244
Comedy Sportz - Site 175 245
Dolly and Me Dress up Tea at Georgell Doll Shop - Site 176 246
MAX Zipline Canopy Tour - Site 177 247
Redwood Road Drive-In - Site 178 248
$&S Shortline Train Park - Site 179 249
SCHEELS - Site 180 250
Thanksgiving Point Special Events - Site 181 252
Tiny Tim's Foundation for Kids - Site 182 253
UTA TRAX & FrontRunner - Site 183 254

17 Ski Areas & Resorts 255

Alta Ski Area - Site 184 256
Brighton Ski Resort - Site 185 257
Powder Mountain - Site 186 258
Snowbasin Resort - Site 187 259
Snowbird Ski and Summer Resort - Site 188 260
Solitude Mountain Resort - Site 189 262
Sundance Mountain Resort - Site 190 263
Wolf Mountain Resort - Site 191 264

18 Sporting Events 265

Ogden Raptors - Site 192 266
Orem Owlz - Site 193 267
Real Salt Lake - Site 194 268
Salt Lake Bees - Site 195 269
Utah Blaze - Site 196 270
Utah Grizzlies - Site 197 271
Utah Jazz - Site 198 272

19 Park City 273

Canyons Resort - Site 199 274
Deer Valley Resort - Site 200 275
The Fieldhouse Splash Pad - Site 201 276
Monkey Mountain - Site 202 277
Park City Mountain Resort - Site 203 278
Park City Museum - Site 204 279
Swaner Preserve and EcoCenter - Site 205 280
Trailside Park - Site 206 281
Olympic Park - Site 207 282
Utah Olympic Park Museums - Site 208 284
Willow Creek Park - Site 209 285

20 Heber City 287

Commemorative Air Force Utah Wing Museum - Site 210 288
Cowboy Campfires (Friday night, Homestead Resort) - Site 211 289
Dairy Keen (Home of the Train) - Site 212 290
Deer Creek Reservoir - Site 213 291
Heber Valley Artisan Cheese (Kohler Creamery) - Site 214 292
Heber Valley Railroad - Site 215 293
Soldier Hollow Cross-Country Ski Resort - Site 216 294

21 Appendices and Index of Sites 295

Downtown Destinations Appendix 1 296
Instructions for Games at Legacy Electric Park Appendix 2 298
Duck Ponds Appendix 3 300
Fishing Locations Appendix 4 301
Ice Rinks Appendix 5 302
Outdoor Movies Appendix 6 303
Family Friendly Theaters Appendix 7 304
Rodeos Appendix 8 305
Online Activity Resources Appendix 9 306
Calendar of Events & Festivals Appendix 10 307
Photo Credits Appendix 11 308
Resources Appendix 12 311
Sites by County Appendix 13 314
Alphabetical Index of Sites 317
About the Authors 320

Introduction

When we first agreed to write this book, we had big dreams of visiting each location together with all of our kids. It didn't take more than a week for us to realize we would never make our deadline unless we split everything up. So, we each researched and visited at least 100 locations over the course of nine months. It's definitely going to be a year our kids will remember. We set the bar high on having fun. Our kids have been troopers; even on the days we had to "force" them to have fun.

The Wasatch Front has become a whole new world to us, after exploring and adventuring with our kids for this book. There are places we would never have known about or visited if we hadn't spent hours researching. Even for those of you born and raised in Utah, we are sure you will find places and activities that you have never heard of or knew little about.

Before you say, "Wow, some people have too much energy and time on their hands," it's important to mention, that we are not high-energy women who thrive on planning activities and outings for our kids. We are in awe of those women. Anyone who knows us can attest that this book really thrust us out of our comfort zone. Having grown up on an island, we are very laid back and enjoy spending time close to home with our kids. So if you too are a homebody, content to be home most of the time, we can sincerely tell you that we know how daunting it can seem to go out adventuring with kids. Between snacks, diapers, bottles, strollers, more snacks, sunscreen, hats and shoes, getting out the door can be overwhelming sometimes. But we have learned that the hardest part is over once you have packed up and pulled away from the house.

Good planning is key to prevent things that can make an outing stressful. You can avoid children having meltdowns by thinking ahead and planning for what you might need. Take into consideration things like water, food, nap schedules, strollers, extra clothes, diaper bags, etc. so that an enjoyable experience does not deteriorate to a frustrating one.

This book only includes places we would recommend to our friends. There were many that didn't make the cut. Our intent in writing this book is to share information that will help you have the most enjoyable experience possible at any of the sites you visit. So now you don't have to spend hours researching, we've done the work for you! Just enjoy the adventures and go have fun!

Map of Site Locations

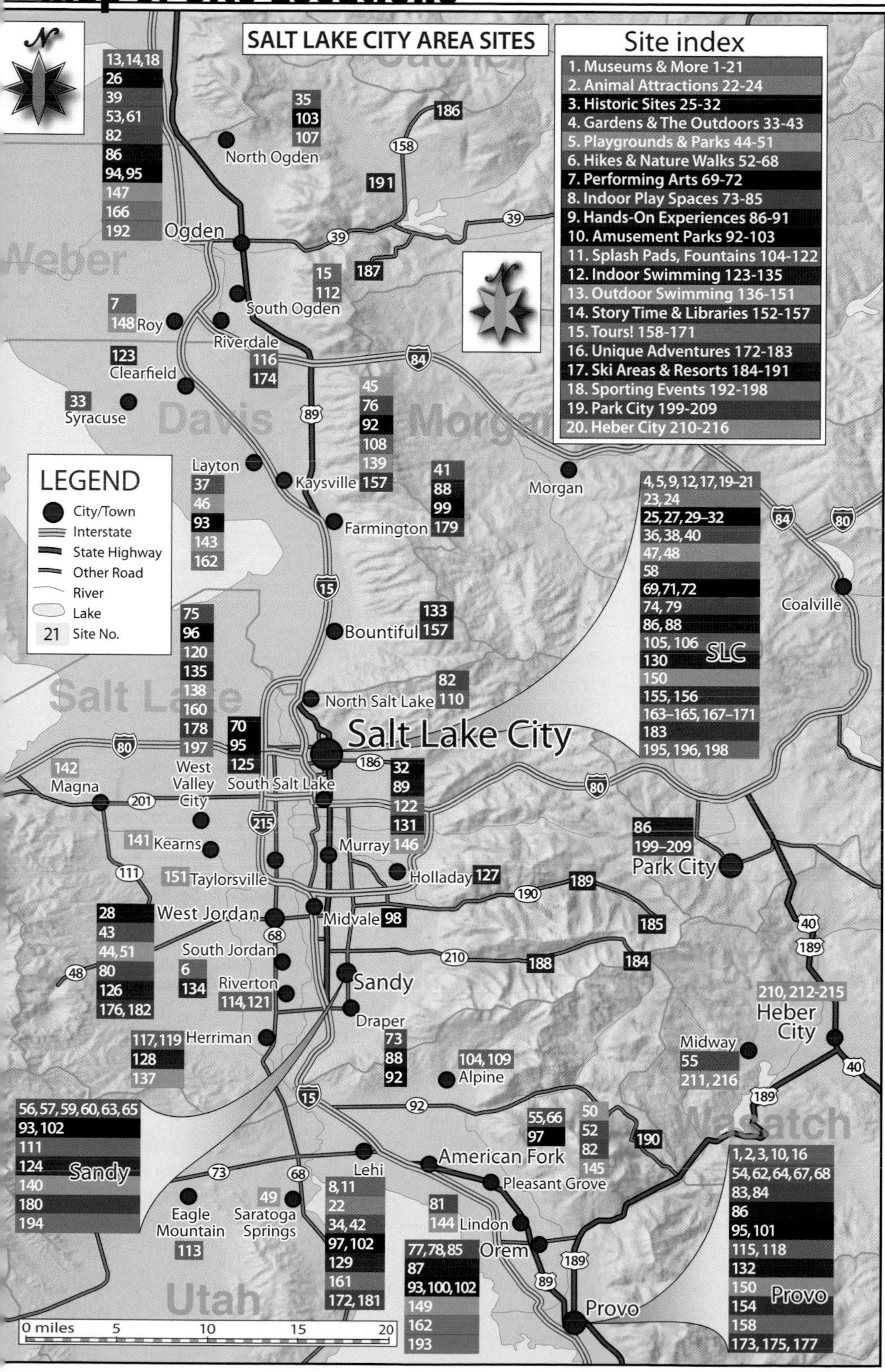

How to Use this Guide

Each chapter is made up of a variety of places that are similar to one another. As you discover your child's interests, it will be easy to find several destinations in the area for exploration and discovery. Each description is similarly organized throughout the book.

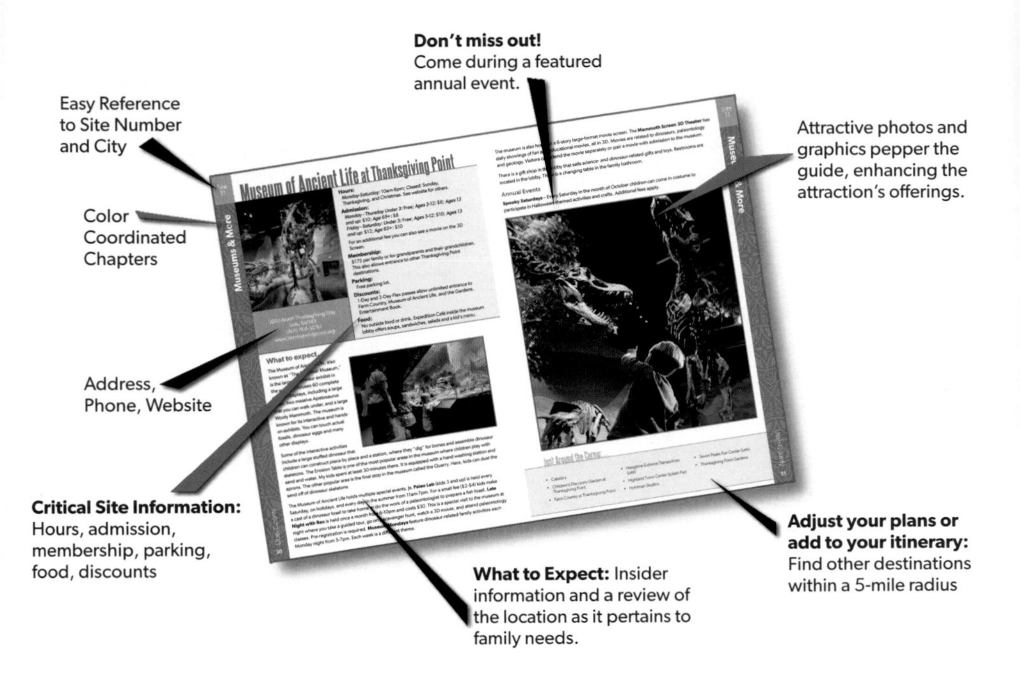

The Basics – Each destination's address, phone number, and website address are listed for easy reference. Following that are hours, admission, membership information, parking, food policy, and how you might be able to obtain discounts for the places that charge admission. Remember, hours and prices may change, so you should call in advance. The memberships and season passes referenced are family memberships, usually for two adults and a certain number of children. Many locations offer free admission to children under a specific age. In those instances, you could purchase an individual or couple admission for a lower rate. Please note that this information is subject to the most change and we encourage you to check the site's website before heading on the road.

What to Expect – A detailed description of the location will help you decide whether or not a certain destination is right for your family. Information that is pertinent to parents of young children is included, such as whether or not restrooms include diaper-changing tables.

Annual Events – Many locations have special celebrations each year that are particularly child-friendly. Some events may celebrate a holiday like Halloween, while others may celebrate something about the facility like its anniversary.

Just Around the Corner – If you have a particularly energetic child, you may want to visit more than one destination in the same day. Maybe you just want to check out another destination on your way home from a favorite spot. Or perhaps you're considering a "staycation" this year and want a variety of activities in a specific part of town. This section will help you fulfill each of these goals. Sites are considered just around the corner if they're within five miles of a given site.

Other Locations – Because many places fit into more than one category, an "Other locations" section relays other sites that are applicable but are located in another chapter. This section may be at the end of the chapter (space provided) but can be located in it's own bar in the middle of a chapter as well.

Keep Your Bags Packed

If you intend to visit a wide variety of places, you might consider keeping a tote box in your trunk with the essential items. Change the box when the weather changes and you'll always be prepared. (Note: If you use plastic water bottles, do not store them in the tote box, particularly in the summer. Studies are showing that the plastic can leach into the water when heated.)

Warm Weather Tote Box:

- ❒ Regular sunscreen
- ❒ Waterproof sunscreen
- ❒ Extra diapers and swim diapers
- ❒ Sun hats, swimsuits, towels, and a change of clothes for you and your child
- ❒ Beach toys like pails, shovels, rakes, sand shapers, and trucks
- ❒ Floaties, goggles, and other swimming accessories
- ❒ Baby powder (for sandbox play)
- ❒ Books, sidewalk chalk, and bubbles
- ❒ Hoodies or light jackets for you and your child
- ❒ A washable tote bag for wet or sandy clothes
- ❒ Bandages and antibiotic cream (Neo to Go sprays on and won't spill in the tote)
- ❒ Insect repellent and anti-itch cream (try Benadryl on the Go for anti-itch)
- ❒ Individually-packaged non-perishable snacks

Cold Weather Tote Box:

- ❒ Lip balm and lotion
- ❒ Sunscreen
- ❒ Extra diapers
- ❒ Extra sweatshirts, coats, hats, and gloves or mittens
- ❒ Short-sleeve shirts for you and your child, for those oddly warm days
- ❒ Swimsuits, towels, and a change of clothes for you and your child for indoor pools
- ❒ Snow boots
- ❒ Hand warmers
- ❒ An inflatable sled
- ❒ Books, coloring books, and crayons
- ❒ A washable tote bag for wet or dirty clothes
- ❒ Bandages and antibiotic cream
- ❒ Individually-packaged non-perishable snacks

Just How Family-Driven is Utah?

Many Utah families, influenced by Mormon culture, have larger than average families. Utah's average family size is highest in America with 3.04 persons per family (although, visitors to Utah will likely experience bigger family encounters).

Census after census (every decade), Utah holds the distinctive spot as youngest state in America, having the youngest median age of 29.2 years, compared to the national median age of 37.2 years. Approximately one third of Utah's population is under 18 years old (also highest percentage).

According to the 2010 Census:

44% of adults in Utah are parents to one or more children, compared to 34% nationally.

31.2% of Utah's population is under 18 years old compared to the national average of 23.7%.

9.3% of Utah's population is under five years old, compared to the national average of 6.5%.

Jell-O:

Also fairly well-known or well-rumored is Utah's ranking as the top consumer of the jiggling snack food, Jell-O! According to Wikipedia, "in 2001, Jell-O was declared the "Official State Snack" of Utah, with Governor Michael O. Leavitt declaring an annual "Jell-O Week." During the 2002 Winter Olympics in Salt Lake City, the souvenir pins included one depicting green Jell-O."

The six counties included in *Playdate with Salt Lake City* comprise over 70% of Utah's total population (population ranked):

1 Salt Lake County
2 Utah County
3 Davis County
4 Weber County
5 Summit County
6 Wasatch County

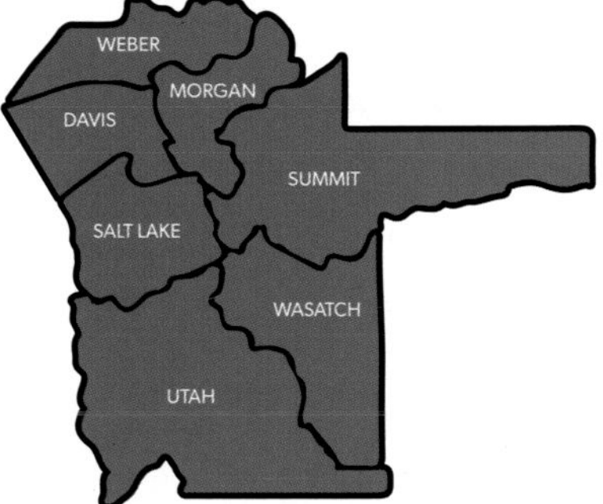

Close to the airport:

Almost all *Playdate with Salt Lake City & Utah's Wasatch Front* adventures are within one hour's drive of the Salt Lake City International Airport.

References:

- *http://www.statemaster.com/graph/lif_ave_hou_siz-lifestyle-average-household-size*
- *http://www.bebr.utah.edu/Documents/uebr/UEBR2011/UEBR2011no2.pdf*
- *http://www.statehealthfacts.org/comparetable.jsp?ind=2&cat=1&sub=1&yr=274&typ=2*
- *http://tax.utah.gov/sales/citycountylist.pdf*
- *http://quickfacts.census.gov/qfd/states/49000.html*
- *http://www.mormonstudies.com/index.php?option=com_content&view=article&id=12:why-do-mormons-tend-to-have-large-families&catid=1:faq&Itemid=2*
- *http://en.wikipedia.org/wiki/Jell-O*
- *http://www.slate.com/articles/life/food/2012/08/jell_o_and_mormonism_the_stereotype_s_surprising_origins_.html*

Museums & More

This chapter highlights a wide variety of museums along the Wasatch front. Some are well-known and others are hidden gems known mostly by local residents. Most museums have evolved to include a children's area or special programs and activities for children. Some of the museums were specifically designed with children in mind, featuring entirely hands-on exhibits. Other museums featured in this chapter may not be places you would think to take your kids, but we have highlighted them and shown how each can be explored and enjoyed with young children. Many offer a regular craft or learning activity. Think about planning your first visit paired with one of these special events. Also, many of these museums cannot be explored completely in one visit. Consider buying a membership so that you can take things slow on your visit and come back frequently.

Courtesy of Ogden Dinosaur Park and Museum

BYU Museum of Art

Hours:

Van Gough to Play Dough
Tuesday and Thursdays: 10am-11am

Adventures in Art
Offered the second and third Saturdays of every month; *Ages 5-7:* 10am-11:30; *Ages 8-11:* 12pm-1:30pm.

Open Studio Offered the first Saturday of every month. Drop in between 10am-noon.

Admission:
FREE!

Parking:
"Visitors Only" parking lot. on the north side of the museum

Food:
No food or drink is allowed. The MOA Café is open Monday-Friday for lunch from 11-2pm.

North Campus Drive
Provo, 84602
(801) 422-8287
www.moa.byu.edu

What to expect...

The BYU Museum of Art (MOA) is one of the largest and most popular art museums in the Mountain West. Open to the public, the museum houses ten exhibition galleries which display some of BYU's permanent collection, traveling shows, and other local or special shows.

The MOA offers three different art workshops for kids and families. Each month the classes are planned around a current exhibit in the museum. Elements of art are explored through books, movement, songs, the five senses, and hands-on art projects. Classes are free but registration is required. You can register online at http://moa.byu.edu/learn/family-programs/ the first business day of the month for classes held the next month.

Van Gogh to Play Dough (For kids ages 2-4): Exploration of the exhibit is engaging and typically involves movement and observation of the art through games or activities. The last 30 minutes of the class is usually spent in hands-on art centers. One adult must attend for every three children.

Adventures in Art (For families) Adventures in Art is a family class offered two Saturdays a month. The activities in this class also include movement and creativity, but are tailored to engage the whole family.

Open Studio (For Families) On the first Saturday of every month, families can drop by anytime between 10am-noon and participate in an art experience. There is no registration required. Families will be asked a question about a specific exhibit theme, and then use their creativity to "answer" the question with an art project.

Just Around the Corner: See opposing page, BYU Museum of Palentology

BYU Museum of Paleontology

1683 N. Canyon Road
Provo 84602
(801) 422-3680
www.ctms.byu.edu/esm

Hours:
Monday-Friday: 9am-5pm;
Monday Nights: 6pm-9pm

Admission:
FREE!

Parking:
Free parking lot.

Food:
No food or drink is allowed in the museum.

What to expect...

Dinosaurs and fossils from the Ice Age and Jurassic Period come alive in the BYU paleontology museum. The excitement lies in the sheer size of the amazing fossils and casts of many dinosaurs, including Allosaurus, Torvosaurus, and Pteranodons. Exhibits include geodes, an enormous prehistoric fish skull, a giant ground sloth, petrified dinosaur eggs, dinosaur footprints, and T-Rex and triceratops skulls, which my kids especially liked. You can call ahead to schedule a tour with one of the student preparators or you can just walk in and eplore at your own pace. Two kind and enthusiastic students gave us an informative tour. The museum is very child-friendly, with many displays marked with a pair of hands signifying that they can be touched. Be sure to take a look through the large glass picture window on the west wall that looks into the lab where the university students are actually working on fossils.

Restrooms without changing tables are located in the entrance of the museum. This museum is stroller friendly.

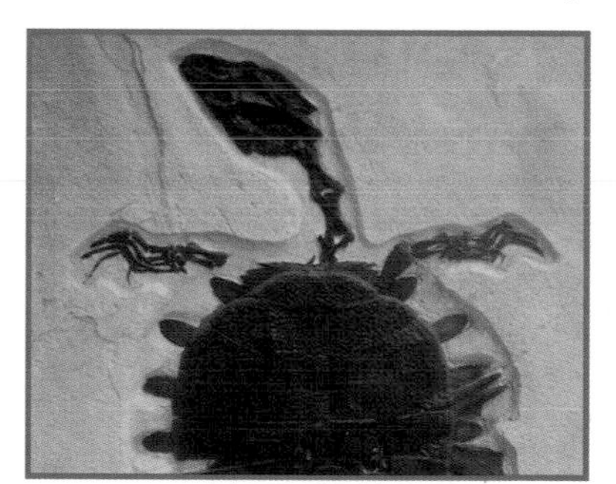

Just Around the Corner...

- BYU Broadcasting
- BYU Museum of Art
- BYU Museum of Peoples and Cultures
- Children's Library at Provo City Library
- Creativity Art Studio
- Color Me Mine (Provo)
- Comedy Sportz
- FatCats (Provo)
- Hang Time Extreme Trampolines (Orem)
- Jake's Archery
- Krispy Kreme (Orem)
- Monte L. Bean Life Science Museum
- Nickel City
- Orem Owlz
- Provo Beach
- Provo Recreation Center
- Royden G. Derek Planetarium
- Scera Pool
- Seven Peaks (Provo)
- Seven Peaks Fun Center (Orem)
- Shops at Riverwoods
- University Mall Tree House Court
- Y Mountain Hike

BYU Museum of Peoples and Cultures

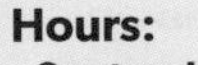

700 North 100 East
Provo, 84606
(801) 422-0020
mpc.byu.edu

Hours:

September-April
Monday, Wednesday, Friday: 9am-5pm;
Tuesday and Thursday: 9am-7pm

May-August
Monday-Friday: 9am-5pm

Admission:
FREE, though group tours carry a small fee. See website.

Parking:
Free parking lot across the street to the east. Park in a museum marked stall, then get a parking pass in the museum office.

Food:
No food or drinks allowed in the museum.

What to expect...

This small museum is housed in an historic building that once served as a men's dormitory. It has been renovated to include a classroom, offices and two small museum galleries. The galleries together cover about 1,100 sq. ft., but the storage area of the museum is home to over 1 million artifacts. The exhibits in the galleries are changed about every year and are assembled and designed by Museum Practices students at BYU as part of their curriculum. All exhibits display and reveal what life is or was like for different people and cultures throughout time. This museum can be visited in about 30-45 minutes.

There is an activity bag that can be checked out from the office that is designed to make the visit more fun for younger children. When we visited, there was also a scavenger hunt worksheet at the front entrance that the kids used to find specific items throughout the exhibits. The **Learning Lounge** is a little room at the back of the gallery which has soft chairs, coloring pages, and several hands-on activities that all of my kids enjoyed. This room is the highlight of the museum for young children.

There is a 45-minute tour offered for a small fee depending on the size of the group. At the end of the tour, the group participates in a hands-on activity in an adjoining classroom. Tours must be scheduled at least a week in advance.

Every Friday at 11am, September through April, the museum offers "Stories from Around the World." After reading a story that highlights a specific culture, kids do a small craft related to the book. It lasts about 30-45 minutes.

Just Around the Corner...

- BYU Broadcasting
- BYU Museum of Art
- BYU Museum of Paleontology
- Children's Library at Provo City Library
- Creativity Art Studio
- Color Me Mine (Provo)
- Comedy Sportz
- FatCats (Provo)
- Hang Time Extreme Trampolines (Orem)
- Jake's Archery
- Krispy Kreme (Orem)
- Monte L. Bean Life Science Museum
- Nickel City
- Orem Owlz
- Provo Beach
- Provo Recreation Center
- Royden G. Derek Planetarium
- Scera Pool
- Seven Peaks (Provo)
- Seven Peaks Fun Center (Orem)
- Shops at Riverwoods
- University Mall Tree House Court
- Y Mountain Hike

Clark Planetarium

110 South 400 West
Salt Lake City, 84101
(385) 468-7827
www.clarkplanetarium.org

Hours:
Monday-Wednesday: 10:30am-10pm; *Thursday:* 10:30am-10pm; *Friday-Saturday:* 10:30am-11pm; *Sunday:* 10:30am-8pm
See website for holiday hours and closings.

Admission:
FREE for *20ish* exhibits; $6-$14 for movies in the *ATK Imax Theatre*, *Hansen Dome* or for *light shows*. See website for show pricing.

Membership:
$45 for two member cards/basic membership; $65 for families (2 adults, 6 kids under 18). Check online for memberships with more expansive benefits.

Parking:
UTA TRAX /bus stop in front. Paid parking at Gateway Winter parking garage. The Planetarium validates $1 for 3 hours.

Food:
Typical movie theater concessions are sold on the 2nd floor.

Discounts:
Visit Salt Lake Connect Pass.

Social:

What to expect...

Clark Planetarium is located at The Gateway in downtown Salt Lake City. Established in 2003, the Planetarium hosts approximately 400,000 visitors every year, 85,000 of which are students.

The Planetarium has 19 interactive and informative exhibits related to space and science. These displays offer: images from the Hubble Space Telescope, a walk on the simulated surfaces of Mars and the Moon (great for photo opportunities), a hands-on exploration of meteorites, a look at a real moon rock, quizzes on your knowledge of the planets, and an exhibit that calculates how much you would weigh on another planet. Newton's Daydream, a kinetic art installation that explores physics, is a popular exhibit. Visitors can get a close-up view and work moving parts on both the second and third floors.

Hansen Dome offers exciting 2D views of the universe from reclined seats. Most children enjoy this, but some younger children can become overwhelmed. Movies last between 35-45 minutes. ATK IMAX Theater is the Planetarium's largest screen, which offers 3D films and shows nature and science documentaries. You can see schedules and buy tickets online or just purchase tickets at the front desk.

Plan on spending an hour exploring the free exhibits. Add another 30 to 45 minutes if you choose to see an Imax, Dome or light show. The unique Planet Fun Store, sells science and space themed toys, games, telescopes, posters and gifts. Restrooms with changing tables are located on the first floor. Scavenger hunt checklists that guide children through the exhibits are available on their website. Click "Education" then "Guides and Handouts."

Annual Events

Breakfast with the Easter Bunny & Egg Hunt – Purchase tickets ahead of time.

See Appendix 1 for Downtown Destinations close to this area

Discovery Gateway: The Children's Museum of Utah

444 West 100 South
Salt Lake City, 84101
(801) 456-5437
www.childmuseum.org

Hours:
Monday-Thursday: 10am-6pm;
Friday-Saturday: 10am-8pm; *Sunday:* 12pm-6pm;
Closed Thanksgiving, Christmas and Easter and 4th of July.

Admission:
Under 1 year old: free; *1 year and up:* $8.50; *65+:* $6

Membership:
An annual family membership for a family of three is $95 (add $20 for each additional person). Introductory 6 month memberships are also available.

Parking:
Park in the Winter Parking Garage at The Gateway Mall. Parking validations can be purchased at the Discovery to Go! store for $1.

Food:
No food, gum or drink is allowed in the museum. However, The Gateway Shopping Center has plenty of food options, including a nearby food court.

Discounts:
Each child who joins the Birthday Club receives a coupon for one free admission during their birthday month. See the website for various seasonal offers and discounts. Entertainment Book. Visit Salt Lake Connect Pass.

What to expect...

Discovery Gateway: The Children's Museum of Utah is located in the open-air Gateway Center. Built on the idea that children learn through play, the museum is an inviting place where kids can engage in imaginative play and hands-on activities. While visiting, children may freely explore six permanent galleries and special temporary exhibits.

The Garden – This area features a giant beehive made up of a maze of tubes. Children insert balls in various chutes and watch as they travel overhead and back down.

Kid's Eye View – Activities include: a construction zone, a play house, a grocery store, a farm, a rock wall, a large water table, toy cars, and a gated play area for ages 3 and under called Hatch, Waddle, and Fly. This area also offers comfortable seating for nursing.

Story Factory – This gallery explores multiple ways to tell stories, including a dress-up theater, the creation of comic strips and an animation station. Children may also send messages to each other from across the museum using the Communication Station.

Media Zone – Kids anchor the news in front of a camera or report the weather using a green screen, and see themselves on a TV monitor.

The Studio – Kids can build using Legos, magnetic building sets, and large building blocks. They can create paper airplanes and fly them in a wind tunnel, create a ping pong ball maze with a series of pipes along a magnetic wall, or build a structure at the earthquake table.

The Terrace – The outdoor terrace located on the top floor includes the Saving Lives exhibit sponsored by Intermountain Healthcare featuring a Life Flight helicopter and a kid-sized Primary Children's emergency department.

Discovery Gateway offers daily classes and weekly workshops at no additional charge. Space is limited, so sign up in advance. For more information, see the website under "Classes & Special Events."

The entire museum is stroller-friendly. Restrooms have changing areas with the option of a family bathroom on the first floor. Hand sanitizer is available throughout the museum. Coin-operated lockers are also available for use. Children under 14 must be accompanied by an adult 18 years and older. The Discovery to Go! Store sells a variety of educational toys, including some of the toys enjoyed in the museum.

Annual Events

Week of the Young Child – April. There are special activities all week related to early childhood education.

Halloween Spooktacular – Special Fundraising Event–October. A non-scary Halloween party with hands-on activities.

Breakfast with Santa – Weekend mornings in December. This includes breakfast or brunch, a visit with Santa, crafts and play in the museum. Extra fees apply.

See Appendix 1 for Downtown Destinations close to this area

The Gale Center of History and Culture

10300 South Beckstead Lane
South Jordan, 84095
(801) 254-3048
www.galecenter.org

Hours:
Tuesday-Friday: 10am-6pm;
Saturdays: By appointment only
Closed: Sundays, Mondays and holidays

Admission:
FREE! Donations welcome.

Parking:
Free parking lot.

Food:
No food or drink is allowed in the museum.

What to expect...

The Gale Center of History and Culture is a local museum and education center. Here visitors can experience and learn about South Jordan's past. Children love this museum for the friendly and interactive nature of its exhibits.

The museum is made up of permanent indoor and outdoor exhibits, as well as changing displays. Exhibits include a school house, a farmhouse, an old-fashioned store, a mine and "Grandma's House." Some of these areas are interactive and include hands-on activities. Children can milk a pretend cow, play with old-fashioned wooden toys, wash and hang clothes, and shop at the store. The outdoor exhibits include old farming machinery, a granary and a dugout. The museum also regularly exhibits the work of local artists.

You can view the museum at your own pace or ask for a tour, which lasts about 45 minutes. Any tour can be tailored to your group and time constraints, just ask. Be aware that you must schedule a visit if your group is larger than five people.

The museum is recommended for children ages 5 and up, but is best suited for children ages 8 and older. Parents are encouraged to follow children closely and to be respectful by keeping exhibits tidy. Although interactive, it is primarily a museum, not an indoor play center. The museum hosts a family activity once a month called Terrific Tuesdays. On a Tuesday evening, once a month, families can enjoy crafts, activities, guest speakers, movies, games, and more. Changing tables are located in the ladies restroom.

Annual Events

Gingerbread Gala – November, Gingerbread creation contest.

Just Around the Corner...

- Accessible Playground at Veteran's Memorial Park
- Airborne
- Classic Fun Center (SLC)
- Color Me Mine (Draper)
- Gardner Village
- Gene Fullmer Recreation Center
- Georgell Doll Shop
- Old Farm Splash Park
- Real Salt Lake
- Scheels
- Tiny Tim's Foundation for Kids
- Urban Park Interactive Fountain
- (West Jordan) Conservation Garden Park
- Wild West Jordan Playground

Hill Aerospace Museum

7961 Wardleigh Road
Hill Airforce Base, 84056
(801) 777-6868

Hours:
Tuesday-Saturday: 9am-4:30pm;
Closed: New Years Day, Christmas and Thanksgiving

Admission:
FREE! Donations are accepted.

Parking:
Free parking lot.

Food:
No food or drink is allowed in the museum.

Social: 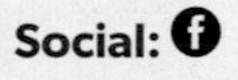

What to expect...

Located on the northwest corner of Hill Air Force Base, this museum gives visitors a close look at more than 90 authentic military aircraft, missiles, aerospace vehicles, and other related artifacts. Many of the volunteers throughout the museum are veterans.

The excitement begins as you drive up to the museum and are greeted by a line of huge cargo airplanes. Visitors can walk around and explore this outside area. The main part of the museum is found in two large hangars filled with dozens of historic aircraft flown from WWI to the present day. My favorite aircraft were the beautiful airplanes used during both World Wars. The exhibits feature military vehicles, ground equipment, helicopters, jet engines, and even a ¾ scale replica of the Wright Brothers 1903 Flyer.

Surrounding the large aircraft are smaller displays with artifacts from specific eras. All of the displays share the history of Hill Air Force Base throughout the wars. These include things like: uniforms, helmets, first aid kits, canteens, flight handbooks, an ejection seat, and an impressive display about the Vietnam War.

The **Aerospace Center for Education** (ACE) is an area of the museum where kids can experience a simulated flight on an airplane and enjoy other hands-on activities. This area is open Wednesdays 9-11am. during the school year, and more frequently during the summer. There are scavenger hunt and activity worksheets found on the website.

Each year on the third Saturday in September, the museum stages an open house called "Food-For-Life Day," during which visitors can view aircraft up close, even getting inside some of them! The suggested "admission price" is one item of non-perishable food (preferably canned), which goes to the Hill AFB Airmen's Attic food pantry.

For more information you can visit the website at www.hill.af.mil/library/museum/index.asp.

Just Around the Corner...

- Clearfield Aquatic Center
- Coleman's Motor-VU Drive-In
- Riverdale Park
- Roy Aquatic Center

John Hutchings Museum of Natural History

55 North Center Street
Lehi, 84043
(801) 768-7180
www.lehi-ut.gov/discover/hutchings-museum

Hours:
Tuesday-Saturday: 11am-5pm;
Closed: Sunday, Monday and Holidays

Admission:
Under 3: Free; *Ages 3-18:* $3; 18+: $4;
Senior Citizens: $3

Membership:
$25 for individuals and $50 for families.

Food:
No food or drink is allowed.

Parking:
There is street parking in front. You can also park along the left side or around the back of the museum.

Discounts:
Families (up to 6 family members) can get in on a group rate of $12; Discounts are also available for scouts and their leaders. Lowered group rates are available by reservation. Sign up to receive their newsletter to become aware of a few free days each year.

What to expect...

John Hutchings Museum of Natural History is an exciting local museum packed full of hands-on and interesting exhibits. If I lived closer to this museum, my children and I would be frequent visitors. In 1956 John Hutchings and his wife donated their large personal collection of fossils, pioneer items, rocks, minerals, shells, stuffed birds, eggs, etc., to benefit the children of Lehi. This collection has been added to over the years and has become a local treasure. Plan for about an hour on your first visit.

The museum is divided into themed exhibit rooms including: the **Bird & Egg Room**, the **Rock and Mineral Room**, the **Fossil & Shell Room**, the **Pioneer Room**, the **Native American Room**, and the **Wild West Room**. During our visit, the kids touched and examined rocks, walked inside a pretend bear cave, hand-ground corn, listened to bird calls, and brushed sand off dinosaur bones. A favorite spot in the museum was the real jail cell with dummy prisoners. You can print out the Scout Self-Guided Tour Worksheet from the website. It includes two questions per room. Answers can be found easily throughout the museum on bright green placards.

This museum is known for its classes, workshops and special events that happen year-round. To receive the most updated information on events, sign up online to receive newsletters. Currently the museum provides a Family Night on the first Monday of the month, youth group nights, home school tours, and field trips.

There is a small gift shop area in the museum with old-fashioned candy, rocks and a few toys. Restrooms are located in the middle of the museum. There are no changing tables.

Annual Events

Night at the Museum – February. See the exhibits all come to life!
Lehi Round-Up Week – In conjunction with Lehi's city celebration, the museum holds activities.

Just Around the Corner...

- American Fork Fitness Center
- Jack and Jill Lanes
- Legacy Recreation Center
- Neptune Park
- Seven Peaks Fun Center (Lehi)

LDS Church History Museum

45 North West Temple
Salt Lake City, 84150
(801) 240-3310
www.history.lds.org

Hours:
Monday-Friday: 9am-9pm;
Saturday-Sunday: 10am-5pm

Admission:
FREE!

Parking:
There are nearby paid parking lots and metered street parking. Street parking is free for two hours on Saturdays and Sundays.

Food:
No food or drink is allowed in the museum.

What to expect...

The Church History Museum is located directly across the street from Temple Square to the west. The history of The Church of Jesus Christ of Latter-day Saints is told through artifacts and displays. Things like clothing, tools, furniture, a covered wagon, and an 1830 edition of the *Book of Mormon*. The second level has some permanent and traveling collections of art.

In the northeast corner of the second level, there is a large **Children's Exhibit.** This exhibit changes every two or three years, but always provides fun, interactive activities for kids. When we went, activities included: fishing off the side of a boat, building huge foam blocks, computer matching games, paper dolls, a farm area, and an area to learn Mexican dancing with full costumes.

Restrooms with changing tables are available. The building is stroller friendly.

See Appendix 1 for Downtown Destinations close to this area

Monte L. Bean Life Science Museum

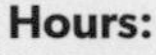

645 East 1430 North
Provo, 84602
(801) 442-5052
mlbean.byu.edu

Hours:
Closed until Spring of 2014. See website for current hours.

Admission:
FREE!

Food:
No food or drink is allowed.

Parking:
Free, but visitors must pick up a parking permit from the museum's front desk.

Social:

What to expect...

The Bean Museum, located on the Brigham Young University campus has been open to the community since 1978. Known for it's exciting exhibits of taxidermy animals, it houses millions of specimens including mammals, birds, insects, shells and plants. The Bean Museum has been a favorite place for my family to visit for many years.

The Bean Museum offers multiple permanent exhibits and displays. You could see the whole museum in about an hour. Add time if you plan to attend an animal show, which I recommend. One of the best things about this museum, compared to going to the zoo to see live animals, is the fact that children can get an up close look at these display animals. They can freely examine their fur, their claws, their teeth and their whiskers, things that are only seen from far away at the zoo.

Since the Summer of 2012, the museum has been under renovation adding 30,000 square feet to the existing building. It will include an orientation theater and several new exhibits. One of which will include the President Boyd K. Packer Gallery presenting his collection of wood carvings, illustrations and paintings of animals and wildlife.

The new museum store will sell toys, books, seashells, games and BYU merchandise. The information desk will also provide educational scavenger hunts for children. Story time has been offered once a week in the past. The museum has also offered daily Public Shows, which are educational and interactive presentations about reptiles, plants and animals. They have also offered Saturday Safari classes for young kids as well as Family Nights. See the website for current shows and times.

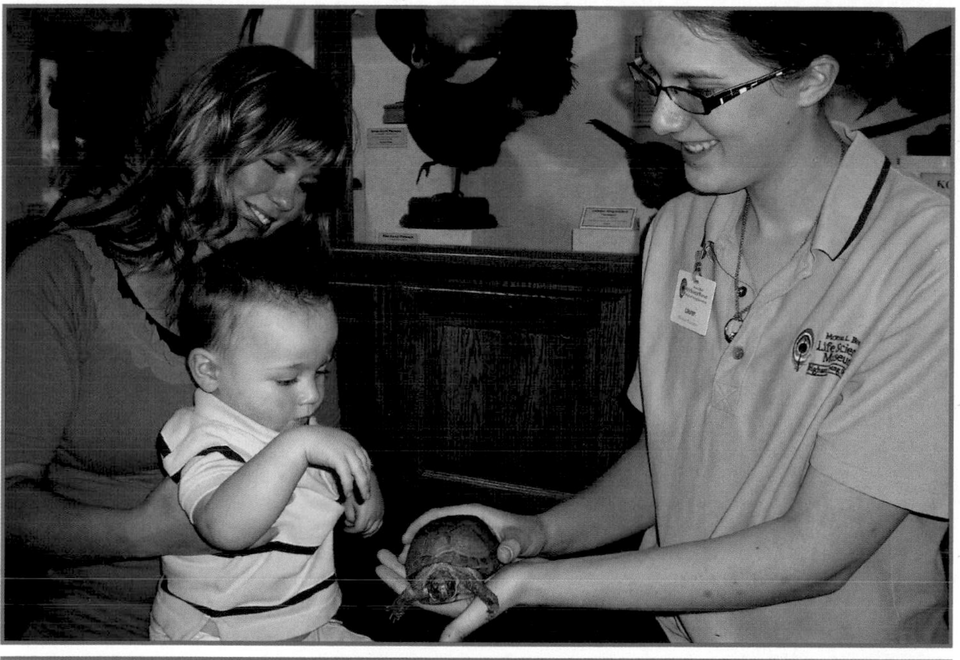

Just Around the Corner...

- BYU Broadcasting
- BYU Museum of Art
- BYU Museum of Paleontology
- BYU Museum of Peoples and Cultures
- Children's Library at Provo City Library
- Creativity Art Studio
- Color Me Mine (Provo)
- Comedy Sportz
- FatCats (Provo)
- Hang Time Extreme Trampolines (Orem)
- Jake's Archery
- Krispy Kreme (Orem)
- Nickel City Fun Center
- Orem Owlz
- Provo Beach
- Provo Recreation Center
- Royden G. Derek Planetarium
- Scera Pool
- Seven Peaks (Provo)
- Seven Peaks Fun Center (Orem)
- Shops at Riverwoods
- University Mall Tree House Court
- Y Mountain Hike

Museum of Ancient Life at Thanksgiving Point

3003 North Thanksgiving Way
Lehi, 84043
(801) 766-5030
www.thanksgivingpoint.org

Hours:
Monday-Saturday: 10am-8pm; *Closed:* Sunday, Thanksgiving, and Christmas. See website for others.

Admission:
Monday - Thursday Under 3: Free; *Ages 3-12:* $8; *Ages 13 and up:* $10; *Age 65+:* $8
Friday - Saturday: Under 3: Free; *Ages 3-12:* $10; *Ages 13 and up:* $12; *Age 65+:* $10

For an additional fee you can also see a movie on the 3D Screen.

Membership:
$175 per family or for grandparents and their grandchildren. This also allows entrance to other Thanksgiving Point destinations.

Parking:
Free parking lot.

Discounts:
1-Day and 2-Day Flex passes allow unlimited entrance to Farm Country, Museum of Ancient Life, and the Gardens. Entertainment Book.

Food:
No outside food or drink. Expedition Café inside the museum lobby offers soups, sandwiches, salads and a kid's menu.

What to expect...

The Museum of Ancient Life, also known as "The Dinosaur Museum," is the largest dinosaur exhibit in the world. It houses 60 complete skeletal displays, including a large T-Rex, two massive Apatosaurus that you can walk under, and a large Wooly Mammoth. The museum is known for its interactive and hands-on exhibits. You can touch actual fossils, dinosaur eggs and many other displays.

Some of the interactive activities include a large stuffed dinosaur that children can construct piece by piece and a station, where they "dig" for bones and assemble dinosaur skeletons. The Erosion Table is one of the most popular areas in the museum where children play with sand and water. My kids spent at least 30 minutes there. It is equipped with a hand washing station and aprons. The other popular area is the final stop in the museum called the Quarry. Here, kids can dust the sand off of dinosaur skeletons.

The Museum of Ancient Life holds multiple special events. **Jr. Paleo Lab** (kids 3 and up) is held every Saturday, on holidays, and every day in the summer from 11am-7pm. For a small fee ($2-$4) kids make a cast of a dinosaur fossil to take home or do the work of a paleontologist to prepare a fish fossil. **Late Night with Rex** is held once a month from 6-10pm and costs $30. This is a special visit to the museum at night where you take a guided tour, go on a scavenger hunt, watch a 3D movie, and attend paleontology classes. Pre-registration is required. **Museum Mondays** feature dinosaur-related family activities each Monday night from 5-7pm. Each week is a different theme.

The museum is also home to a 6-story large-format movie screen. The **Mammoth Screen 3D Theater** has daily showings of fun and educational movies, all in 3D. Movies are related to dinosaurs, paleontology and geology. Visitors can attend the movie separately or pair a movie with admission to the museum.

There is a gift shop in the lobby that sells science- and dinosaur-related gifts and toys. Restrooms are located in the lobby. There is a changing table in the family bathroom.

Annual Events

Spooky Saturdays – Every Saturday in the month of October children can come in costume to participate in Halloween-themed activities and crafts. Additional fees apply.

Just Around the Corner...

- Cabela's
- Children's Discovery Garden at Thanksgiving Point
- Farm Country at Thanksgiving Point
- Hangtime Extreme Trampolines (Lehi)
- Highland Town Center Splash Pad
- Holdman Studios
- Seven Peaks Fun Center (Lehi)
- Thanksgiving Point Gardens

Natural History Museum of Utah

301 Wakara Way
Salt Lake City, 84108
(801) 581-4303
www.nhmu.utah.edu

Hours:
Daily: 10am-5pm; *Wednesdays:* 10am-9pm; Last admission is 30 minutes before closing; *Closed:* Thanksgiving and Christmas

Admission:
Under 3: Free; *Ages 3-12:* $8; Ages 13-24: $9; *Ages 25-64:* $11; *Age 65+:* $9; *University of Utah students, faculty and staff with valid ID:* Free.

Membership:
$95 for two adults and up to six dependent children or grandchildren. Other memberships available.

Parking:
There is free parking next to the Museum. It is an uphill walk from the parking lot to the museum. Drivers can drop passengers off at the turnaround.

Food:
No food or drink is allowed in the museum galleries. The Museum Café buys locally and offers a variety of breakfast pastries, Panini sandwiches, salads, and kid's meals with dino-shaped sandwiches.

Discounts:
There are a number of free days each year as part of Salt Lake County's Zoo Arts & Parks funding. See the website for current days. Reserve your ticket one week in advance. There are group rates. Visit Utah Connect Pass.

Social:

What to expect...

The Natural History Museum of Utah is a beautiful building set against the foothills above Salt Lake City. It is located on the University of Utah Campus right next to Red Butte Garden. The building itself, called the Rio Tinto Center, is a unique structure built to follow the contours of the hillside and blend into the environment. It is also covered in standing seam copper from the Kennecott Utah Copper Mine.

Exhibits – This museum allows visitors to explore science and nature related to Utah. There are five levels of galleries with interactive displays throughout the museum. Exhibits include: Sky, Native Voices, Life, Land, First Peoples, Gems and Minerals, Great Salt Lake, Past Worlds, Our Backyard, and Utah Futures. Many areas use art, games, buttons, lights and more to engage visitors. Displays that children may touch are clearly marked. Some of the displays include: a long walk-way full of mounted dinosaur skeletons, a small dino-dig sandpit, see-through floors with dinosaur skeletons, and a little archaeological dig site. Don't miss the beautiful views of the Salt Lake Valley out on the terrace as part of the Sky Exhibit.

Our Backyard – This is a room created especially for toddlers. It has a long water table, a cave, dress-ups, and an area for study and exploration.

Classes & Programs – The museum offers a wide variety of classes for kids. There are live animal observations of **Utah's Animals** such as the Utah salamander and the North American bullfrog. These encounters are offered on the first and third Saturday of every month from 2-3pm. **Bug Brigade** is offered every second and fourth Saturday of every month from 2-4pm. Kids have the opportunity to learn about, observe, and handle live bugs. **The Chickadee Society** is a preschool story time held the second and fourth Thursday of every month from 11-11:30am. It includes science-themed stories, activities, and more. All of these programs are free with admission to the museum. The museum also offers Spring Break Day Camps and week-long summer camps.

The Museum Store sells unique art, handmade items, t-shirts, toys, books and gifts. A Mother's Room/Family Restroom with a changing station is located on the 2nd level just past the museum store and café.

Just Around the Corner...

- Color Me Mine (SLC)
- Fort Douglas Military Museum
- Gilgal Garden
- Liberty Park
- Red Butte Garden
- The King's English
- This is the Place Heritage Park
- Tracy Aviary
- Utah's Hogle Zoo

Ogden Dinosaur Park and Museum

1544 East Park Boulevard
Ogden, 84401
(801) 393-3466
www.dinosaurpark.org

Hours:
Hours are seasonal. Check website.

Admission:
Under 2: Free; *Ages 2-12:* $5; *Ages 13-17:* $6; *Age 18-61:* $7; *Age 62+:* $6.

Food:
Outside food and drink is permitted in the park. The outdoor Cretaceous Café is open during the summer and serves food from 11am-5pm.

Discounts:
Lowered rates are offered to homeschoolers; see website. Membership to Tracy Aviary applicable to the Dinosaur Park for free on weekdays. Entertainment Book.

Social:

What to expect...

Get ready for an unforgettable dinosaur adventure when you visit the Ogden Dinosaur Park and Museum. This unique park features a large museum and 8 acres of beautiful, landscaped walking trails with large dinosaur sculptures lurking throughout. There are many hands-on activities inside and outside the museum.

Museum

The museum features complete full-size dinosaur skeletons, bones and teeth. Upstairs on the second floor is an animatronic display with dinosaurs that move and make sounds. It seemed so real that my 3-year-old didn't want to get too close.

The **Education Center** located in the museum, offers art projects, puzzles, videos, reading areas, and other activities related to dinosaurs. A large glass window allows visitors a look into a working dinosaur laboratory where scientists and technicians prepare recently excavated bones and teeth for display.

One activity that costs extra, but was worth the money (unless you have lots of kids), is the **Gem Mine**. It's like a treasure hunt! For $7, your child gets to spend 10 minutes in the gem mine digging in pea gravel with shovels and buckets to find colorful precious stones. Whatever they find is theirs to keep. They will come away with a little satchel full of gemstones. My kids LOVED this activity.

The Park

A lot of thought and creativity went into the planning of this amazing park. Over 100 life-size dinosaur sculptures are positioned throughout the walking trails. Speakers strategically placed throughout the trails play dinosaur sounds, which add to the ambiance. Toddlers may even be a little frightened by the sounds.

The **Kid's Quarry** is a sandpit where the fossil of a stegosaurus can be uncovered with a brush. The **Gold Sluice** gives kids the opportunity to pan for gold. There is a very big **playground** area that features dinosaur-related play structures. Kids can slide down a pterodactyl's beak, or climb through a triceratops skull. Shaded picnic tables and benches can be found throughout the park.

Just Around the Corner...

- Birdsong Trail
- Color Me Mine (Ogden)
- FastKart Speedway (Ogden)
- FatCats (Ogden)
- Fort Buenaventura
- Ogden Nature Center
- Ogden Raptors
- Ogden River Parkway
- Ogden's Union Station
- Ott Planetarium
- Peery's Egyptian Theater
- Riverdale Park
- Treehouse Children's Museum

Ogden Union Station

2501 Wall Avenue
Ogden, 84401
(801) 393-9886
www.theunionstation.org

Hours:
Monday-Saturday: 10am-5pm;
Closed: New Years Eve, New Years Day, Thanksgiving, Christmas Eve and Christmas.

Admission:
Ages 3-12: $3; *Ages 13-17:* $4; *Ages 18-61:* $5; *Age 62+:* $4.

A Family Day pass is $15 for two adults and up to four kids.

Parking:
There is free parking in the north and south lots in front of the Station.

Food:
No food or drink is allowed in the museums. The Union Grill Restaurant is open Monday-Saturday from 11am-10pm.

What to expect...

Ogden Union Station was constructed in 1923 and served as a train station until its closing in 1977. It has since been restored and is now home to four museums, two art galleries, and the The Union Grill Restaurant. The large front doors open to the beautiful Grand Lobby that used to serve as the main terminal room of the train station. Admission includes all four museums and is paid in the gift shop located on the northeast side of the Grand Lobby.

Utah State Railroad Museum: This is the largest museum of the four and contains historic photographs, maps, artifacts, and displays, many of which are interactive. There are all kinds of things for kids to touch and experience, including a look into a real train caboose. The last part of the museum, which was my kids' favorite, features a model railroad. Four electric model trains move through beautifully designed scenes complete with model people and animals.

The Browning-Kimball Classic Car Museum: The Classic Car Museum displays beautifully preserved cars from "The Golden Age" of motorcar history. The collection showcases the different body styles, wheels, running boards, and even headlights of cars throughout that time. The oldest car is a 1901 single cylinder Oldsmobile. It only takes about 15 minutes to tour the small one room museum.

The John M. Browning Firearms Museum: This museum, located on the second floor, contains dozens of glass display boxes showcasing the evolution of guns. You can see original models of firearms designed by John M. Browning. Hundreds of firearms on display include rifles, pistols, shot guns, machine guns and cannons.

The Eccles Rail Trains: This is a collection of actual locomotives including switch engines, boxcars and cabooses. They are located outside of the building to the south and can be viewed for free. There are dozens of train cars hooked together on the tracks. It's worth getting close to them to experience their sheer size. If you ask the host at the information desk, an employee may be able to come out and allow you the chance to get inside the trains.

Be sure to check out the **Utah Cowboy and Western Heritage Museum**, which is a new addition to Ogden Union Station that opened after our family visited.

Ott Planetarium

Weber State Campus
1551 Edvalson Street
Ogden, 84408
(801) 626-6871
www.ottplanetarium.org

Hours:
From 12pm-5pm every other Saturday during the summer and once a month during the school year.

Families and groups can make reservations for a field trip on the website. The rates are reasonable and you can pick a program to view.

Admission:
FREE on specific dates and times. See the website for a schedule of free public events.

Parking:
Free parking lot.

Food:
No food or drink is allowed in the planetarium.

What to expect...

Located on Weber State campus, this planetarium is a little known jewel. Every other Saturday in the summer and once a month during the school year, the planetarium hosts Science Saturday.

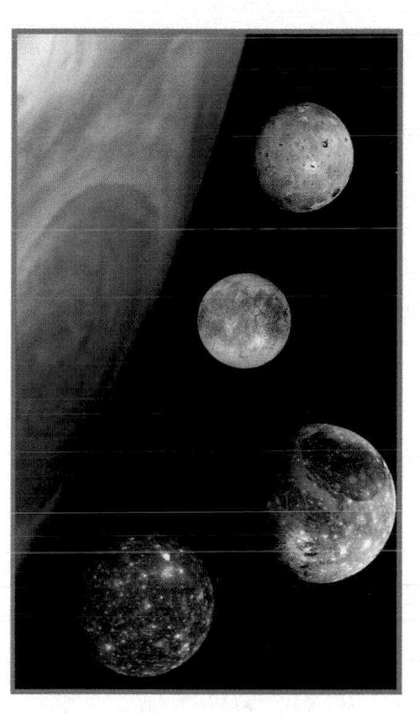

Science Saturday is an outreach program that is taught primarily by university students from a variety of science fields. Planetarium shows run every half hour and with such a variety that you could see three different shows in one day. With a newly updated system, the planetarium shows give a unique look at our solar system.

Additionally, there are wonderful mini-classes throughout the day offering kids a hands-on experience with science. Class content and activities range in subjects from botany and physics to biology and chemistry. Each class lasts about 15-20 minutes. Some activities have been: looking at a real human brain, exploring different smells, outlining bodies on large paper and drawing in the nervous system, and exploring the reasons for the seasons. The university students make the classes fun for the kids. Classes are different each week so check the website for current information.

While visiting the planetarium, plan time to also visit the small natural science museum on the main floor of the building featuring displays of skeletons, amphibians, dinosaur fossil replicas, and precious stone. The outside perimeter of the museum features several hands on science-themed games and activities. My kids really enjoyed the games and begged for more time to explore them all.

Restrooms without changing tables are located on the first and second floors.

Just Around the Corner...

- Birdsong Trail
- Color Me Mine (Ogden)
- FastKart Speedway (Ogden)
- FatCats (Ogden)
- Fort Buenaventura
- Nature Park
- Ogden Dinosaur Park and Museum
- Ogden Raptors
- Ogden River Parkway
- Ogden's Union Station
- Peery's Egyptian Theater
- Riverdale Park
- Treehouse Children's Museum

Royden G. Derrek Planetarium

BYU Campus
Eyring Science Center
Campus Drive, 84602
(801)-422-3849
www.planetarium.byu.edu

Hours:
See website for specific times and shows.

Admission:
Weekday shows: $1, *Friday night shows:* $2.

Parking:
See website for parking instructions.

Food:
No food or drink is allowed.

What to expect...

The Royden G. Derrek (BYU) Planetarium runs an outreach program that offers shows to the public. Because all shows are created by students, they change from month to month. More outreach shows are offered during the semester when the university students are on campus. December and the months of May through August offer limited shows.

The shows cover subjects such as the solar system, star formations, black holes, the moon, etc. As the lights go down, sit back in the large reclining chairs and look at the solar system as you never have before.

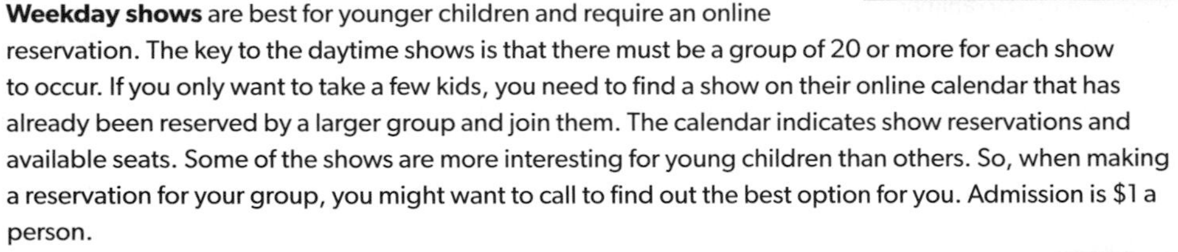

Weekday shows are best for younger children and require an online reservation. The key to the daytime shows is that there must be a group of 20 or more for each show to occur. If you only want to take a few kids, you need to find a show on their online calendar that has already been reserved by a larger group and join them. The calendar indicates show reservations and available seats. Some of the shows are more interesting for young children than others. So, when making a reservation for your group, you might want to call to find out the best option for you. Admission is $1 a person.

Thursday night shows are at 7:30pm. This show is specifically offered for scout and church groups. Again, there must be at least 20 people in a group for the show to happen. Admission is $1 a person.

Friday night shows are open to the public and do not require a reservation. These shows are usually most interesting to adults as they cover more in-depth topics and I would not recommend taking young children. Tickets can only be bought the evening of the show at the planetarium and are $2.

Just Around the Corner: See pg 29 Monte L. Bean Life Science Museum

The Leonardo

209 East 500 South
Salt Lake City, 84111
(801) 531-9800
www.theleonardo.org

Hours:
Sunday-Wednesday: 10am – 5pm;
Thursday-Saturday: 10am – 10pm
Hours can change seasonally. See website for current hours.

Admission:
Under 6: Free; *Age 6 – 11*: $7; *Age 12 – 17*: $8, *Adults:* $9; *Seniors, Students, Military:* $8. Does not include special engagements.

Membership:
$45 for 1, $65 for two, $85 for four, or $150 for six.

Parking:
UTA Trax drops you off near the SLC Library (on the same square). There is metered parking on the surrounding blocks. Paid underground parking is available below the SLC Library off of 400 South. Look for elevators up to the library square near the red wall in the parking garage.

Food:
SALT Bistro offers contemporary, locally sourced and organic American cuisine. Offering soups, salads, sandwiches, dinner entrees, fresh pastries and full espresso bar. Brunch every Sunday from 10:00am – 3:00pm.

Discounts:
Group discounts available for groups of 15 or more. Visit Salt Lake Connect Pass.

Social:

See Appendix 1 for Downtown Destinations close to this area

What to expect...

The Leonardo's mission is to "inspire creativity and innovation." Combining art, science, and technology you are encouraged to think, create, and collaborate. My children loved the exhibits so much, we spent four hours on our first visit; plan on spending at least two! In my opinion, this museum is best for kids ages seven and older.

The museum changes exhibits regularly and often plays host to special traveling exhibits. I highly recommend looking at the well-maintained website for updated information on current exhibits before your visit. Click "Exhibits" on the home page. While we were there we enjoyed a number of interactive displays. One display we enjoyed was a huge piece of art that went high above our heads and twisted around portions of the gallery. The children were allowed to touch and explore it. There was also an exhibit related to animation that included a green screen; computers with a program that allows you to "paint" with paint brushes on the screen; and still-animation work stations with toys that you use to create moving stories. Every exhibit was engaging and fun. Exhibits change often at The Leonardo, so be aware that the exhibits I mentioned may not be there when you go. Again, I suggest studying the website for current exhibits and activities before going.

The museum offers two exciting work rooms. **Lab at Leo** provides In house artists to assist your budding painters, sculptors, and sketchers. In addition, check the class list on the website (click programs then lab@leo). **The Tinkering Garage** is a space for visitors to create simple machines, learn basic principles of circuits and motors, participate in "cardboard engineering," and much more.

The Leonardo offers a number of special programs, classes, summer camps, and even museum sleepovers. Also, throughout the year there are special events tied to traveling exhibits including art and science workshops, and other fun enriching activities. Stay up-to-date on these special offerings by signing up for the e-newsletter through their website.

Entry to the museum faces the SLC Library (not the street). The Leo Store sells jewelry, clothing, books, art supplies, science kits, home décor and more.

Treehouse Children's Museum

347 22nd Street
Ogden, 84401
(801) 394-9663
www.treehousemuseum.org

Hours:
Monday: 10am-3pm (September-May)
10am-5pm (June-August);

*Tuesday, Wednesday, Thursday & Saturday:*10am-5pm;

Friday: 10am-8pm; See the website for holiday hours.

Admission:
Babies under 1 year: Free; *Ages 1-12:* $6; *Ages 13 and up*: $5.

Membership:
Prices range from $50-$100, depending on the number of children in the family.

Parking:
Free parking is available surrounding the museum. There is also parking at the Junction Parking Terrace (enter from Grant Avenue or 23rd Street).

Food:
No food or drink is allowed in the museum.

Discounts:
On Track to Reading on Mondays (September through May) offers reduced admission for children aged 1-5 ($3), and for adults aged 18+ ($1). *Alphabet Soup* on Friday nights from 6-8pm offers reduced admission for children 1-17 years ($3) and adults ($1). Visit the website for a printout coupon of $1 off admission. Entertainment Book.

What to expect...

Ogden's Treehouse Museum is a non-profit organization dedicated to helping families "step into stories." Since 2006 the museum has been located in the beautiful Elizabeth Stewart Treehouse Museum, which provides more than 28,000 sq ft of space for fun, hands-on exhibits and engaging programs.

The Tree – The museum's hallmark attraction is a big tree in the center of the building. At the base, children can crawl through tunnels, sit and read, or begin a climb up a flight of stairs inside the trunk to the second floor. The upper tree includes a safe overlook through branches and leaves.

Learning – Each exhibit features opportunities for imaginative play, as well as deeper level learning. Many exhibits provide dress-ups for active learning through role-playing, as well as more advanced activities, such as matching symbols, locating places, creating stories, and making music or art. Programs provide another layer of learning through interactive stories, the arts, and the humanities.

The Art Garden – Located on the 2nd floor, children may stop in and create an art project under the direction of the encouraging and helpful staff.

Exhibits – Exhibits inlcude: The 1920's Fire Truck with costumes and books, the Big Red Barn where young visitors can "milk" Oreo the cow or collect eggs from the chickens, and the One World Village which includes dress-ups, games and stories from places like China, Mexico, Germany and Mongolia.

At the Pioneer Days Rodeo, children can ride a rocking, hand-carved horse or bull, and at the Pioneer Schoolhouse they can practice their figures, read from a McGuffey Reader, or even be the teacher. To learn more about Utah and our country, visitors can play a game at the Mapping Utah exhibit or at the Great American Map, exhibits featuring giant, informational floor maps. And there's more: the Music Room filled with marimbas and drums, the Oval Office with an exact replica of the President's Resolute Desk, the Days of the Knights area which includes a castle playscape, thrones with dress-ups, a giant chess set, and the Royal Stage.

Treehouse offers a number of regular programs throughout the year. **On Track to Reading**, a reading readiness program for pre-K unsing interactive activities, songs, and art, is offered on Mondays September through May (excluding major holidays.) Alphabet Soup, offered Friday nights, involves the whole family in literacy activities through stories, songs, theater, art, science, and history. **RAMPed Up Art**, offered daily in the museum's Art Garden, explores a variety of art mediums that reflect the art and stories found in children's books.

Children under 18 must be accompanied by an adult. Lockers are available in the lobby for $1. Restrooms are located on both levels including changing tables, child-sized toilets and child-sized sinks. Treehouse does not allow strollers in the Museum. They do make exceptions for sleeping babies, multiple babies or medical conditions.

Annual Events

Treehouse Troupe Plays – Saturday evenings in November, January & March. Kid-friendly plays and fairy tales by professional actors.

Fairy Tale Ball – The evening of the first Saturday in May. Each year features a different fairy tale. Enjoy dancing to a live band, a show in the Treehouse Theater, games and more.

Enchanted Woods – Weekends during the month of October. Kids can come dressed in costume and follow a themed non-scary adventure through the museum.

New Year's Eve Party – Held during the day on New Year's Eve.

Just Around the Corner...

- Birdsong Trail
- Coleman's Motor-VU Drive-In
- Color Me Mine (Ogden)
- FastKart Speedway (Ogden)
- FatCats (Ogden)
- Fort Buenaventura
- Ogden Dinosaur Park and Museum
- Ogden Nature Center
- Ogden Raptors
- Ogden River Parkway
- Ogden's Union Station
- Ott Planetarium
- Peery's Egyptian Theater
- Riverdale Park

Utah Museum of Contemporary Art

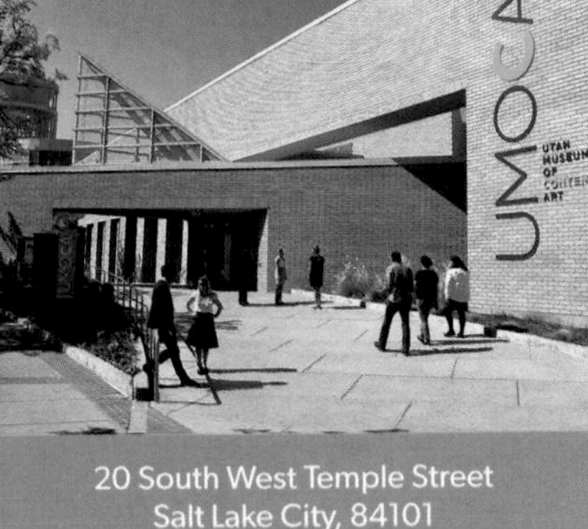

20 South West Temple Street
Salt Lake City, 84101
(801) 328-4201
www.utahmoca.org

Hours:
Tues-Thurs & Sat: 11am-6pm; *Friday:* 11am-9pm

Admission:
Free for Salt Lake County residents and everyone on Family Art Saturday. New rates are in effect 2014.

Food:
No food or drink allowed in the museum. There are many food options across the street at City Creek.

Parking:
Metered parking is available on West Temple and on 100 South between West Temple and Main Street. Paid parking is available to the public across the street at the Marriott Hotel (free for UMOCA members with validation) or at City Creek (park near Nordstrom). TRAX drops you off half a block away at the Temple Square Station.

What to expect...

The Utah Museum of Contemporary Art, known as UMOCA (pronounced "you-mocha") displays multiple rotating exhibits throughout the year in four gallery spaces. Nothing in the museum is permanent, so each exhibit is displayed for a short period of time. While we were there we observed a kid-friendly exhibit called "Mr. Winkle." The display included photographs of an adorable little dog in interesting poses and costumes. We also enjoyed examining a display of a tower-like wall of hundreds of books piled high, representing how obsolete books have become in our time.

The best way for young children to experience the museum is to attend the museum's **Family Art Saturday**. On the second Saturday of each month from 2-4pm families may visit UMOCA and participate in a craft related to one of the exhibits. The activity is always something interesting, fun and free! I suggest entering the museum and going directly to the craft room to experience the activity. Afterward, take a walk through the exhibits that interest you and your children. See the website for information on current and upcoming exhibits.

Restrooms with changing tables are located on the main floor.

See Appendix 1 for Downtown Destinations close to this area

Utah Museum of Fine Arts

410 Campus Center Drive
SLC, 84112
(801) 581-7332
www.umfa.utah.edu

Hours:
Tuesday, Thursday & Friday: 10am-5pm;
Wednesday: 10am-8pm
Saturday & Sunday: 11am-5pm
Closed Mondays
Every third Saturday of the month the hours are 1-4pm.

Admission:
FREE!

Parking:
Free parking in lot east of the museum building.

Food:
No food or drink is allowed in the museum. There is a museum café.

Discounts:
Visit Salt Lake Connect Pass. Entertainment Book.

What to expect...

Boring Saturday afternoons can be transformed with a fun trip to the monthly art activity at the Utah Museum of Fine Arts. Every third Saturday of the month, families with children are allowed free entrance into the museum (does not include special exhibits). No registration is required. Let the worker at the front desk know you are there for the free activity, and you will receive a special treasure hunt map that will lead you to three different works of art in the museum. The selected artwork relates to the specific art activity being offered that day and will help give kids inspiration for their own creation. After you have explored the galleries, you can head to the Education Center where the hands-on fun begins.

There is no formal instruction period, just walk in and a staff member will give you the supplies that you need and instructions on what to do. The large art room is filled with tables holding all the necessary art supplies to create the project. Most of the activities are easy enough for kids ages three and up. Some may be a little more difficult and require an adult's help. We made clothespin puppets the day we went. The studio was full of families, but turnover is quick, so you shouldn't have to wait.

Check out **Learning Backpacks** for free at the front desk. The themed backpacks have games and activities that make it fun for children to explore the different exhibits. Restrooms are near the art room. No changing tables are available.

Other museum experiences featured in this book:

- Fort Buenaventura
- Fort Douglas Military Museum
- Heber Airport Museum
- Park City Museum
- Temple Square
- This Is The Place Heritage Park
- Utah Olympic Park Museums
- Utah State Capitol

Just Around the Corner...

- Color Me Mine (SLC)
- Fort Douglas Military Museum
- Gilgal Sculpture Garden
- Liberty Park
- Natural History Museum of Utah
- Red Butte Garden
- The King's English
- This is the Place Heritage Park
- Tracy Aviary
- Utah Museum of Fine Art
- Utah's Hogle Zoo

Utah Pioneer Museum

300 N Main Street
Sal Lake City, 84103
(801) 532-6479
www.dupinternational.org

Hours:
Monday-Saturday: 9am-5pm (Wednesdays until 8pm)
Closed Sundays

Admission:
FREE!

Parking:
There is a small, free parking lot on the north side (back) of the museum.

Food:
No food or drink is allowed in the museum.

What to expect...

The Utah Pioneer Museum houses an enormous collection of pioneer era artifacts. Many items were carried across the plains with Mormon pioneers and paint a fascinating picture of what life was like in that time.

There are three floors in the building and an attached carriage house with two floors. The three floors of the main building contain items like furniture, pianos, pocket watches, china, dental equipment, tools, kitchen utensils, wedding dresses, and much more. There are dozens of glass display cases on each floor, as well as small themed rooms decorated as they would have been in the 1800s. My kids' favorite themed rooms were: the small school room display with slates and small school desks, the general store display, and the children's toy display. My four-year-old daughter's favorite display was the "Doll Room." It contains glass cases full of dozens of dolls, some dating back to the early 1800s.

The Carriage House is accessed through the basement of the main building. The displays focus on large outdoor items like an original pioneer wagon, carriages, handcarts, bathtubs, an early washing machine, an early Salt Lake City street car, and a beautifully restored fire truck from the early 1800s.

This is not a "hands-on" museum for kids. However, it is very kid-friendly in that everything is behind protective glass, so there is nothing children can damage.

I would highly recommend printing off the **scavenger hunt game** for kids that you can find on their website (Click "Education" then "School Tours") which was really what made it fun for my kids. My older boys scurried around trying to see who could find the specified objects first, like a baby carriage, pioneer croquet game, a wooden leg, and a pioneer camera. I would plan on an hour to an hour and a half.

There is an elevator available. The lobby houses a small gift shop and snack shelf with candy bars and small cookie packages. The volunteer staff is friendly and helpful. Cameras and video cameras are not allowed.

Animal Attracttions

Children have a natural curiosity and interest in animals. They love any opportunity to observe them up close. This chapter shares some of the great animal destinations along the Wasatch Front. Each of these places is open year-round and allows children to see unique animals outside of their everyday world. They are more crowded in the summer, but the animals tend to be more active and visible in the winter.

There are other locations in the book that also include animal attractions, so be sure to search the list at the end of the chapter for other ideas.

Hogle Zoo Courtesy of Brittany Bezanson

Farm Country at Thanksgiving Point

3003 North Thanksgiving Way
Lehi, 84043
(801) 768-2300
www.thanksgivingpoint.org

Hours:
Monday-Saturday: 10am-8pm;
April-October: 10am-5pm
Closed (November-March): Sundays, Thanksgiving, Christmas and New Years Day

Admission:
Monday-Thursday: Under 3: Free; *Age 3 -12:*$4; *Age* 13+:$6
Friday-Saturday: Under 3: Free; *Age 3 -12:*$5; *Age* 13+:$7
Admission includes entrance, a wagon ride, and a pony ride (only for ages 3-12).

Membership:
$175 per family or two grandparents and their grandchildren. Allows entrance to ALL Thanksgiving Point venues, 50% off for guests, and more.

Parking:
Free parking lot.

Food:
Visitor's Center gift shop sells drinks, snacks, and treats.

Discounts:
1-Day and 2-Day Flex passes allow unlimited entrance to Farm Country, Museum of Ancient Life, and the Gardens.

What to expect...

Farm Country at Thanksgiving Point is a real, working farm. It is a great place to get an up-close and personal experience with farm animals!

The Visitor's Center sells snacks, drinks, and farm-themed toys and offers enjoyable interactive displays.

The Farm can be accessed through the back door of the Visitor's Center. See jersey cows, pigs, goats, turkeys, donkeys, horses, sheep, llamas, bunnies, and chickens. Visit all of the animals at your own pace, feeding and petting as you go. Bring quarters for animal feed machines. Admission includes one pony ride for kids and one wagon ride per person.

Visitors may milk a cow every day at no additional charge. Milking starts at 5pm in the summer and 4pm in the winter. Everyone who would like is allowed a turn! Family Night on the Farm is on Monday nights for an additional fee. These nights offer visits with the animals, crafts, games, and more.

Restrooms with a changing table as well as a hand-washing station are located inside the Visitor's Center.

Annual Events

Lamb & Wool Festival – April. Participate in games, entertainment and activities.

Baby Animal Birthday Celebration – May. Meet the Spring babies on the farm.

Dairy Days – June. For $5 participate in milk-related activities.

Pig-n-Pork Day – August. Food, games, crafts, and activities related to pigs.

Barnyard Boo – October. Non-scary Halloween crafts, games and stories.

Youth Education Classes – All summer, see website for list of classes.

Just Around the Corner...

- Cabela's
- Children's Discovery Garden at Thanksgiving Point
- Hangtime Extreme Trampolines (Lehi)
- Highland Town Center Splash Pad
- Holdman Studios
- Museum of Ancient Life
- Seven Peaks Fun Center (Lehi)
- Thanksgiving Point Gardens

Tracy Aviary

589 East 1300 South
Salt Lake City, 84105
(801) 596-8500
www.tracyaviary.org

Hours:
Daily: 9am-5pm;
Closed: Thanksgiving and Christmas; Open late on Mondays during the summer months.

Admission:
Under 3: Free; *Ages 3-12:* $5; *Adults:* $7; Students, seniors, and military: $6

Membership:
$60 for a family of two adults and two children. $100 for a family of two adults and up to six children. Membership reciprocates with other sites in and out of Utah.

Parking:
Free parking lot.

Food:
The gift shop sells snacks, ice cream, and drinks. Outside food is permitted. Enjoy a lunch on one of the many picnic tables. Do not feed the ducks or other birds in the Aviary.

Discounts:
Military and group discounts available. See website for other deals such as Winter Wednesdays for $1. Pass of All Passes. Visit Salt Lake Connect Pass. Entertainment Book.

What to expect. . .

See Appendix 1 for Downtown Destinations close to this area

Tracy Aviary displays a large variety of birds in a friendly setting. These exhibits allow you to see unique birds such as the Bald Eagle, American White Pelicans, Chilean Flamingos and Great Grey Owls.

Exhibits include things like the Rare Bird Exhibit, Owl Forest, the South American Pavilion, Destination Argentina, Birds of Prey of the Americas, and the Kennecott Wetland Immersion Experience. The Owl Forest also provides a climbing structure for children to see the birds from a different view. If you are interested in feeding the birds, there is duck food available in the gift shop as well as in quarter machines throughout Tracy Aviary for feeding waterfowl (ducks, swans, etc.). Please do not feed any birds anything other than this special food. You may also feed the Sun Conures in an interactive exhibit for $3 per person ($2 each for members).

Children's Discovery Garden is located near the Backyard Birds Exhibit. It includes a play area for young children with a large sandbox and plenty of bird-themed photo opportunities.

Daily activities offer a more intimate experiece. They include Keeper Talks and Bird Shows or Free-flight Encounters. Pelican Encounters and Amazon Adventures each cost an additional $3 ($2 for members). These are more intimate and hands-on experiences with the birds

Location & Entry – Tracy Aviary is located in the southwest corner of Liberty Park and is best accessed through the north park entrance on 900 South and 600 East. The entrance fee is paid inside the gift shop, which sells a variety of snacks, gifts, fair trade items, and products made by local artists.

Family restrooms with changing tables are located just inside the Aviary at the Visitors Center. Wagons can be rented for $3. Tracy Aviary seasonally offers Book & Bird, a story time where children get to meet the bird highlighted in a book. See the website under "upcoming events."

Annual Events

Breakfast with the Birds – Annual fundraiser, held every summer. Families welcome.

Halloween Hoot – Saturdays in October and Halloween day. Meet birds up close, do some crafts, and participate in story time. Come in costume for 50% off. See website for details

Utah's Hogle Zoo

2600 East Sunnyside Avenue
Salt Lake City, 84108
(801) 582-1631
www.hoglezoo.org

Hours:
Open Daily; *March 1 - October 31:* 9am-5pm;
November 1 - February 28: 9am-4pm;
Closed: Christmas and New Year's Day.

Admission:
Under 3: Free; *Age 3-12:* $9.75; *Age 13-64:* $12.75;
Age 65+: $9.75; All credit cards accepted

Membership:
$79 for two named adults and their children under 18 (or grandchildren). Other memberships available. Zoo membership offers reciprocity with other nationwide zoos and aquariums. See the website for a list of locations.

Parking:
Free parking lot.

Food:
You may bring your own food and drink and picnic. The zoo also has multiple concession areas with kid-friendly options.

Discounts:
On the website, click "Your Zoo Visit" and "Discount Coupons" for current deals. Discounted group rates are also available for groups of 20 or more. Visit Salt Lake Connect Pass.

What to expect...

Utah's Hogle Zoo is one of Salt Lake City's most popular destinations. Hundreds of animals from many parts of the world call Hogle Zoo home, including African elephants, Amur tigers, giraffes, primates, and animals native to Utah such as Mountain King snake, river otters, bald eagles and more. A few special exhibits include:

Rocky Shores – This features a polar bear, grizzly bears, sea lions, harbor seals, sea otters, and bald eagles.

Asian Highlands – This exhibit features five endangered Asian cat species living in a recreated Himalayan village.

Elephant Encounter – This exhibit features African elephants and two white rhinoceros.

World of Flight Bird Show – This is a 30-minute show featuring trained birds of all sizes. (May-Sept.)

African Savanna – A new African savanna featuring giraffes, zebras, African lions, ostriches and more will open in the spring of 2014. The train ride will re-open offering up close views of the animals as you ride around the savanna. Watch for this exciting new area of the zoo to develop.

Other attractions include a **large spinning granite globe fountain** just inside the entrance that children can touch, a large elephant sculpture near the elephant exhibit that spouts water from hs trunk, and the **Conservation Carousel**, which costs $2 per person. Enjoy the new **Lighthouse Point Splash Zone** located near the entry to Rocky Shores. Ride the curly slide inside the lighthouse or frolic in the splash area — watch out for the blow hole!

Water mists spray visitors on hot days in various locations in the park. The large gift shop sells plenty of zoo merchandise, sunscreen, and batteries. Strollers and wagons can be rented (for $6-$8). Restrooms with diaper-changing tables are located throughout the zoo. A mother's room in the restroom near the entrance of the zoo provides a private place for nursing.

Annual Events

Popular Annual Events (see website for more)

Party for the Planet: An annual party to celebrate Earth Day in April.

Enrichment Day: This mid-Summer event allows zoo visitors to get up-close and personal with the animals and their zookeepers.

Boo at the Zoo: Safely Trick-or-Treat across the Zoo for Halloween. Free with paid admission.

Zoo Lights: November 30 – December 31, starting at 5:30pm until 8:00, open until 9 Thursday - Saturday. Fees apply. Enjoy over 200 animated light displays along with nightly entertainment, live reindeer, and Santa's station presented by Macy's. Pick up a deep fried s'more and warm up in the all new Beastro.

Just Around the Corner...

- Color Me Mine (SLC)
- Fort Douglas Military Museum
- Gilgal Sculpture Garden
- Liberty Park
- Natural History Museum of Utah
- Red Butte Garden
- The King's English
- This Is The Place Heritage Park
- Tracy Aviary
- Utah Museum of Fine Art

Local Pet Stores

Other locations with animal attractions in this book:

- Antelope Island
- Bean Life Science Museum
- Cabela's
- Cold Springs Trout Farm
- Heber Artisan Cheese
- Lagoon
- Ogden Nature Center
- Scheels
- This is the Place Heritage Park
- Wheeler Historic Farm

What to expect...

Pet Stores are great places for kids to see and enjoy animals. Most pet shops sell birds, fish, reptiles and rodents, as well as more unique animals. The animals are on display throughout the store in cages and aquariums. At Petsmart, you can even adopt cats and dogs from the Humane Society or bring an animal home for a trial weekend. Your child will love this quick, local trip to the pet store. (So much that they'll probably beg you to bring something home!) Find a store to visit in your neighborhood. Below some of the local places to check out:

Animal Ark
33 West Center Street, Orem, 84057

Jay's Jungle Pet & Supply Store
272 West Center Street, Provo, 84601

Living Safari
6540 South State Street, Murray 84107 or
8695 South Highland Drive, Sandy, 84093

Mark's Ark
4875 South Redwood Road, Taylorsville, 84123

Petco
Over a dozen stores along the Wasatch Front.
Find the location nearest you at www.petco.com.

Pet Planet
11968 South Redwood Road, Riverton, 84065

Pets & Such
3680 West 3500 South, West Valley City, 84120

PetSmart
A dozen stores along the Wasatch Front. Find the location nearest you at www.petsmart.com

Pet Village & Bird World
3649 South Highway 89, Bountiful, 84010

Go One Step Further

The Loveland Living Planet Aquarium Did you know that you can see sharks, jelly fish, sea otters, and penguins in Utah? Visit The Living Planet Aquarium! This exciting animal attraction is in the process of moving to a larger location in Draper. Please see the aquarium's website for updated information: www.thelivingplanet.com.

Historic Sites

Here in Utah, our historic sites are only about 150 years old, usually dating back to the 1800s during the time Salt Lake was settled by the Mormon pioneers. The great thing about our century old historic sites is that they have been well-preserved and contain many original characteristics and artifacts. Some of the sites have been repurposed, but maintain some portion of their historic significance.

Fort Buenaventura Courtesy of Emily Smith Robbins

Site 25

Cathedral of the Madeleine

331 East South Temple
Salt Lake City, 84111
(801) 328-8941
www.utcotm.org

Visiting Hours:
Monday-Friday: 7:30am-8:30pm;
Saturday-Sunday: 7:30am-7:30pm

Tours are offered but must be scheduled 4-6 weeks in advance.

Admission:
FREE!

Parking:
There is free street parking or you can drive up the hill behind the cathedral to their free parking lot.

Food:
No outside food or drink is allowed.

What to expect...

Who needs to go to Europe to tour beautiful historic cathedrals when we have one in downtown Salt Lake City? The Cathedral of the Madeleine was constructed in the early 1900s and is on the National Register of Historic Places. It is impressive from the outside with tall sandstone towers and sculpted gargoyles, but even more so from the inside.

The interior décor was inspired by gothic art of the middle ages. The dramatic high ceiling pulls your eyes up toward the beautiful arches and murals overhead. Dark wood paneling on the walls is offset by the ornate coloration of the columns and murals. The wonderful acoustics of the church intensify and cause the dramatic sounds of the organ to resonate. If you are lucky, someone may be practicing the organ while you are there. The spectacular stained glass windows were made in Germany and installed during the original construction of the Cathedral. The windows depict key events in the life of Christ, from the Annunciation to the Coronation of Mary. The circular transept stained glass windows are magnificent.

You can schedule a tour or wander freely throughout the cathedral when Mass is not in session. Taking pictures is allowed when Mass is not is session. See their website for daily Mass hours.

Restrooms without changing tables are located in the basement.

Fort Buenaventura

2450 A Avenue
Ogden, 84401
(801) 399-8099 or 399-8491
www.co.weber.ut.us/parks/forb/

Hours:
Daily from 9am to dusk.
The office for canoe rental is open from 8am-8pm

Admission:
$1 paid at the visitor center.

Canoe Rental:
$3 for half hour or $5 for an hour per canoe.

Parking:
Free parking lot.

Food:
Outside food and drink permitted. There are many picnic tables to use.

What to expect...

Utah history tells the story of "Mountain Men," tough guys like Jim Bridger. Fort Buenaventura keeps that story alive. Now a county park, the property once belonged to one of the earliest Mountain Men named Miles Goodyear. A replica fort has been built in the exact location of the original, which was used as a trading post in the 1840's. Some Saturdays there is a small trading post store open which sells all kinds of goods relating to the 1800s.

The central feature of the park is a large pond. The Weber River runs alongside the park. Activities involving the pond are the highlight of the park, in my opinion. Canoes are available for very reasonable rental, which also includes lifejackets. The pond is stocked with fish so you are sure to catch something. Kids ages 11 and under don't need a fishing license. Bring your own fishing poles.

A small visitor center houses a Mountain Man museum with artifacts from the 1800s like old metal animal traps, hunting knives, a beaver skin top hat, and a handmade buffalo hide coat.

Under the canopy of huge cottonwood trees, the park offers picnic tables, walking and biking trails, and camping. There are several large Tee-pees that can be rented for overnight camping, though not for the faint of heart! Most trails are paved and stroller friendly. There is a playground area with a climbing structure and slides. Restrooms are located in three different areas of the park. A ranger takes care of the park and is available to help with any questions.

Special Events:

Easter Rendezvous takes place annually every Easter weekend. The park turns into a re-creation of the fur trading era with trappers, American Indians, and mountain men. Events include Dutch oven cooking contests, canoe races, rifle shooting, a frying pan toss, and kids' games. Periodic clothing encouraged.

The Ogden Music Festival is held each year in June. Planned and promoted by the Ogden Friends of Acoustic Music, the festival features nationally known top-quality musicians on an outdoor state. Many activities are available for the kids. Visit www.ofoam.org for more information.

Just Around the Corner...

- Birdsong Trail
- Color Me Mine (Ogden)
- Colman's Motor-VU Drive-In
- FastKart Speedway (Ogden)
- FatCats (Ogden)
- Ogden Dinosaur Park and Museum
- Ogden Nature Center
- Ogden Raptors
- Ogden River Parkway
- Ogden's Union Station
- Ott Planetarium
- Peery's Egyptian Theater
- Riverdale Park
- Treehouse Children's Museum

Fort Douglas Military Museum

32 Potter Street (U of U campus)
Fort Douglas, 84113
(801)-581-1251
www.fortdouglas.org

Hours:
Tuesday-Saturday: Noon-5pm. *Closed:* Thanksgiving and Christmas.

Admission:
FREE! Donations are welcome.

Parking:
Free parking directly in front of the museum.

Food:
No food or drink is allowed.

What to expect...

The Fort Douglas Military Museum chronicles Utah's military history from the time it was established through all of the major world wars and even conflicts of today. Camp Douglas was first established in 1862 as a civil war post to help insure the delivery of overland mail and telegraphs from Indian attack. A few years later, after more permanent structures had been erected, it was renamed Fort Douglas. From that time, it remained an active military post until 1967.

The museum is housed in two of the old sandstone barracks built in 1875. It has been beautifully renovated and expanded to include galleries of all major wars of this century. The exhibits include many artifacts directly related to Fort Douglas throughout its long history such as uniforms, helmets, weaponry, medicine bottles, coinage, war medals, and much more. There are some hands-on displays that kids will enjoy, as well as wonderful life-sized mannequin displays.

Outside the museum is a grassy shady area called Cannon Park. There, you will see a number of cannons and other large artillery machines. Probably the most impressive outdoor display is the line of real life tanks and helicopters located behind the museum. Although climbing on the vehicles is not allowed, it is exciting to get such a close look.

This is not a large museum, which actually makes it perfect for young children. We spent about 30 minutes there, though I could have spent much more time. Tours are free, but must be scheduled one week in advance. Restrooms without changing tables are available.

Just Around the Corner...

- Color Me Mine (SLC)
- Gilgal Sculpture Garden
- Liberty Park
- Natural History Museum of Utah
- Red Butte Garden
- The King's English
- This is the Place Heritage Park
- Tracy Aviary
- Utah Museum of Fine Art
- Utah's Hogle Zoo

Gardner Village

1100 West 7800 South
West Jordan, 84088
(801) 566-8903
www.gardnervillage.com

Hours:

January-March *Monday-Thursday:* 10am-6pm; Friday-*Saturday*: 10am-8pm

April-December *Monday-Saturday:* 10am-8pm; Closed Sundays. See website for holiday hours.

Admission:

FREE!

Parking:

Free parking lot. Sometimes large events require parking attendants. In this case, parking fees apply.

Food:

Archibald's Restaurant and Naborhood Bakery serve meals. Taste Culinary Boutique offers snacks and drinks.

What to expect...

Gardner Village is a one-of-a-kind shopping experience, offering 22 boutiques and specialty shops in a quaint setting. Shops sell items including, home décor, quilting goods, holiday decorations, furniture, art, dolls, clothing, toys, kitchen items, as well as baby and children's clothing and gifts.

The signature building at the front of Gardner Village is an old flour mill, originally built by Utah pioneer, Archibald Gardner. The mill has been turned into Archibald's Restaurant and Country Furniture & Gifts. Other historic buildings were later brought in to serve as boutique style shops. Shopping here is like walking through an old Utah village with winding brick pathways, antique pioneer fixtures, beautiful landscaping, and a picturesque pond yet with the latest trends and styles.

I specifically recommend three stores that appeal to children. Storybook Nook sells games, classic toys, and books. Sweet Afton's is a specialty candy shop that sells a large variety of candy including homemade fudge, taffy, jellybeans, licorice, homemade lollypops, old-fashioned candy bars and drinks. Georgell Doll Shop features all kinds of dolls and doll accessories. Other stores of interest include Sassy Babies and Spoiled Rotten Children's Boutique. Restrooms with changing tables are located near Celebrations by Modern Display.

Annual Events...

Easter Brunch – Buffet served on Easter Sunday for the whole family. Fees apply.

Wasatch Front Farmer's Market – Every Saturday from June-October. Live music, a farm-fresh breakfast, 90+ farmers selling fresh produce, art, an animal train, and more.

Breakfast with a Witch – August-October. Children can come dressed up for a buffet breakfast with a witch. Whimsical witches mingle and take photos.

Witchapalooza Music Dinner Theater – August through the end of October. A unique Halloween-themed music dinner show. Buy tickets in advance. Best for children 8 and older.

Witch Displays – Mid-September through the end of October. Bring children in costume for great photo opportunities and to do a witch scavenger hunt. Print your hunt online before you come.

North Pole Elf Displays – Mid-November-December. Go on an elf scavenger hunt.

Just Around the Corner...

- Accessible Playground at Veteran's Memorial Park
- Classic Fun Center (SLC)
- Gale Center of History and Culture
- Gene Fullmer Recreation Center
- Georgell Doll Shop
- Jump 'N Bounce
- South Jordan Recreation Center
- Tiny Tim's Foundation for Kids
- (West Jordan) Conservation Garden Park
- Wild West Jordan Playground at Veteran's Memorial Park

Temple Square

15 East South Temple
Salt Lake City, 84150
(801) 240-4872
www.visittemplesquare.com

Hours:
9am-9pm daily

Admission:
FREE!

Parking:
Paid parking is available under *City Creek Center* and under the *Conference Center*, though these options can be expensive. There is metered street parking all around *Temple Square* and free street parking north of Temple Square if you are willing to walk a few blocks. One fun suggestion would be to take *TRAX*. It lets you off right next to Temple Square and the ride itself is an adventure for kids. Check the TRAX website for time schedules.

Food:
There are many food options across the street at City Creek or The Nauvoo Café, The Garden restaurant, and The Lion House, which are all located on Temple Square.

What to expect...

Historic Temple Square is located in the heart of downtown Salt Lake City. It spans 35 acres and is the world headquarters for the Church of Jesus Christ of Latter-day Saints. There are so many things to see and experience at Temple Square. Adults could easily spend 3-4 hours and not do or see everything there is to experience. However, young children may fizzle out after a couple of hours. With that in mind, here are a few tips and ideas for a fun trip to Temple Square with young children.

Children are welcome at Temple Square. Every tour is stroller friendly with the exception of the Beehive House. There are bathrooms with changing tables in practically every building. Tours of Temple Square are offered every 10 minutes starting at the flagpole. You can also just wander freely about the beautiful grounds and enjoy them at your leisure.

The central feature of Temple Square is the beautiful **Temple**, completed in 1893 by early Mormon pioneers. The temple was an amazing architectural achievement for its time, and continues to inspire awe at the magnitude of the building project accomplished by a people with very few resources over a period of 40 years. Although there are well over one hundred LDS temples worldwide, the Salt Lake Temple has become an iconic, international symbol for the church because of its distinct architecture and unique history. The temple can only be entered by faithful members of the Mormon church, therefore, it is the only building on temple square that cannot be toured inside. A large model of the Salt Lake Temple is available to visitors in the South Visitor's Center, showing the beautiful interior of the entire building.

North and South Visitor Centers: The exhibits in these two different buildings can be enjoyed at your own pace or guided. The model of the temple in the South Visitor center is a favorite of kids, as well as the 15 minute guided tour of "God's Plan" in the North Visitor Center.

Legacy Theater: Every hour and a half a movie called *Joseph Smith the Prophet of the Restoration* is played in the Joseph Smith Memorial Building on an enormous screen. This might be most appropriate for children age 6 and older as there are some very dramatic real events portrayed.

Reflection Pool: The reflection pool, found in the middle of Temple Square, is a favorite stopping spot for young children and features an infinity pool that little hands can splash in. The gardens surrounding the pool and all over the rest of Temple Square add to the beautiful serenity of the grounds.

The Beehive House: The Beehive House was once home to the Mormon prophet Brigham Young. It was built in 1853 and has been restored and decorated to appear as it would have during Brigham Young's time. The tour includes views of completely furnished and decorated period rooms like a kitchen, a

bedroom, a playroom, a gathering room, and a family store. Strollers cannot be used on the tour because of the many staircases in the house. Tours run every ten minutes from 9:30am-8:30pm Monday-Saturday and last about 30 minutes.

Dining: There are several dining options on Temple Square. The Roof and the Garden restaurants are located on the top floor of the Joseph Smith Memorial Building with spectacular views of Temple Square and Downtown Salt Lake City. On the ground floor of the same building is the Nauvoo Café, which offers sandwiches, soup, and salads. The most kid-friendly choice would probably be The Lion House Pantry, located next to the Beehive House. It offers a cafeteria line style service with several delicious menu choices including á la cart items.

Carriage Rides: Outside the walls of Temple Square on South Temple, you can hire a carriage driver to give you a tour through some of the downtown Salt Lake City streets. Carriage rides are offered 6 days a week, Monday through Saturday, from 6-11pm. During the summer season, carriage rides are also available on Saturdays from10am-4pm. Rides last 30-60 minutes and range in price from $40-$80. Carriages can seat 4 adults and 2 small children.

See Appendix 1 for Downtown Destinations close to this area

Other historic related activities in this book:

- Gilgal Garden
- The Gale Center of History and Culture
- Heber Airport
- Hill Aerospace Museum
- Memory Grove Park
- Mormon Tabernacle Choir
- Ogden Union Station
- Park City Museum
- Peery's Egyptian Theater Tour
- Provo City Library
- Temple Quarry Trail

This is the Place Heritage Park

2601 East Sunnyside Avenue
Salt Lake City, 84108
(801) 582-1847
www.thisistheplace.org

Hours:
Monday-Saturday: 9am-5pm;
Sunday: 10am-5pm

Admission:
Admission is seasonal. Check the website for pricing.

Parking:
Free parking lot.

Food:
Outside food and drink is permitted. The Huntsman Hotel houses a café and an ice cream parlor.

Discounts:
Visit Salt Lake Connect Pass. Entertainment Book.

What to expect...

This is the Place Heritage Park gives visitors the chance to take a step back in time to see what life was like for early Utah pioneers. Many historic log homes from around the state have been relocated to the park and many of the buildings and shops have been recreated to appear as they would have in their day. The homes and structures are placed along small dirt streets, recreating what a pioneer village might have been like. Visitors can wander freely through the park, stopping at the various cabins and shops for a demonstration or brief activity. New attractions are constantly being added to the park, so even if you have come before, there is probably something new you haven't seen.

In the **School House**, children can sit in the old desks, use a slate board and chalk, and learn about how pioneer children were educated and some of the punishments they endured for misbehaving. At the **Shaving Parlor**, not only will the barber give kids an old fashioned shave, he'll pull a tooth too, since he is also the village dentist! At the **Gardiner Cabin**, kids can try washing clothes on a wash board, plowing in the garden, or try their hand at hoop rolling. The **Petting Corral** gives kids the chance to get close enough to touch farm animals and even take a pony ride. **Panning for Gold** happens on the far east side of the park where kids are given a pan to sift for gold out of a steam. They can then trade their gold pieces for candy at **The Bank**. The **Tithing Office building** offers pioneer crafts like making a simple pioneer doll or arrowhead necklace. There are many other shops to visit like the hat shop, the blacksmith, the leather shop, and the printing shop. Sometimes there is someone out in front of the school teaching kids to play and participate in **pioneer games** like potato sack racing and tug of war.

There is a **large train** that makes a circuit around the park stopping along the way where you can be dropped off or picked up. Ask what time the train robbery will take place so you can be there to watch. Up the hill, kids can ride the **mini train**, which goes along a little track around a pond. There is also a really fun **playground** with miniature size cabins and houses. **Brother Brigham's Donuts** is found in the social hall. You can watch as homemade donuts are made and then purchase some if you want. The small donuts are a favorite treat for my kids. A new feature at the park is a splash pad where kids can cool off.

Included in the price of regular admission are **three activities of your choice** of the following: a pony ride, making a pioneer craft, and a ride on the miniature train. You could do all three, or take three pony rides, three train rides, etc.

My biggest piece of advice for the best experience is to visit during the summer session, called Heritage Season, when all of the various village cabins are open. There are a lot of fun events year round that are definitely worth the trip, but the most typical attractions and sites are only all open during the summer. I would also suggest getting there as early as possible because hot summer afternoons take away from the fun of the park. You might want to look at the virtual map tour before coming so you can get a general idea of the layout of the park.

Spring is called **Baby Animal Season**, when you can see all the new baby animals born on the farm. Here are some of the other annual events that happen at the park. Find detailed descriptions of each event on the website.

Annual Events

October: Haunted village & Little Haunts.

December: Candlelight Christmas

June: Mountain Man Living History Camp

July: Pioneer Days and Liberty Days

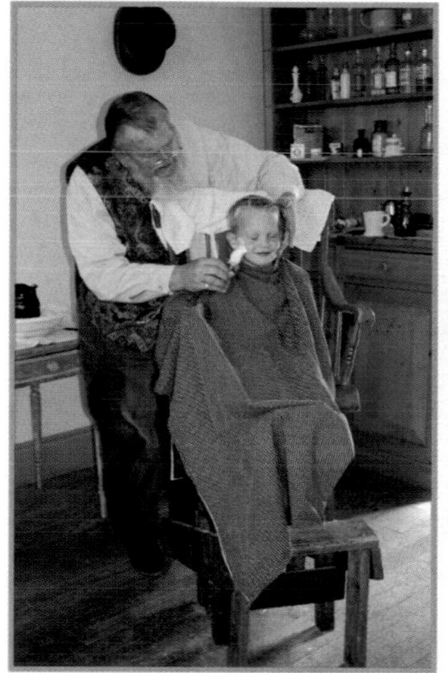

Just Around the Corner...

- Color Me Mine (SLC)
- Fort Douglas Military Museum
- Gilgal Sculpture Garden
- Liberty Park
- Natural History Museum of Utah
- Red Butte Garden
- The King's English
- Tracy Aviary
- Utah Museum of Fine Art
- Utah's Hogle Zoo

Utah State Capitol

350 North State Street
Salt Lake City, 84114
(801) 538-1800
www.utahstatecapitol.utah.gov

Hours:
Monday-Friday: 7am-8pm;
Saturday, Sunday & holidays: 8am-6pm

Guided Tour Hours:
Monday-Friday: 9am-4pm with tours given on the hour.

Admission:
FREE!

Parking:
Free visitor parking is available on the east side of the capitol building.

Food:
Outside food and drink is allowed.

What to expect...

The Utah State Capitol sits prominently on Capitol Hill overlooking downtown Salt Lake. Almost 100 years old, it has been the home of Utah government since 1916.

The actual building itself is what will be most impressive to young children. The gorgeous architecture, marble staircases, columns, and large murals all feel very grand. You can explore the Capitol Building in one of two ways, with either a guided or self-guided tour.

Guided tours are offered Monday-Friday. The tour usually lasts 45 minutes to an hour. Walk-in guests are welcome, but groups of 10 or more must make a reservation.

Self-guided tours can be taken at anytime during the hours that the Capitol Building is open. This is what I would recommend for those visiting with young children. Kids are interested in looking at most things, but may not have the attention span for the hour-long tour. The State Capitol website provides a really fun **bingo game** that has pictures of architectural details, symbols, and art found throughout the building for children to find. My kids really got into this activity. It was a very fun way for them to explore the building. Print this game off at home before coming because it is not available at the capitol. Click on "Plan a Visit" and then click "Children's Activities" and then click "Games" and you will find it. You can find games, quizzes, word searches, coloring pages, stories, and worksheets about the Capitol Building and Utah history on the website.

See Appendix 1 for Downtown Destinations close to this area

The State Legislature is not in session during the summer months, so if you would like to visit and get a peek at a session of the Senate or the House, make sure to go sometime from the end of January to the beginning of March. It is also the busiest time.

STATE OF UTAH

Wheeler Historic Farm

6351 South 900 East
Salt Lake City, UT 84121
(385) 468-1755
www.wheelerfarm.com

Hours:
Open dawn till dusk every day;
Office hours are *Monday-Saturday:* 9am-5pm

Admission:
FREE!

Parking:
Free parking lot.

Food:
Outside food and drink is permitted. There are picnic tables located throughout the farm and lots of grassy areas to spread out a blanket.

What to expect...

Wheeler Farm is a 19th century farm homestead that is listed on the National Register of Historic Places. Once privately owned, this working farm is now run by the City and County of Salt Lake and offers farm-related activities. Once in the parking lot, there is no clear entrance. Walk towards the big barn and you will see the main entrance behind it.

Wheeler farm has a collection of **animals** used for agricultural purposes. It is not a petting zoo, but kids will still get a close-up look at horses, cows, sheep, pigs, chickens, and turkeys. Feeding the animals is not allowed. Ducks are the only exception to that rule.

Wagon Rides, a popular summer activity, are offered every half hour on the hour and cost $2 a person. The wagon is pulled by a large tractor, which takes you through the outer region of the farm and surrounding woodland. Ride tokens are sold at the Activity Barn all year and at the Rosebud Country Store during the warm months. Tokens should be bought at least 15 minutes ahead of time, and can be used at any time during the day. During the winter months, wagon rides are available as weather permits, often closing down entirely for the months of December through February.

Cow Milking Demonstrations take place Monday through Saturday at 5pm. Attendance tokens ($1) can be purchased at the Activity Barn or Rosebud Country Store. It's your chance to give milking a try.

Historic House Tours of the Victorian Farm Home, built in the late 1800s, are offered Monday through Friday at 3pm. The home features over six thousand historic artifacts from the 1890's through the 1940's. The tour lasts about an hour, and costs $4 for adults and $2 for children.

Feeding the ducks and geese is a major highlight of the farm experience. You can purchase a small bag of feed for 50 cents at the Activity Barn or Rosebud Country store.

A creative, tree-house looking **Play Structure** has been added near the parking lot. Plan to play here.

The **Rosebud Country Store** is only open during the warm months (usually March-October, check website). Besides purchasing duck food, milk demonstration tokens, and wagon ride tokens, the store offers penny candy, all kinds of snacks, treats, and drinks.

Restrooms with changing tables are located in the Activity Barn and a couple of other places throughout the farm.

Just Around the Corner...

- Holladay Lions Fitness and Recreation Center
- Jungle Jim's Playland
- Lake Shore Learning
- Mountview Park
- Seven Peaks Fun Center (SLC)

Gardens & Outdoors

Many children today have little contact with the natural world around them. They are spending more and more time indoors, in front of electronics and TV monitors. A recent study found that nearly half of preschoolers in the U.S. don't get outside at least once a day for parent-supervised playtime. Add to that, the statistic that children ages 2-11 watch an average of 30 hours of television a week, and it might inspire you to take a good look at this chapter. It is full of outdoor destinations that you might never have guessed exist in our Utah desert. Lush green gardens, thriving nature centers and unique sculpture gardens are just some of the sites listed.

http://abcnews.go.com/blogs/health/2012/04/03/too-few-kids-getting-outdoors-with-mom-or-dad/

http://blog.nielsen.com/nielsenwire/media_entertainment/tv-viewing-among-kids-at-an-eight-year-high/print/

Great Salt Lake Shorlands Preserve Courtesy of Meilani Smith Kongaika

Antelope Island

4528 West 1700 South
Syracuse, 84075
Entrance Gate: (801)773-2941
Visitor's Center: (801)725-9263
www.stateparks.utah.gov/park/antelope-island-state-park

Hours:
Open daily. See the website for seasonal hours.

Visitor's Center & Fielding Garr Ranch Hours:
April 15-September: 14th 9am-6pm;
September 15- April 14th: 9am-5pm;
Closed: Thanksgiving and Christmas

Admission:
$10 vehicle pass for up to 8 passengers; Checks and cash accepted for self-service check-in. Discover, Visa, MasterCard, checks, and cash accepted if entrance is staffed.

Annual Pass:
$75 for access to all Utah State Parks (pass does not cover the Davis County causeway fee of $3 to enter Antelope Island).

Parking:
Free parking anywhere on the island.

Food:
Picnic tables are available throughout the park for your own food or drinks. Island Buffalo Grill sells hamburgers, fish, hotdogs, and more at a large beach pavilion (indoor and outdoor seating).

What to expect...

Antelope Island is the largest of nine islands in the Great Salt Lake. As one of Utah's State Parks, Antelope Island is one of the best ways to view and experience the lake. After visiting twice, I've come up with several recommendations for enjoying Antelope Island with a young family.

Take Antelope Drive directly west into Syracuse as far as you can go. You will arrive at the State Park entrance. Pay your fee at the fee station, then drive directly onto the island through the causeway. Follow signs to the **Visitor's Center**. The parking area provides great views of the island, the Great Salt Lake, and the Wasatch Mountains across the way. The Visitor's Center itself offers a gift shop and a brief learning experience about the island. Plan to spend about 30 minutes exploring exhibits and watching the 18 minute video about the island.

From the Visitor's Center take a left coming out of the parking lot and drive a short distance to **Bridger Bay Beach**. This is the best location to experience the water of the Great Salt Lake. I do not recommend swimming in the lake with kids. Swarms of gnats sit along the water's edge and there is a foul scent in the air. It is also a long walk down to the water and back. If you and your children decide to walk down to the water, park in the lot next to the Buffalo Grill, and walk down the metal ramp. This makes it much easier to traverse the slope of deep sand. When we were there we talked to two families about their experience swimming. One said that they would never recommend it. The other said it was worthwhile, just to say that you experienced it. The water—several times saltier than ocean water—provides a unique swimming experience. I recommend taking in the views and possibly walking to the water's edge with children 8 and up. The parking area provides bathrooms, free showers, and private, quarter-operated showers for visitors to wash off the sand and salt.

Once you are done at the beach, take a drive back to the front entry and turn to the right (rather than leaving the island) following signs to **Fielding Garr Ranch**. Antelope Island is home to a variety of wildlife including bison, coyotes, antelope, deer, bobcat, and many kinds of birds and waterfowl. The wildlife can be spotted easily from your car on this scenic drive. If you are lucky, you will spot huge herds of bison! Once you reach the ranch, eat lunch or a snack in the grassy, shady picnic area just below the parking lot. When kids are done eating they can wander the little ranch and explore the old artifacts, tools, and buildings. Be sure to visit the island during the ranch's hours of operation. If the ranch is closed, you lose access to a larger portion of the road.

Restrooms with changing tables are located in the Visitor's Center and at Fielding Garr Ranch. Bathrooms can also be found at Bridger Bay Beach. Horseback rides are available on the island through R & G Horse and Wagon. Rides are by reservation only and can be done on the beach or at the ranch. For reservations or more information go to *www.randghorseandwagon.com*.

Antelope Island is known for seasons when gnats swarm. See the website for warnings about the gnat activity. When we were there the gnats were swarming heavily and we made the mistake of opening our car door for a quick picture of some animals, letting them into our car. Yuck! Be aware of these seasons if you plan to swim or hike. Visitors are encouraged to wear long sleeves, pants, hats, and fine mesh head nets for protection during these swarming seasons.

The park hosts multiple special events every month of the year including guided hikes, junior ranger workshops, art exhibits, discussions, star gazing, and more! For information on any special events, go to the website and click on "Events."

Annual Events

Easter Egg Hunt – April. Bridger Bay Beach. Candy, prizes, and kite fliers for kids ages 12 and under. Breakfast with the Easter Bunny at Island Buffalo Grill ($5 per person).

Great Salt Lake Bird Festival – May. Get information at www.greatsaltlakebirdfest.com

Cowboy Legends Cowboy Poetry and Music Gathering – May.

Children's Discovery Garden at Thanksgiving Point

3900 N. Garden Drive
Lehi, 84043
(801) 768-4999
www.thanksgivingpoint.org

Hours: Open April through October
Monday-Saturday: 10am-8pm; *Closed:* Sunday

Admission:
Monday - Thursday: Under 3: Free; *Age 3-12:* $4; *Age 13 and up:* $6; *Senior 65+*: $4
Friday-Saturday: Under 3: Free; *Age 3-12:* $6; *Age 13 and up:* $8; *Senior 65+*: $4

Membership:
$175 per family, or for two grandparents and their grandchildren. This allows entrance to ALL Thanksgiving Point venues, 50% off for guests and more.

Parking:
Free parking in front of the garden entrance.

Food:
Concessions are available or bring a picnic.

Discounts:
1-Day and 2-Day Flex passes allow unlimited entrance to Farm Country, Museum of Ancient Life, and the Gardens.

What to expect...

The Children's Discovery Garden at Thanksgiving Point, a popular spot separate from the larger gardens, is specifically designed for children to experience and enjoy nature. The entry features a large Noah's Ark structure that spouts water where kids can splash and play. Water runs from Memorial Day to Labor Day. I recommend bringing swimming suits and towels. There are a few benches and a grassy area if you want to bring a blanket.

The Garden features a hedgerow maze worthy of Alice in Wonderland, a man-made cave with crawling tunnels for kids to explore, a large koi pond, a waterfall, animal sculptures, interactive learning displays, a large climbing structure, and more.

Nature Explorer Classroom is an area that is even more interactive. Some activities include: a lookout tower; a large sand pit, a small man-made river and pond for floating foam "boats," nature's tic tac toe played with rocks and sticks, "Build and Stack" area with large pieces of wood, and "Jump and Balance," (an area with stumps and logs for play).

Restrooms are located at the front entrance. Benches are placed throughout the garden and everything is stroller friendly. My five- and three-year-olds enjoyed every part of the garden but spent the bulk of their time in the sand pit and floating boats down the river. I suggest bringing your own sand toys for the sand pit.

Just Around the Corner...

- Farm Country at Thanksgiving Point
- Hangtime Extreme Trampolines (Lehi)
- Highland Town Center Splash Pad
- Holdman Studios
- Museum of Ancient Life
- Seven Peaks Fun Center (Lehi)
- Thanksgiving Point Gardens

Cold Springs Trout Farm

2284 Fruitland Drive
Ogden, 84414
(801) 782-7282
www.coldspringstroutfarm.com

Hours:
Summer hours:
Monday-Saturday: 9am-dusk (April 1 - October 31);
Winter hours:
Saturdays: 11am-dusk (November 1 - March 31)

Admission:
There is no entrance fee. You pay for the fish you catch according to the length of the fish. (Ex. An 8-10 inch fish costs $2.50.)

Parking:
Free parking lot.

Food:
Outside food and drink is permitted.

What to expect...

If you are a little squeamish about fish like I am, this is the perfect way to let your kids experience fishing without any of the dirty work. You don't need a fishing license and are guaranteed to catch a trout without the usual long wait. Cold Springs Trout Farm is a family owned and operated business that was started in 1924. The grounds are absolutely beautiful. Three different ponds are available for fishing, with each pond holding different sizes of trout. Cost, is determined by the length of the trout, so you can choose to fish in a pond that fits within your budget.

Simple fishing poles are provided and easy for kids to use. There is no need to bait the hook. A small piece of leather that resembles fish pellets is enough to entice the fish. You can purchase a little cup of fish food pellets for 25 cents.

I'm so queasy I didn't even want to pull the hooks out of the fishes' mouths. Lucky for me, the nice young men working in the cleaning station took the hooks out of the fish's mouths, something they will do for anyone who asks. My kids all caught a fish and desperately wanted to keep fishing.

Once you have caught all you want, take the bucket of fish to the cleaning station to pay for what you caught. For an additional 50 cents a fish, you can have the trout filleted. Restrooms and picnic tables are available on site.

Finding this location is not difficult, but you may think you are going the wrong way as you pass through a residential neighborhood and turn up a driveway that turns into an alley that ends in the parking lot of the Trout Farm.

Just Around the Corner...

- Harrisville City Park
- Toad's Fun Zone

Gilgal Sculpture Garden

749 East 500 South
Salt Lake City, Utah 84102
(801) 972-7800
www.gilgalgarden.org

Hours:
Open daily from 8pm-5pm.

Admission:
FREE!

What to expect...

Gilgal Sculpture Garden is a hidden city park full of unique sculptures and stones. Formerly known as the secret garden of Salt Lake, many people do not know about it because it is tucked away behind businesses and homes. This slightly strange place is not a destination as it only takes about 10 to 15 minutes to walk through. But, if you are in the area on your way to something else, stop in and take a look.

The garden was built by Thomas Battersby Child Jr. over a period of 18 years until his death in 1963. He felt that it was an expression of his religious beliefs through symbolism and art. Gilgal means circle of stones and the garden contains 12 original sculptures and over 70 engraved stones with poems, scriptures and quotes. I suggest taking the "Interactive Tour" on the website before going. Each sculpture is pictured on the tour with a paragraph or two about the meaning behind each one. Some of the more memorable sculptures include a sphinx with the head of Joseph Smith, a large bird house, and the self-portrait of Child wearing brick pants.

See Appendix 1 for Downtown Destinations close to this area

There are no bathrooms on the property. Although the posted hours say that it is open daily from 8am-5pm, sometimes the garden gates are still closed for whatever reason.

The Great Salt Lake Shorelands Preserve

3200 West
Layton, 84041

Hours:
Open daily; *April-September:* 7am-8pm;
October-March: 8am-5pm

Admission:
FREE!

Parking:
Free parking lot. The parking area is inside the gate at the end of the dirt road and near the entry to the walkway.

Food:
There are no obvious places to picnic here. You could bring a snack and sit on one of the benches along the boardwalk.

What to expect...

The Great Salt Lake Shorelands Preserve is a unique place to visit. It is the resting place for thousands of birds as they migrate to and from Central and South America. The land on the Preserve is a system of marshes, mudflats, ponds, pools, and sloughs. A mile-long boardwalk circles over the area to allow you to walk right through this rare ecosystem. On your visit, you can take a nature walk along the boardwalk, visit the beautiful open-air Visitor's Center, read the interpretive and educational signs, and climb the tower for a better view.

Photo by Robert Johnson, Standard-Examiner

Boardwalk – The boardwalk is a 1-mile loop that will take you through the Visitor's Center and all the way around to the Tower. Plan for about 45 minutes to 1 hour to take the loop at a leisurely pace. The boardwalk is suitable for strollers and has educational signs, kiosks, and benches. You can watch for birds and wildlife as you go. We went on a hot afternoon in September and didn't see many birds. Staff who give educational tours indicate that there are more birds in October and April. Mornings and evenings are the best time to visit.

Visitor's Center – This wooden, open-air building is itself a work of art. Take a minute to view its many varied angles. Inside you can read about the birds that visit the Preserve, learn about the ecosystem and about The Nature Conservancy.

Tower – The 30-foot high tower is an open-air structure with stairs that lead up to a look-out deck. Bring binoculars to watch for birds and enjoy the view.

Guided tours and group reservations are available by special request. Call The Nature Conservancy Office at (801) 531-0999 for more information. Restrooms are located at the entrance to the boardwalk near the parking lot. There are no changing tables.

Just Around the Corner...

- Clearfield Aquatic Center
- Get Air Sportsplex
- Krispy Kreme (Layton)
- Legacy Electric Park
- Layton Surf 'n Swim

International Peace Gardens

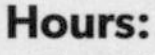

1000 South 900 West
Salt Lake City, 84104
(801) 938-5326
www.internationalpeacegardens.org

Hours:
May - September: Open from dawn to dusk daily.

Admission:
FREE!

Parking:
Free parking near the entrance inside Jordan Park.

Food:
Pavilions and picnic benches are located in Jordan Park, just outside the entrance to the garden.

What to expect...

The International Peace Gardens is a large, gated garden inside Jordan Park. The gardens feature 26 different nations through plants, structures, flags, and monuments. I highly recommend a visit, as great photo opportunities and learning experiences abound. The location of the gardens sometimes feels isolated, so I suggest you bring a friend just to feel completely secure.

Conceived in 1939 and dedicated in 1952 the Peace Gardens were founded as a lesson in peace and understanding between nations. One of the prominent features is a circle of 84 Peace Poles with the repeated statement in multiple languages that states "May Peace Prevail on Earth." These were moved to the gardens from the Olympic Village after the 2002 Winter Olympic Games. Each pole represents every competing nation.

The gardens are full of unique structures. Memorable features include pagodas, a little house, a huge mountain, a bust of Ghandi, small bridges, a miniature Eiffel Tower, a large cross, and more. Benches, flowers, tall trees, and vines line the quiet pathways. The Jordan River Parkway runs along the outer edge of the gardens.

See Appendix 1 for Downtown Destinations close to this area

Jordan Park offers playgrounds, swing sets, pavilions, a baseball diamond, and a skate park. Restrooms can be accessed within the park. There are no changing tables.

Ogden Nature Center

966 West 12th Street
Ogden, 84404
(801) 621-7595
www.ogdennaturecenter.org

Hours:
Monday-Friday: 9am-5pm; *Saturday:* 9am-4pm;
Closed: Sundays and holidays

Admission:
Under 2: Free; *Age 2-11:* $2; *Age 12-54:* $4; 55+: $3.

Annual Pass:
$45 for a family or grandparents membership.

Food:
Outside food is permitted. Shady picnic areas are plentiful. The gift shop sells snacks.

Parking:
Free parking lot.

Social:

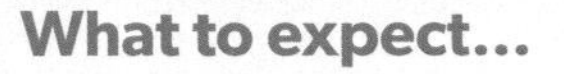

What to expect...

Ogden Nature Center is a jewel just off the freeway in the middle of Ogden City. This large nature preserve and education center, tucked away from a busy street, covers 152 acres of land in a quiet setting. Established in 1975, the Nature Center is a place where people can enjoy and learn about the natural world year-round. Plan for at least three hours on your first visit. There is so much to see and this kind of adventure requires a slow pace.

Birdhouse Trail – Start your adventure right out of the parking lot. Make your way to the gift shop/entrance by walking a short pathway through a unique display of birdhouses. The birds on display have been permanently injured or imprinted and can no longer take care of themselves in the wild. These animals are cared for by the Ogden Nature Center with state and federal permissions. Salamanders, snakes, tortoises and other animals are also on display.

Nest Gift Shop – Pay entrance fees inside the Nest Gift Shop. The shop sells nature-themed toys, books and gifts, as well as snacks. Visitors may check out binoculars or explorer backpacks from inside the gift shop. Choose from several themes such as Plants, Insects and Spiders, Ponds, or Birds. These backpacks contain a variety of books and activities related to their subjects.

Nature Activities – Ogden Nature Center offers a variety of nature activities and experiences for visitors. These include: walking trails, live bird exhibits, a tree house, observation areas, three ponds, and other wildlife areas. A human-sized mouse hole and bear den are both meant to be natural play areas for children. Children also get excited about the roaming live turkeys as well as the occasional squirrel or deer sightings.

Live Bird Exhibit – The large exhibit of live birds cannot be missed. Explore this collection of eagles, hawks, owls, and more. Many of these large birds of prey were injured and rescued, then donated to the Ogden Nature Center. Salamanders, snakes, and other animals are also on display.

Nature Trail – On our visit, we took the trail that goes out to the tree house which is a very manageable nature walk for younger children. I recommend bringing snacks for the stop at the tree house. The path is mostly dirt and rocks. Strollers can be used on the path, but it is bumpy. I recommend a jogger stroller or backpack baby carrier for taking children ages three or younger. The tree house is a fun ending point and is ramped with a look-out deck and a picnic table nearby. See the website for a map of the Nature Center, including trails.

Ponds – There are many ponds on the property, each offering something unique. Arrowhead Pond offers a tucked in bird blind and Teal Pond offers an observation tower/bird blind for quietly viewing wildlife.

L.S. Perry Education Building – Indoors at the more recently built Education Building children and adults can participate in nature-based workshops or community classes. The Nature Center offers a weekly education class called Wild Wednesdays at 3:45pm. These are hands-on and kid-friendly workshops about a wide variety of nature and animal-themed topics. Preschool Discovery Days are offered two days a month. The Nature Center offers many summer camp programs as well as camping opportunities. See the website calendar for specific days and times as well as for other classes and events. Staff at Ogden Nature Center, many of whom are volunteers, are helpful, well-informed, and love working with kids.

Wear closed-toed shoes, hats, sunscreen, and bug spray in the warm months. Restrooms with changing tables are adjacent to the gift shop.

Just Around the Corner...

- Birdsong Trail
- Color Me Mine (Ogden)
- FastKart Speedway (Ogden)
- FatCats (Ogden)
- Fort Buenaventura
- Ogden Dinosaur Park and Museum
- Ogden Raptors
- Ogden River Parkway
- Ogden's Union Station
- Peery's Egyptian Theater
- Riverdale Park
- Treehouse Children's Museum
- Toad's Fun Zone

Red Butte Garden

300 Wakara Way
Salt Lake City, 84108
(801) 585-0556
www.redbuttegarden.org

Hours:
Opens 9am daily. Closing hours change seasonally. See website for current hours and closings.

Admission:
Under 3: Free; *Age 3-17:* $6; *Age 18-64:* $10; *Age 65+:* $8; *U of U Faculty/Staff:* $6; *U of U Students:* Free with valid ID.

Garden Membership:
Memberships range from $35 to $65 for one, two, four or eight people.

A Red Butte Garden membership allows admission to other botanical gardens across the country.

Parking:
Free parking in front of the Visitor Center.

Food:
Visitors can picnic anywhere in the garden. Tables and benches are available as well as lawn areas.

Discounts:
Several free days occur each year. Check the website for current days. Half-price winter admission Dec-Feb. Entertainment Book. Visit Salt Lake Connect Pass.

What to expect...

Red Butte Garden, located on the University of Utah Campus, is a beautiful Botanical Garden and Arboretum open year-round. Plan to spend at least an hour exploring. There are at least 11 themed gardens and nearly four miles of hiking trails to enjoy. Themed gardens include: a Rose Garden, an Herb Garden, a Medicinal Garden, a Fragrance Garden, and a Children's Garden. The grounds also include a waterfall, a creek, and a relaxing pond with ducks. Stroller-friendly pathways lead to picnic areas and benches for resting.

The Children's Center, located a short walk from the Visitor's Center, is full of exciting features for kids to explore. In the summer, children can take a reprieve from the heat in a cool fountain that spouts up from the ground. Other features include: a child-sized maze, three large lizard sculptures, crayons with coordinating colored flowers growing out of the tops, and a sandbox area for digging in red sand. Bring a swimsuit if desired or a change of clothes so that children may play freely.

Other gardens and outdoor activities in this book:

- CLAS Ropes Course & Canoeing
- Fort Buenaventura
- Hikes & Nature Walks Chapter
- Playgrounds & Parks Chapter
- Ski Areas & Resorts Chapter
- Swaner EcoCenter
- Temple Square

For **first time visitors** with children, the staff suggests taking the long way to the Children's Garden (about a 45 minute leisure walk). This way the kids will happily end their visit in the Children's Garden. Veer left when entering the main garden and take the pathway around to the Water Pavilion at the pond, then walk back up through the Fragrance, Medicinal, and Herb gardens. Finally, rest and play in the Children's Garden.

Garden Adventure classes are offered in the Sprout House (located in the Children's Garden) for kids ages 4-7 for a small fee. Pre-registration is required and space is limited. Red Butte Garden also offers summer camps, family nights, and overnight campouts.

Restrooms with changing tables are located in the Visitor Center and in the Sprout House. Prepare for seasonal weather conditions and always bring sunscreen, hats, and water. Tram tours are offered as part of admission from May through September, 10am-1pm.

Annual Events

Outdoor Concert Series – May-September. Additional fees apply.

Family Nights – Monday nights in June and July.

Sundance Institute Summer Film Series – July & August

Garden After Dark – October, a family-friendly Halloween Celebration. Additional fees apply.

Holiday Open House – First weekend in December.

Check the website for more information about events, classes, workshops, lectures, and our art and floral exhibits.

Just Around the Corner...

- Color Me Mine (SLC)
- Fort Douglas Military Museum
- Gilgal Sculpture Garden
- Liberty Park
- Natural History Museum of Utah
- The King's English
- This is the Place Heritage Park
- Tracy Aviary
- Utah's Hogle Zoo

Robert N. Hasenyager Great Salt Lake Nature Center

1700 West Glovers Lane (925 South)
Farmington, 84025
(801) 589-2373
www.greatsaltlakenaturecenter.org

Learning Center hours:
Monday-Friday: 8am-4:30pm;
Open some Saturdays;
Closed: Sundays and Holidays

Trails and paths are open throughout the year even if the Learning Center is closed.

Admission:
FREE!

Parking:
Free parking lot.

Food:
Outside food permitted.

What to expect...

The Robert N. Hasenyager Great Salt Lake Nature Center, located along the southeast shore of The GreatSalt Lake, is the perfect place to explore Utah's wetlands, observe a large variety of birds, take a nature walk, or enjoy a quiet, natural environment. The Nature Center covers nearly 300 acres and includes the Learning Center, six ponds and nature trails.

The Learning Center, staffed by Utah Division of Wildlife Resources Education Specialists and volunteers, is used for educating school groups, but is also open to the public to enjoy hands-on exhibits. Decks with bird-spotting scopes are available for members of the public to use upon request.

Bird Watching is a great activity at the nature center. You will notice a set of tall posts with large nests atop platforms that serves as a place for Great Blue Herons to nest in the spring and summer.

Nature trails allow visitors to observe and experience the area without disrupting nesting sites and damaging habitats. The main trail, a 1.3 mile loop past ponds and viewing decks, is marked with a sign that says "Walk, Bike and Wheelchair Trail."

Farmington Bay Waterfowl Management Area (WMA) adjacent to the Nature Center encompasses and additional 18,000 acres of wetlands for you to explore. After visiting the Learning Center and walking the trails, take a drive through this expansive area. The entry is located just one road east of the Nature Center on 1325 West. Drive out to Goose Egg Island, a small hill at the northwest edge of the WMA. Cars may drive right onto the island to a great lookout point with a picnic area. Many birds and wildlife can be viewed without ever leaving your car. There are educational signs and pullouts along the way to help you learn more about the area. During the nesting season from March 1 through September 15, you can only walk or bike beyond a gate at Goose Egg Island. At other times you can drive about two miles further down along the ponds of the WMA.

Restrooms can be accessed on the edge of the parking lot at the Nature Center. There are no changing tables. Dogs are not allowed during nesting season from March 1 through September 15, but are allowed along the trails on a leash from September 16 through February. Pick nicks on the deck are fine, but it is requested you pack out your garbage.

Just Around the Corner...

- Lagoon
- S&S Shortline Train Park

TIPS

- Bring your binoculars
- Baby jogger/strollers
- Wear closed-toe shoes
- Check bird activity on website

Annual Events

Bald Eagle Day – February The Center's biggest event of the year. View Bald Eagles with spotting equipment set up along Farmington Bay WMA's main dike road. In February you can sometimes see up to 400 Bald Eagles.

Tundra Swan Day – March. View swans with spotting equipment set up along Farmington Bay WMA's main dike road. In March around 10,000 Tundra Swans pass through as they migrate to the Arctic. For specific dates see the Utah Division of Wildlife Resources online events calendar at http://wildlife.utah.gov/calendar/month_calendar/2013/10/-.htm

Thanksgiving Point Gardens

3900 North Garden Drive
Lehi, 84043
(801) 768-4999
www.thanksgivingpoint.org/visit/gardens/about.html

Hours:
Open from the end of March through October: 10am-8pm; Closed Sundays

Admission:
Monday - Thursday. *Under 3:* Free; *Age 3-12:* $8; *Age 13-64:* $10; *Age 65+:* $8

Friday & Saturday. *Under 3:* Free; *Age 3-12:* $10; *Age 13-64:* $12; *Age 65+:* $10

Membership:
$175 per family, or for two grandparents and their grandchildren. Allows entrance to ALL Thanksgiving Point venues, 50% off for guests and more.

Food:
Trellis Café, located in the Gardens Visitor's Center serves an affordable lunch menu with indoor and outdoor seating. Snacks and drinks are sold in the gift shop. Concessions and vending machines are available in the Gardens.

Discounts:
1-Day and 2-Day Flex passes allow unlimited entrance to Farm Country, Museum of Ancient Life, and the Gardens. Entertainment Book.

What to expect...

One of the biggest surprises Thanksgiving Point has to offer is its gardens. Driving by on the freeway you would never guess there are 55 acres of manicured gardens on the property. The Gardens feature 15 themed gardens, stately lawns, beautiful waterfalls, and surprises around every corner. Be sure to grab a map on your way in; it is easy to miss large portions of the garden without one.

The 15 themed gardens are created like rooms and separated by thousands of trees, shrubs and grasses. Visit each garden on a leisurely walk along paved and pebble pathways. My children's favorite is the Secret Garden. They love the tunnel-like canopy of roses leading to the doors that you must enter to get into the garden. It is completely enclosed and has a fountain inside (although water play is not permitted). Other kid-friendly features throughout the gardens include a river with bridges, a large koi pond, and an art piece merry-go-round with flowers and plants growing on and around the horses.

The Light of the World Garden is a unique place worth visiting. It contains beautiful sculptures that depict the miracles and teachings of Jesus Christ, created by artist Angela Johnson.

The Gardens are home to the largest man-made waterfall in the Western Hemisphere. It was very exciting to stand on the bridge above this massive water feature. The water flows down to a large pool and acts as a beautiful backdrop to an outdoor amphitheater.

Consider bringing a stroller for kids five and younger. Also bring sunscreen, hats, and water. All restrooms have changing tables.

Annual Events

Tulip Festival – April. 250,000 Tulips in an amazing display!

Labor Day Luau – September. Luau-style dinner with entertainment in the gardens.

Dog Days in the Gardens – October. Dogs, usually prohibited, get in for FREE.

Just Around the Corner...

- Children's Discovery Garden at Thanksgiving Point
- Farm Country at Thanksgiving Point
- Hangtime Extreme Trampolines (Lehi)
- Highland Town Center Splash Pad
- Holdman Studios
- Museum of Ancient Life
- Seven Peaks Fun Center (Lehi)

(West Jordan) Conservation Garden Park

8275 South 1300 West
West Jordan, 84088
(801) 565-4400
www.conservationgardenpark.org

Hours:
May 5- September 30 *Monday-Saturday:* 8am-8pm;
October 1- April 30 *Monday-Friday:* 8am-5pm

Admission:
FREE!

Parking:
Free parking lot.

Food:
Food and drink are permitted in the garden.

What to expect...

The Conservation Garden Park is owned and operated by the Jordan Valley Water Conservancy District. The purpose of the garden is to educate the public on water conservation. Even if you don't think you would be interested, or you are already very water-wise, I promise you will enjoy a visit to this beautiful garden. It's gorgeous and peaceful.

The Conservation Garden offers interactive exhibits and landscape ideas. Four themed paths (Design, Irrigation, Planting, and Maintenance) highlight different parts of landscaping and how to make them more water-wise. There are beautiful landscape design ideas and over 800 plants throughout the garden. Some displays include: grass and soil varieties, sprinkler options, and natural alternatives for pest control.

Although children may not understand the educational purpose behind the garden, they will enjoy the interactive displays and winding paths that ramble through the garden. The paths break off to secret destination points like a bench under an arbor. Large stepping-stones are the only invitation kids need to follow a trail and find out where it ends. My favorite area is a long path covered by arching shade trees.

Restrooms are located in the Education Building as well as the back of the garden. Because there are so many plant varieties represented, the landscape changes monthly as different perennials are in bloom. Although the garden is not huge, it's definitely a place where kids will feel like they are adventuring and discovering.

Just Around the Corner...

- Accessible Playground at Veteran's Memorial Park
- Classic Fun Center (SLC)
- Gale Center of History and Culture
- Gardner Village
- Gene Fullmer Recreation Center
- Georgell Doll Shop
- Jump 'N Bounce
- South Jordan Recreation Center
- Tiny Tim's Foundation for Kids
- Wild West Jordan Playground at Veteran's Memorial Park

Playgrounds & Parks

No matter how much money you spend to make your backyard entertaining for your kids, they will always jump at the chance to go to the local park. Many cities have dedicated a lot of planning and resources to building amazing community parks. Each park highlighted in this chapter was chosen for a unique element that sets it apart from run-of-the-mill playgrounds. Each offers something distinct, fun, and out of the ordinary. These parks are worth a planned visit, even if you live far away. All are ideal for picnics and some even have ponds for feeding ducks. For a complete list of duck ponds see the Duck Pond list in Appendix 3.

Liberty Park Courtesy of Rachel Clarke

Accessible Playground at Veteran's Memorial Park

1985 W. 7800 S.
West Jordan, 84084
(801) 569-5700
www.wjordan.com

Hours:
Daily from dawn to dusk.

Admission:
FREE!

Parking:
Free parking on the street in front of the playground.

Picnic Areas:
Picnic tables as well as pavilions are located nearby.

What to expect...

The Accessible Playground at Veteran's Memorial park is a unique play structure built specifically for children with special needs. This is one of two fully accessible playgrounds in Salt Lake City. (The other is located in Liberty Park). Although the playground was built for kids with special needs, all children will enjoy playing here.

The playground was purposefully paired with the Miracle League Baseball Field that has a smooth rubber surface. On Saturdays during the warmer months, you might catch a baseball game. Kids play baseball despite physical or mental challenges. It is really inspiring to watch kids with walkers and wheelchairs round the bases.

The playground has many specialized features to serve children within the autism spectrum, those with limited sight, and those with limited ranges of motion. The floor is a safety surface that makes it possible for mobility devices to easily access the play areas.

The main play structure includes a wide ramp, deck, bridge, and a glider that accommodates two wheelchairs at a time. The playground also offers four types of swings, three spinning seats, and a sensory play center with visual, auditory, and tactile activities. One of my children's favorite elements is the roller table which allows children to move along conveyer belt-like rollers, just like a suitcase at the airport.

Restrooms without changing tables are located on the other side of the baseball field. There are few trees in this area and although shade canopies are built into the playground, shade still feels scarce. I suggest going during cooler times of the day.

Just Around the Corner...

- Classic Fun Center (SLC)
- Gale Center of History and Culture
- Gardner Village
- Gene Fullmer Recreation Center
- Georgell Doll Shop
- Jump 'N Bounce
- South Jordan Recreation Center
- Tiny Tim's Foundation for Kids
- (West Jordan) Conservation Garden Park
- Wild West Jordan Playground at Veteran's Memorial Park

Castle Heights Playground at Nicholls Park

1200 East Nicholls Rd.
Kaysville, 84039
(801) 546-0861
www.fruitheightscity.com

Hours:
Daily from sunrise to sunset.

Admission:
FREE!

Parking:
Free parking lot and streetparking.

Picnic Areas:
Picnic tables,benches, and two large pavilions are available, or you can spread a blanket on the lawn. A vending machine sells bottled drinks near the restrooms.

What to expect...

Castle Heights Playground is a unique play structure located in Fruit Heights and was designed by elementary school children in 2003 to look like a castle. It includes four slides, a boat, a train, swings (including an accessible swing), rock climbing walls, a tire swing and a tree house. There is also a toddler zone with baby swings and two small sand pits. My children all loved this playground as it lends to a lot of imaginative play. Also, behind the playground is a ravine with a river. Unless children know it is there they wouldn't notice it because of brush and trees that line the edge. The playground is designated for children ages 5-12 and the tot lot area is for ages 2-5. It has recently been repainted and looks bright and inviting. One drawback is that the structure is large enough that sometimes you can lose sight of your children.

Nicholls Park also offers three baseball diamonds, a smaller playground, two large pavilions, and sand volleyball. Bathrooms can be accessed to the west of the playground. The bathrooms are not very nice and do not have changing tables.

Just Around the Corner...

- Boondocks (Kaysville)
- Cherry Hill
- Get Air Sportsplex
- Heritage Park
- Lagoon
- Layton Surf 'n Swim
- S&S Shortline Train Park
- Three Little Monkeys (Kaysville)

Legacy Electric Park

325 North 3200 West
Layton, 84041
(801) 336-3900
www.laytoncity.org

Hours:
Dawn to dusk

Admission:
FREE!

Parking:
Free parking lot.

Picnic Areas:
There is a large pavilion nearby and lots of grassy areas.

What to expect...

Upon first glance this park may not seem like anything special, but with a little investigating and playing, this park comes alive through technology-driven games and activities. As one of a handful of parks like this in the United States, it is definitely a very unique play experience.

There are no signs with instructions on how to activate or play the games. The games are designed to be intuitive so that kids can figure out the games by themselves. But, we had a difficult time determining how to work the game controller and what certain symbols meant. We could tell there was something fun to do, we just didn't know how to do it. It was very frustrating to all of us. However after a phone call to the Parks Department, we were given information about how to play the games and then my kids LOVED it and didn't want to leave. So, to save you frustration and maximize playing time, I have included a list of the games with instructions on how to play them straight from the manufacturer.

There are a total of 10 games available between the three different play structures. Each game is designed to develop specific abilities like agility, speed, memory, and teamwork. My kids' favorite was a game played on the climbing structure called Castle, which is basically Capture the Flag. We were there with cousins and they all had fun working together.

This park is designed for children age 5 and up. Most of the games require teamwork, so being there with one or two kids would not be as fun. Toddlers cannot play most of the games, but my daughter had fun running around, playing in the adjoining sand box, sitting in the spinner bowls and sliding down a small slide. Restrooms without changing tables are nearby. Please note that the park is on the property of the Jr. High and is often used during lunch break.

Just Around the Corner...

- Clearfield Aquatic Center
- Get Air
- Great Salt Lake Shorelands Preserve
- Krispy Kreme (Layton)
- Layton Surf 'n Swim

Liberty Park

600 East 900 South
Salt Lake City, 84104
(801) 972-7800
www.slcparks.com

Hours:
Closes daily at 11pm.

Admission:
FREE!

Parking:
Free parking surrounds the perimeter of the park. There is also a parking lot on the west side.

Picnic Areas:
Concessions are sold in the summer near the center of the park. There are picnic tables and grills throughout the park.

What to expect...

Liberty Park is a large city park that covers 80 acres and offers many activities. Founded in 1882, it's the oldest park in the city, which is why it has so many huge, shady trees.

Rotary Play Park – One of the main attractions at Liberty Park is this large playground, located in the northwest corner. It is one of two handicap accessible playgrounds in Utah (the other is found in West Jordan). Features include: swings, sand tables and sand pits, slides, climbing structures, and ramped play structures.

Splash Pad – At the center of Rotary Play Park is a colorful splash pad. Surrounding areas are covered with turf and large rocks where supervising adults can sit and watch.

Seven Canyons Fountain – This unique fountain is located in the center of the park. Seven small streams representing each of the seven canyons along the Wasatch Front run down into a pool of water representing the Jordan River. Children may play inside this fountain. Signs posted at the fountain say, "No diapers, training pants, pull ups, or dogs allowed in the water." The stream currents are gentle, narrow, and perfect for floating little boats or toys, so bring something for floating if that would interest your children.

Liberty Lake – Located in the southeast corner of the park, it is great for feeding ducks.

Carnival Rides – On the west side of the park, there are a few carnival rides open during the summer months. Some of the rides have seen better days, but still work fine. You can choose from a carousel ride, a small Ferris wheel, airplanes or cars.

See Appendix 1 for Downtown Destinations close to this area

Other Amenities – The park also features a community pool, tennis courts, basketball courts, bocce ball, horseshoe pits, volleyball, and other play structures. Tracy Aviary and the old Chase Home (historic pioneer house) are also housed in the park.

Memory Grove Park

375 North Canyon Road
Salt Lake City, 84103
(801) 972-7800
www.slcparks.com

Hours:
None posted.

Admission:
FREE!

Parking:
There is limited street parking on North Canyon Road. Only cars with authorization to enter the park gates may park inside. I suggest parking above the park along the east side of the State Capitol and walking down the trail/steps.

Picnic Areas:
There are picnic tables and grassy areas in the park.

What to expect...

Memory Grove Park is a unique oasis at the bottom of City Creek Canyon. It is a beautiful place to watch dogs at play, let children wade in the creek, or have a picnic. The park is located just below the east side of the State Capitol. Multiple pathways lead down into the park, which makes it a popular starting point for city residents to walk their dog or jog into City Creek Canyon.

Memory Grove Park serves as a repository of war memorials. Each pays tribute to Utahans who lost their lives at war. Memorials include: a picturesque pagoda, a fountain, a flag, various plaques, a meditation chapel, and other monuments. Every memorial is unique. We took particular interest in reading plaques with the names of people who died at Pearl Harbor. We also enjoyed looking at the replica of the Liberty Bell.

The park is a popular spot for walking dogs because of an Off Leash Area within the park. While we were there we observed a variety of dogs walking and playing with their owners. A number of them jumped into the small pond at the bottom of the creek. The park is also a popular place for bridal/engagement photos, so don't be surprised if you see a bride on the grounds. There is a nice reception hall in the park called Memorial House, often used for weddings. Bathrooms are located near the Memorial House.

Neptune Park   Courtesy of Meilani Smith Kongaika

Neptune Park

452 West 400 North
Saratoga Springs, 84045
(801) 766-9793
www.saratogaspringscity.com

Hours:
Dawn to dusk

Admission:
FREE!

Parking:
Free parking lot off of 400 North.

Picnic Areas:
There is a large pavilion with barbecue grills and a soda machine near the restrooms.

What to expect...

Neptune Park is a gathering place for the Saratoga Springs Community. It features unique play equipment, soccer fields, basketball courts, a large pavilion, and an outdoor stage.

The playground's signature piece of play equipment is called the Neptune XXL. Standing 30 feet high, it is the tallest of its kind and one of only three in the world! This pyramid is made up of a system of ropes for climbing. Although it seems dangerous, the ropes were built not only for climbing, but also for catching someone if they fall. You can use your own judgment based on your child's abilities. My 6-year-old nephew made it to the top and back without incident. Other children in our group went as far as they dared, then worked their way back to the ground on their own.

The playground is full of other unique play equipment including: a rock climbing structure that looks like a caterpillar, stand and spin toys, a large spinning wheel, three kinds of swings, a stand and swing pendulum, slides, a playhouse, a bouncy see saw and much more. You really have to experience all of this fun equipment to see how unique and exciting it is. Some of the play equipment even attracts teenagers because it's so inviting and fun.

A pavilion sits right next to the playground and serves as the best shade. Restrooms are located next to the pavilion, but there are no changing tables.

Just Around the Corner...

- American Fork Fitness Center
- Jack and Jill Lanes
- John Hutchings Museum of Natural History
- Legacy Recreation Center
- Nolan Park

Novell Children's Discovery Park

Manilla Park
1550 North 100 East
Pleasant Grove, 84062
(801) 785-6172
www.plgrove.org

Hours:
Daily dawn to dusk.

Admission:
FREE!

Parking:
Free parking lot.

Picnic Areas:
There are picnic tables in the adjoining garden courtyard.

What to expect...

This park is unlike any I've ever visited. As we pulled up in the car, my kids were so excited by what they saw that they raced to unbuckle themselves. They fled the car so quickly that I was left standing with sunscreen in hand and no child in sight. What makes this playground so unique? First of all, unlike most playground equipment, Novell Discovery Park is made of wood. It has an intricate layout of tall lookout towers and platforms connected by walkways, bridges, planks, and stairs.

The second thing that makes it unique is that the park was designed with a learning theme. All the activities in the park relate to one of five areas of science: paleontology, geology, natural science, physics, and astronomy. Kids can try to balance on the earthquake platform, dig up fossils in the dinosaur sand pit, climb into a rocket ship, or follow animal tracks. There are a few different areas to experiment with sound, including echo boxes, xylophones, and speaking tubes located at several spots around the play area. Just find two tubes with matching numbers and kids can talk to each other across the playground through the tubes.

Benches are positioned around the outside of the play area, but if you have a toddler you will have to follow them pretty closely as it is hard to see at all times because of the towers and walls. The park also has two swing sets including one with baby seats. Right off of the play area is a pretty little garden and courtyard with trees, picnic tables, and benches. Restrooms are nearby, just beyond the garden area.

Just Around the Corner...

- Battle Creek Falls Hike
- Jump On It
- Lindon Aquatics Center

Wild West Jordan Playground at Veteran's Memorial Park

1985 West 7800 South
West Jordan, 84084
(801) 569-5700
www.wjordan.com

Hours:
Daily dawn to dusk.

Admission:
FREE!

Parking:
Free parking on the street in front of the playground.

Picnic Areas:
Picnic tables as well as a pavilion are located near the playground. Or, just bring a blanket and eat in a shady area on the lawn.

What to expect...

The Wild West Jordan Playground is located inside Veteran's Memorial Park. The children, residents, and businesses of West Jordan collaborated to create this fun and unique playground. In fact, children from West Jordan's public schools gave their ideas and 400,000 pennies to help make the playground possible.

Built to portray the history of West Jordan, the playground is composed of miniature buildings made to resemble and represent real businesses from the city's past. The playground also includes placards that teach visitors about these places and their role in the area. Features include: a train, a horse drawn wagon, various shops, a boat, petroglyphs, a mine, painted murals, and a police station with a jail. The tot lot is designated for ages two to five and includes baby swings, an accessible swing, a bouncy horse, and more. The larger area is designated for ages five to twelve and includes taller climbing structures, slides, swings, a tire swing, and a rock-climbing wall.

Wild West playground is well-maintained and very secure, with a surrounding fence. The park is also under 24 hour video surveillance by police. Bathrooms without changing tables are located directly behind the play structure.

Other playgrounds and parks related activities in this book:

- CLAS Ropes Course & Canoeing
- City Creek Play Area
- Fort Buenaventura
- Ogden Dinosaur Park Museum
- Provo Towne Centre Play Area
- Splash Pads Chapter
- Trailside Park
- University Mall Treehouse Court
- Wheeler Historic Farm
- Willow Creek Park

Just Around the Corner...

- Accessible Playground at Veteran's Memorial Park
- Classic Fun Center (SLC)
- Gale Center of History and Culture
- Gardner Village
- Gene Fullmer Recreation Center
- Georgell Doll Shop
- Jump 'N Bounce
- South Jordan Recreation Center
- Tiny Tim's Foundation for Kids
- (West Jordan) Conservation Garden Park

Hikes & Nature Walks

One of the best things about Salt Lake City and the areas along the Wasatch Front is the fast and easy access we have to the mountains. A short drive will transport you from busy city life to picturesque canyons and valleys. There are endless possibilities for enjoying the mountains year-round.

This chapter highlights kid-friendly hikes all along the Wasatch Front. We recommend hiking with young children in the summer and fall. If you choose to hike in the spring be aware that some areas will still have snow with cold temperatures and rivers, streams, and waterfalls are much stronger and higher. When hiking in the summer, choose a cool time of day to hike. August is a great time of year to hike because the wildflowers are in bloom up in the mountains and of course, the fall is always great because of the gorgeous colors and cool temperatures.

This chapter is for families who are just getting started in their attempt to hike with kids. Seasoned hikers might find these hikes too easy or too popular for their taste, but we felt it was important to take the perspective of first-time or novice hikers since we ourselves had never experienced hiking with our kids. Some of the "hikes" are actually easy nature trails and it should be easy to differentiate between the two as you read. We outline a suggested age for each hike. But you know your kids best. If you think they could handle a specific hike, go for it!

Courtesy of Meilani Smith Kongaika

Tips for hiking with kids:

- Always tell someone where you are going and bring a cell phone.
- Bring lots of water. It can be very hot and tiring to hike for kids (and for you too!), especially in the hot summer.
- Bring snacks. It's always nice to have something on hand to eat at the top or along the way at a rest point.
- Bring a friend. Kids sometimes behave better and have a more enjoyable time when a friend is along for the journey.
- Wear good sneakers. Hiking boots/shoes are not necessary for any of these hikes. Some of the nature trails can be done in flip flops, but it's a good rule to hike in close-toed shoes to avoid tripping and sliding.
- Wear sunscreen and bring hats.
- Take breaks when necessary and have fun! Enjoy the scenery and watch for any signs of wildlife, including insects and bugs.

Site 52

Battle Creek Falls Hike

Hours:
Dawn to dusk

Distance:
1.2 miles out and back.

Time:
1 hour

Suggested Age:
5 and older.

Picnic Areas:
There is a pavilion at the trailhead, but it is not an ideal spot to picnic.

Directions to Trailhead:
The trailhead begins at the end of 200 South in Pleasant Grove. Park where the street dead ends then begin the hike up to the right of the Kiwanis Park entrance. A wooden sign that says "Battle Creek Tr." marks the trailhead

Parking:
The parking area is located at the top of 200 South.

1700 East 200 South
Pleasant Grove, 84062

What to expect...

Battle Creek Falls is an easy hike to an impressive waterfall. The waterfall sprays in two ribbons down a tall cliff straight into a creek bed. Plan for about an hour of hiking with young children from start to finish. We took a two-year-old who walked almost the entire hike on his own with a few breaks to play by the river or to take a drink. The trail follows beside the creek and is well maintained. For the first part of the hike, the creek bed is completely dry because the river is diverted higher up.

My kids were a little grouchy at the start because of the heat and lack of scenery. But the minute we came to the water, their spirits were lifted and the outing became really fun. The hike is uphill with a few steep areas and spots of shade. The steepest portion of the hike is the last five minutes leading to the top of the waterfall. Be sure to watch your children closely. Also, on the way down, don't miss the little pathway leading to the bottom of the falls. Although there is no pool of water for swimming, children will enjoy throwing rocks and splashing in the water. There are vault toilet restrooms just past the pavilion at the trailhead, but I would avoid using them if possible.

Just Around the Corner...

- Jack and Jill Lanes
- Manila Creek Pond
- Novell Children's Discovery Park

Birdsong Trail

Ogden, near the mouth of the canyon.

Hours:
Dawn to dusk

Distance:
1 mile.

Time:
1 hour.

Suggested Age:
5 and up.

Picnic Areas:
There is a picnic table at the end of the trail.

Directions to Trailhead:
Find Rainbow Gardens (a restaurant and gift shop) at the mouth of Ogden Canyon. Park in the Rainbow Gardens parking lot and walk under the sign at the corner that says "Rainbow Trail." Turn left at the bulletin board. A wood post with the sign "Birdsong Trail" signals to make a quick right and you are on the trail.

Parking:
Free parking lot at Rainbow Gardens. Park in the southwest corner of the parking lot.

What to expect...

The Birdsong Trail runs along the east bench in Ogden between Rainbow Gardens and 20th Street. It promises sweeping views of the Ogden Valley and quiet walks through forests and meadows. Information on the trail describes the trail passing by six springs and a pond. We hiked in the last few days of the summer and only saw one spring and a very small pond, but I assume that the other springs are active earlier in the season. Despite that, the hike was still very enjoyable and worthwhile.

The Birdsong Trail is named for the many birds that frequent the forest along the path. I recommend hiking during the early morning hours to be able to spot birds along the trail. Within 15 minutes from beginning, you will reach the main spring and pond. The entire area is shaded and has a bench. To finish the hike, follow the rest of the trail another 15 minutes through forest and meadow until you hook up to the end point on Fillmore Avenue and 20th Street. There is a covered picnic bench for resting and snacking. This area offers great views of the Ogden Valley and is a good spot for pictures. At this point, you may have someone pick you up, or just return the way you came.

The trail is narrow so you often have to walk single file. Also, be aware that this trail is used by mountain bikers. Just step aside to allow them to pass. Dogs are allowed on this trail as long as they are on a leash. You may use the restrooms at Rainbow Gardens if needed. The gift shop is a good place to buy a few snacks and water from vending machines.

Just Around the Corner...

- Color Me Mine (Ogden)
- FastKart Speedway (Ogden)
- FatCats (Ogden)
- Fort Buenaventura
- Ogden Dinosaur Park and Museum
- Ogden Nature Center
- Ogden Raptors
- Ogden River Parkway
- Ogden's Union Station
- Ott Planetarium
- Peery's Egyptian Theater
- Riverdale Park
- Treehouse Children's Museum

Bridal Veil Falls

Provo Canyon

Hours:
5am-11pm (Provo river park trail hours)

Distance:
0.5 mile

Time:
About 15 minutes from the parking lot to the falls.

Trailhead:
Access the trailhead by driving through Provo Canyon on US Highway 89. At about mile 4 on the east side, there is a turn off for Bridal Falls Park where you will find a paved parking lot adjoining the small park. The paved trail begins at the park.

Parking:
Free parking lot.

What to expect...

Provo Canyon is known for the beautiful double waterfall that cascades down the mountainside resembling a bride's long white veil. This nature walk leads to a shallow pool at the base of the falls, perfect for wading and exploring.

The trail begins at the small grassy park adjoining the parking lot. The park has picnic tables and room enough to pass a football or kick a ball. It would be fun to pack a picnic to eat at the park before taking the short walk to the bottom of the falls. Most of the trail is limited to pedestrian traffic only. Beautiful trees arch over the path creating a shady canopy for much of the walk. The Provo River runs along the side of the trail, but not close enough to make you nervous about kids falling in.

Once at the bottom of the falls, you can enjoy the view from a wide wooden deck built out over the shallow water. Kids can kick off their shoes and wade out into the rocky stream. There are lots of little rocks to throw into the water and big rocks to climb on. The pool at the base of the falls is not deep at all, so it is easy for children to wade through and you don't have to be nervous about kids that can't swim. If you are planning to let your kids play for a while, bring along a couple of camping chairs so you can comfortably relax and enjoy the beautiful scenery. If you don't bring a chair, you can dangle your legs over the edge of the wooden landing. The paved trail is entirely stroller-friendly.

There are a few portable toilets in the parking lot where the trail begins. This is a popular hike for families, so the parking lot fills up on Monday nights and weekends.

Just Around the Corner...

- Max Zipline Canopy Tour
- Stewart Falls
- Sundance Mountain Resort
- Timpanogos Falls

Cascade Springs Nature Trail

American Fork Canyon,
7 miles off of the Alpine Loop

Hours:
Closed at dusk

Distance:
Variable. There are three loops that go around the springs. Each takes about 15 minutes.

Time:
30 min-1 hour.

Picnic Areas:
Picnicking is not permitted at Cascade Springs. Picnic areas are plentiful closer to the mouth of either American Fork or Provo Canyon.

Directions to Trailhead:
You can approach Cascade Springs from either American Fork Canyon, Provo Canyon (Sundance) or Soldier Hollow. Signs are easy to follow. It takes 45 minutes to get to the Springs from American Fork Canyon.

Parking:
There is a large upper parking lot and a smaller lower parking lot. Parked cars must display a recreation pass in the windshield. Pay $6 (good for 3 days) either at the fee station at the mouth of American Fork Canyon or at the self-service fee box in front of the lower parking lot.

What to expect...

Cascade Springs was one of the most unique outdoor destinations we visited for this book. The entire area is surrounded by paved or boardwalk trails, making it completely accessible for people of all ages. It's amazing that in this remote area, deep in the mountains, wheelchairs and strollers can be used.

On your way into the canyon, make sure to ask for a free map at the fee station. The road is winding, and as a result, your stomach may turn a little, but it is worth the drive for the scenery alone. The most popular time of year to drive this road is in the early fall when all of the leaves are changing.

Park at the lower parking lot if possible. A gazebo with interpretive signs makes a great start to your journey. You can enter by a steep trail from the gazebo or a gentler slope off to the right. The trail is made up of three small loops. Each takes 15 minutes or less, and I recommend doing all of them. The first is the Pools Loop which is a raised boardwalk that winds around the lower pools and cascades. The water is clear enough to see fish swimming in the ponds. This is the most accessible loop. The second is the Cascade Loop which travels along the cascading river. This is a steep trail, but still very possible to push a stroller along one side, and the other side of this loop does have stairs. The last loop is the Springs Loop. This upper trail is fairly level and circles where the springs begin to surface.

You can start the trails at either the upper or lower parking lot. Both have restrooms, although the lower parking lot provides better facilities. Free Ranger-Guided Tours of Cascade Springs are offered twice weekly throughout the summer. These are open to all ages. Check the calendar on the website for details: *www.nps.gov/tica.*

Just Around the Corner...

- Soldier Hollow
- Stewart Falls
- Sundance Mountain Resort
- Timpanogos Cave
- Timpanogos Falls

Cecret Lake Hike

Little Cottonwood Canyon, Sandy

Hours:
None posted.

Distance:
2.5 miles round trip

Time:
2-2½ hours

Suggested Age:
5 and up

Picnic Areas:
This isn't the best hike to bring a full picnic, as there aren't many ideal picnic spots.

Directions to Trailhead:
Drive all the way up Little Cottonwood Canyon 11.2 miles to the Albion Basin Campground. Parking is available in the free parking lot to the left of the entrance and fee booth of the campground. The canyon road is paved to the Alta Ski Resort, but the last couple of miles take you over a well-maintained gravel road. After parking, follow small wooden signs to the trail, which begins across the road from the parking lot and runs along the west side of the campgrounds.

Parking:
Free parking lot at trailhead and Albion Campgrounds. The parking lot is well-marked.

What to expect...

The hike up to Cecret Lake will transport you from the noisy congested valley to the crisp air and peaceful mountains of Little Cottonwood Canyon. The trail is well marked and maintained. Follow the signs from the trailhead, keeping to the main, wide dirt trail. Other small trails zigzag through the main trail, but stick to the most obvious trail.

This hike is not through heavily forested areas, rather through beautiful mountain meadows with scatterings of alpine fir trees. If you are there in the first few weeks of August, you will be greeted by hundreds of colorful wildflowers.

The trail is mostly a gradual incline and easy to walk. It is ideal for using a backpack baby carrier as there are no low hanging branches. Kids will have no problem navigating the trail. The toughest part of this hike comes just before you reach the lake. The last 10 minutes take you up a rocky slope with several switchbacks. But, as you reach the summit, you will be rewarded with an amazing view of the lake and surrounding mountains. It only takes a couple more minutes to hike down to the water's edge. Swimming is not allowed, but my kids found plenty of exploring and climbing to do. We took a picnic, but there really wasn't an ideal spot nearby to set it up. We sat on the rocks to eat and watched the chipmunks aggressively scurry around after our crumbs.

My five-year-old daughter walked the trail but complained of being tired a lot and needed to be carried a couple of times. It really was a pleasant hike, easy enough to be enjoyable for kids, but hard enough to make them feel it was an accomplishment. Vault toilets are only a short walk from the parking lot.

Just Around the Corner...

- Alta Ski Area
- Lisa Falls
- Snowbird Ski and Summer Resort
- Temple Quarry Nature Trail

Donut Falls

Big Cottonwood Canyon, Sandy

Posted Hours:
The gate that leads to the trailhead is open 7am- 10pm.

Distance:
1 mile roundtrip

Time:
1 hour roundtrip

Suggested Age:
All ages!

Picnic Areas:
There are no picnic tables. You can bring a snack and eat near the falls. Watch out for friendly chipmunks.

Directions to Trailhead:
Go about 9 miles up Big Cottonwood Canyon until you reach the Mill D Trailhead sign. There is parking on both sides of the street and a bathroom. Turn right (south) down a paved road through a gate and past summer homes. It will turn into a dirt road and soon you will arrive at the small trailhead parking lot. The hike begins between the bathrooms and the information boards.

Parking:
There is a small parking lot at the trailhead with room for only about 16 cars. Many people park along one side of the dirt road leading up to the parking lot. Be aware of the No Parking signs.

What to expect...

Take Note: All lakes, rivers, and waterfalls up Big Cottonwood Canyon are part of a watershed. You may not swim or take pets to these places. The water is processed to become drinking water.

Donut Falls is one of the most popular hikes in Salt Lake City and a perfect place to hike with young children. Along the trail we observed many babies in backpacks and toddlers walking at their own pace. The trail is, for the most part, very wide and slopes gently. It is also pretty well-marked. Because so many people are on this trail, you are sure to feel safe and comfortable.

The first portion of the trail takes you through a forested area with large pines and aspens along either side. About half-way through the trail, you will cross a wooden bridge over the river. The hike ends coming down over a large boulder to the river bottom. Kids can sit and scoot over it, or just be handed down. At that point you are inside the canyon walls where the falls come down to the riverbed. We were there in September and the falls were smaller, but still rewarding to see. The nice thing at that time of year is that the river is low, making it easier to cross if you would like.

It is called Donut falls because the water gushes through a donut-shaped hole in the mountain. It seemed that you have to climb up the boulders to see it well. And although many people were climbing up, this did not seem like a safe idea to me. We couldn't view the donut from the river bottom, nor from the ridge off to the left. But we still enjoyed the scene and felt satisfied that we made it. Restrooms are at the trailhead. There are no changing tables.

Just Around the Corner...

- Brighton Ski Resort
- Hidden Falls
- Silver Lake Trail
- Solitude Mountain Resort

Ensign Peak Hike

166 Ensign Vista Drive
Salt Lake City, 84103

Posted Hours:
Daylight to dark.

Distance:
1 mile roundtrip

Time:
1 hour roundtrip

Suggested Age:
5 and older

Picnic Areas:
Ensign Downs Park, just down the street, offers picnic benches, a grassy area, and a playground.

Directions to Trailhead:
Take State Street up to the Capitol. Veer right around to the side of the Capitol onto Capitol Boulevard. Turn left onto Edgecomb Drive and wind up the road where the street turns into Ensign Vista Drive. You will find the trailhead to your left. The signs say "Ensign Peak Nature Park."

Parking:
There is street parking in front of the entry on Ensign Vista Drive. No parking is allowed in this area from 10pm to 6am.

See Appendix 1 for Downtown Destinations close to this area

What to expect...

A hike up to Ensign Peak promises beautiful views of the Salt Lake Valley and the Great Salt Lake. Ensign Peak is a high point, marked with a monument on the small mountain top behind the State Capitol. Brigham Young and other leaders of the Mormon Church hiked to this point two days after entering the Salt Lake Valley. There they surveyed the area and raised a flag.

The bottom of the trail has two resting and learning areas. Ensign Peak Memorial Garden is a gated garden with benches, shade, and historic signs. Across the street, Ensign Peak Nature Park marks the entry to the trail and offers more interpretive signs. This entire area is stroller-friendly, with ramps and cemented walkways. The hiking trail starts from the Nature Park. It begins as a cemented sidewalk that leads to a very close view of the Valley, called Vista Mound. I recommend this early viewpoint for everyone, especially for families with young children and strollers. Just past this point, the trail becomes a dirt path that quickly becomes steep. At this point, follow the well-marked trail up to the Peak. There are resting areas along the way with cement seats and spots of shade.

This hike takes you through dry areas with little vegetation and the sun really beats down on you. Be sure to bring lots of water. It was very dry when we hiked, but many people complain about the trail being muddy after it has rained. The views are definitely worth the hard work of getting to the top, so be sure to bring a camera. There are no restrooms at the trailhead.

Hidden Falls

Big Cottonwood Canyon, Sandy

Hours:
None posted.

Distance:
A roadside attraction that is an easy stroll just off the main road.

Time:
15 minutes total for visiting the falls.

Suggested Age:
All ages!

Picnic Areas:
There are no picnic areas near the trail.

Directions to Trailhead:
Go about 4 miles up the canyon until you see signs for the Mill B Trailhead. This is located at the bottom of the S Curve in the road. Don't park in this parking lot, but in the lot just above it on the inside of the curve. Go up the stairs near the sign board. Then cross the street and do not go up the stairs you see to the right. Instead, follow the riverbed on either side to the waterfall.

Parking:
After you see the sign for Mill B Trailhead, pass the first parking lot and turn up the S Curve in the road slightly then quickly turn into the upper parking lot. You may see cars parked along the street as well.

What to expect...

Hidden Falls is a beautiful roadside attraction and is definitely worth a quick visit on a trip to Big Cottonwood Canyon. You can park and be at the falls within five minutes. It seems silly to call this a hike, but it is a nice destination that requires a little walking.

We went in September, so the riverbed was very low and easy to cross. The waterfall was not big, but still beautiful. Going in the spring can make it much more difficult to hike. A log crosses the river for hikers to use when the river swells.

Hidden Falls is also home to a popular bolted rock climbing wall, known as the Pile Wall. We were able to watch some rock climbers in action on our visit. There is also a locked, abandoned mine off to the right, in the side of the mountain just before the falls. There is a hole big enough for little ones to climb through, so be cautious. There are no restroom facilities.

Take Note: All lakes, rivers, and waterfalls up Big Cottonwood Canyon are part of a watershed. Do not swim or take pets to these places. The water is processed into drinking water.

Just Around the Corner...

- Brighton Ski Resort
- Donut Falls
- Silver Lake Trail
- Solitude Mountain Resort

Lisa Falls

Little Cottonwood Canyon, Sandy

Hours:
None posted.

Distance:
0.5 mile round trip

Time:
30 minutes

Suggested Age:
3 and up

Picnic Areas:
There are some large rocks at the base of the falls where you could sit and enjoy a picnic or snack.

Directions to trailhead:
Drive 2.7 miles up Little Cottonwood Canyon, starting from the Park-and-Ride lot at the mouth of the Canyon. Shortly after passing the large traffic arm marked "B," there is a turnout on both sides of the road, park in either one. The trailhead is on the north (left) side of the road. Look for a small, but well-worn path.

Parking:
There is free parking on either turnout, north or south of the road, near the start of the trail.

What to expect...

This hike is short and sweet, which makes it ideal for families with young children. Because the trail is almost completely shaded, this hike could be done comfortably at any time of day. The dirt trail is freckled with rocks, which makes the mild climbing even easier. Our five-year-old daughter hiked independently and our three-year-old daughter needed just a little help. A backpack baby carrier would be ok on this trail; I didn't seem to notice too many low branches or limbs. The trail is easy to follow, just keep an eye out for a small fork in the trail as you get closer to the falls. Stay left and you are almost there.

The falls come down on the steep flat face of a granite slab and create a trickling stream below. The water will be higher and the waterfall bigger earlier in the season. At the falls, there are spots to rest and rocks to climb on and explore. This hike could easily be added on to another hiking excursion because it is so easy and quick. However, it could definitely stand alone as its own outing if you take some time at the falls to let the kids run around.

Just Around the Corner...

- Alta Ski Area
- Cecret Lake Hike
- Snowbird Ski and Summer Resort
- Temple Quarry Nature Trail

Ogden River Parkway

The mouth of Ogden Canyon through downtown Ogden.

Posted Hours:
One hour before sunrise to one hour after sunset.

Distance:
9.6 miles long (choose the distance you desire along the parkway).

Time:
Variable

Suggested Age:
All Ages!

Picnic Areas:
Benches and picnic tables are all along the parkway. The parkway passes by multiple parks with playgrounds, picnic benches, and grassy areas.

Directions to Trailhead:
Start anywhere along the trail. Suggested starting points include: 18th Street and Washington Boulevard, 1700 Monroe Boulevard, East end of Park Boulevard, or the mouth of Ogden Canyon.

Parking:
Park your car at a park along the parkway or on the street, depending on your starting point.

What to expect...

Ogden River Parkway extends 9.6 miles from the mouth of Ogden Canyon through downtown Ogden. It is a paved walkway that follows the Ogden River and is used for walking, jogging, biking, roller blading, or just relaxing near the river. The path is smooth and wide with a dividing line for two-way traffic. Many parts of the path are shaded even at noon. My children rode their scooters and enjoyed stopping to look at the river and playing at a nearby playground.

Multiple locations line the Parkway including (from east to west): Rainbow Gardens, George S. Eccles Dinosaur Park, Big Dee Sports Park, El Monte Golf Course, MTC Learning Park, Lorin Farr Swimming Pool and Rampage Park, Lorrin Farr Park, Lorin Farr Skate Park, Ogden Pioneer Stadium, West Stadium Park, Peleton's Restaurant and Bingham Cyclery, Gode Ski Lake, Kayak Park, Miles Goodyear Park, King Fisher Aviary, and Fort Buenaventura. You can start the path at any of these points. Rules prohibit skateboards, horses, and alcoholic beverages on the Parkway. Dogs must be on a leash along the path. Restrooms are located in parks along the trail.

Just Around the Corner...

- Powder Mountain
- Snowbasin
- Wolf Mountain Resort

Provo River Parkway

See below for suggested access points

Hours:
5am-11pm

Admission:
FREE!

Parking:
There are free parking lots at both parks mentioned below.

Food:
There are lots of picnic areas at both parks and along the trail.

What to expect...

The Provo River Parkway is a walking and biking trail that stretches 15 miles from Vivian Park in Provo Canyon all the way to Utah Lake. The trail is paved the entire way with dashed lines dividing the lanes of traffic. There are many beautiful areas of the trail, but if you would like to enjoy just part of it and want a good idea of where to go, I have two recommendations. Both of these recommendations are located on areas of the trail that are far removed from traffic and the city.

The parkway starts at Vivian Park in Provo Canyon. This area of the trail is especially beautiful, as the mountains and trees of the canyon surround it. Vivian Park has a playground, restrooms, fishing pond, pavilions, and lots of grassy areas. You could start there and then walk the trail down the canyon as far as you want until you decide to turn back. If you want to bike the trail, you could start at Vivian Park and go down the canyon about 2½ miles to the base of Bridal Veil Falls. The only hard thing for kids is that the way back to the park is uphill.

Another great spot along the trail is called Reams Wilderness Park. Just past the parking lot there is a bridge that takes you across the river to the park. There, you can feed the ducks and play on the playground. Many picnic tables are scattered throughout the park and there is also a large pavilion. If you want to take a little walk up the trail, there is another park and playground about a 10-minute walk up the trail.

This is a very popular and well-used trail. The Provo River runs really high and fast in the spring, so you may feel more comfortable visiting later in the summer if you have adventurous kids. Restrooms are located at both Vivian Park and Reams Wilderness Park.

Suggested Access Points

Paul Ream Wilderness Park
1600 West 500 North
Provo, 84601

Vivian Park
Approximately 5.8 miles up
Provo Canyon

Photo courtesy of Emily Smith Robbins

Silver Lake Trail

Brighton Ski Resort,
Big Cottonwood Canyon, Sandy

Posted Hours:
June through October. Parking lot gate closes at 9pm.

Distance:
0.8 mile loop around the lake.

Time:
30 minutes-1 hour.

Suggested Age:
All ages!

Picnic Areas:
There are a handful of picnic areas just off of the parking lot.

Directions to trailhead:
From the mouth of Big Cottonwood Canyon, drive 14 miles (about 20 minutes) to the top of the canyon. You will be forced to turn right at a fork in the road. The parking lot will be to your right.

Parking:
Park in the free parking lot in front of the Solitude Nordic Center and Silver Lake Information Center.

What to expect...

Take Note: All lakes, rivers, and waterfalls up Big Cottonwood Canyon are part of a watershed. You may not swim or take pets to these places. The water is processed to become drinking water.

Silver Lake is a beautiful place to enjoy the mountains, go fishing, feed ducks, or just take a walk. This is my favorite location that our family visited for this book. Utah's mountains have so much to offer and Silver Lake makes them accessible to everyone. It is an easy way for young children, seniors, and the disabled to enjoy a natural location high in the mountains.

The trail begins around the right side of the Information Center (at the parking lot). It is a stroller- and wheelchair-accessible boardwalk that meanders over a meadow and along the front end of the lake. Along the back of the lake, the path becomes a dirt trail. There are educational signs throughout. I highly recommend taking the whole loop. The views are beautiful and the walk is easy. Don't forget bug repellent and a jacket in case it gets chilly. You can also bring along fishing gear and go fishing on docks that jut into the lake. (A fishing license is needed for anyone over the age of 12).

The Solitude Nordic Center & Silver Lake Information Center is run by the Forest Service in the Summer and by Solitude Ski Resort in the Winter. It is open every day all summer from 11am-5pm and offers maps and more information about the area. Restrooms are near the parking lot. There are no changing tables.

Just Around the Corner...

- Brighton Ski Resort
- Donut Falls
- Hidden Falls
- Solitude Mountain Resort

Stewart Falls

Provo Canyon,
Sundance Mountain Resort

Hours:
Sundance chair lift hours change seasonally.
See the website for current hours.

Distance:
3 miles (Sundance trailhead) or 3.5 miles (Aspen Grove Trailhead)

Time:
2.5-3 hours

Suggested Age:
8 and older (because of length)

Picnic Areas:
There are picnic areas at both trailheads.

Parking:
The Aspen Grove trailhead has a parking lot (must have a receipt in your window) or there is street parking. Sundance Mountain Resort also offers large, free parking lots.

What to expect...

Aspen Grove Trailhead: Drive up Provo Canyon. Turn onto the Alpine Loop and drive just past Aspen Grove. Right after the fee station (pay $6 for parking) turn left into a large parking lot. The trailhead begins in the southwest corner, near the bathrooms. Turn south at a sign that says "Stewart Cascades."

Sundance Chair Lift Trailhead: Drive up Provo Canyon and follow signs to Sundance Mountain Resort. Take the 25 minute chair lift ride to the top. Off to the north (right side) of the lift look for a set of red signs. One says "Stewart Falls Trail" and points towards the start of the trail.

Stewart Falls is one of the more difficult hikes for kids in this book. Though, the scenic 200-foot waterfall provides an exciting reward after all of their hard work. There are two ways to reach the falls.

Aspen Grove – This trail is slightly longer to hike than the Sundance trail. It is also a little more difficult because it goes up a ridge on an incline at the beginning. Despite the slight extra difficulty, many families take this trail because it is cheaper than paying to go up the lift. The path is well-maintained and well-marked. Once you reach the top of the falls, watch your children carefully. They will need help as they climb down the steep descent to the base of the falls. Children may splash and play in the water.

Sundance Mountain Resort – Grab a trail map from the Sundance Chair Lift pay station as you pay for your tickets. It will be useful as you traverse the hike. Lift rides cost $11 for adults and $9 for kids ages 6-12. Children age 5 and under are free. Take the lift up to Ray's Summit. Then take the obvious, signed trail that winds off to the right. The trail is well-marked and easy to follow. After spending time at the falls, you can turn around and return the way you came, taking the lift ride back down (be aware of lift hours). But I recommend that you follow the Sundance trail that takes you back southeast to the base of the resort. It is the easier way because it continues downhill.

Just Around the Corner...

- Cascade Springs Nature Trail
- Timpanogos Falls
- Sundance Mountain Resort

Temple Quarry Nature Trail

Little Cottonwood Canyon, Sandy

Posted Hours:
7am-10pm. The parking lot is closed during winter months.

Distance:
0.3 mile loop

Time:
15 minutes. Spend as much time as you want; we were there about an hour.

Suggested Age:
All ages!

Picnic Areas:
There are no picnic tables, but you could eat on benches along the trail.

Directions to Trailhead:
The trailhead can be found at the point where two roads meet: South Wasatch Boulevard and Little Cottonwood Road. Take I-215 to 6200 South. Follow signs to Alta Ski Area and turn up Little Cottonwood Road. The trailhead is directly to the right as you hit the mouth of the canyon. A gate and a sign mark the entrance to the parking area.

Parking:
There is a free parking lot directly in front of the trail.

What to expect...

Temple Quarry Nature Trail is an easy nature walk for all ages. The trail highlights the area where Mormon settlers quarried granite stone for the Salt Lake City Temple. Markers along the trail give information on how the rock was quarried and taken into the valley. Look for marks on the rocks showing the remnants of work done by early pioneers. The nature walk also includes beautiful mountain views with oak and maple trees lining the path. The entire trail is paved and stroller-friendly.

There are three entrances to the trail off the parking lot. The trail loops from one end of the small parking lot to the other. Restrooms can be found in the parking area. Changing tables are not available.

Just Around the Corner...

- Alta Ski Area
- Cecret Lake Hike
- Lisa Falls
- Snowbird Ski and Summer Resort

Timpanogos Caves

American Fork Canyon
(801) 756-5238
www.nps.gov

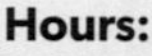

Hours:
May–September: 7am-5:30pm.

The first hike time to the caves is 7:20am and the last hike time is 4pm.

September-part of October: 8am and 3:30pm

Admission:
Entrance to American Fork Canyon $6 per vehicle.

Admission to Caves: *Under 3:* Free; *Ages 3-5:* $3; *Ages 6-15:* $5; *Ages 16+:* $7

Visitor Center and Ticket Reservations
(801) 756-5238.

Parking:
Free parking lot at visitor center.

Food:
Food and drink is allowed along the trail, but not in the caves. On-site concessions sell pizza and burgers near the visitor center. There is a large covered area with tables and chairs for eating.

What to expect...

Located in the Wasatch Mountains of American Fork Canyon, the Timpanogos Caves system is comprised of three natural limestone caves connected by man-made tunnels. The caves are famous for their large variety of cave formations like helictites, stalagmites, stalactites, cave columns, and cave popcorn.

Tours of the caves (20 person max) are offered every day during the open season. Although tickets may be bought on site, I recommend calling the reservation number listed above. You will be asked to give a time that you will start your hike to the caves, and then you will be assigned a tour time 1½ hours from your start time. It takes about 1 hour to hike up to the caves, so the given hour and a half should be plenty of time to make it up to the caves by your assigned tour time. If you are hiking with little kids, you can check in at the visitor center and start a little earlier.

The trail up to the caves is paved the entire way, however strollers and wheelchairs are prohibited. The trail is a constant gradual slope up which gets steeper throughout the 1,100 foot elevation gain. There are benches to rest at various points along the way and it is shady for some parts of the trail. Although the path is wide and perfectly safe, there are steep drop-offs at times. I saw a lot of young children on the hike and most seemed fine, but there were some who were whining and crying a bit. For this reason, I would suggest ages 6 and up for this hike. If you feel that your 3-5-year-old could do it, they probably can. We were definitely glad we left our little girls at home with Grandma.

Once at the entrance to the caves, you can sit on benches and wait for the 45 minute tour to begin. The inside of the caves reveal the effects of centuries of water seeping through the rock and leaving mineral deposits that have built up for thousands of years creating stalagmites, stalactites and other formations. Nothing in the cave can be touched. There are a few points where you have to duck down low to get through the passageway. The caves have lights along the pathway, but it is a good idea to bring a flashlight. You will also want to **bring a jacket** as the temperature in the caves is about 40 degrees.

Restrooms are located at the visitor center and also up near the cave. There is no water available once you leave the visitor center, so be sure to fill up your water bottles.

Just Around the Corner...

- Cascade Springs Nature Trail
- Creekside Park
- Highland Town Center Splash Pad

Timpanogos Falls

Provo Canyon, along the Alpine Loop.

Hours:
None posted

Distance:
About 2 miles out and back

Time:
1.5-2 hours

Suggested Age:
8 and up

Picnic Areas:
The trailhead begins at a picnic ground.

Directions to Trailhead:
Drive up Provo Canyon. Turn onto the Alpine Loop and drive just past Aspen Grove. After the fee station, turn left into a large parking lot. The trailhead begins going straight west up a small set of stairs, next to the bulletin board.

Parking:
There is a paid parking lot (put your receipt in the front window). Pay $6 at the fee station or at the self-serve station in the parking lot. You may also park on the street.

What to expect...

The Timpanogos Falls hike is a beautiful trail on the east side of Mount Timpanogos. It is one of the more difficult hikes in this book. This hike is actually the first portion of a much longer hike that takes you all the way to the summit of Mount Timpanogos. This is a popular hike for more avid hikers and many take the trail at 2am hoping to catch the sunrise from the top. I understand that there are many falls along the hike, but the first two are easiest for kids to reach.

Begin the hike by walking west from the parking lot. You will see a sign that says "Mt. Timpanogos Tr." Just beyond the sign you will pass a check point for hikers going up the mountain. Sign in at the check point on the clipboard. This is a safety measure during busy months to help keep track of hikers. Then follow obvious signs for "Mt. Timpanogos Tr." that lead up the mountain. The falls come into view at about 30 minutes into the hike and you will reach it by about 45 minutes. The falls are always more full in the spring than the fall. We went in the fall and the changing leaves were breathtaking. The second falls come into view within minutes of starting up the trail again. Turn around and you will catch a view of the two falls together. It takes about 10 to 15 minutes to reach the second falls, which is even more beautiful than the first. Return back the way you came.

I recommend this trail for ages 8 and up because of the length and elevation gain. The trail goes up at a constant incline and can be quite tiresome. The trail is also narrow, making it difficult to walk side by side. While we were there, we observed two families with young children including a child in a backpack.

Vault toilet restrooms are located at the trailhead parking lot.

Just Around the Corner...

- Cascade Springs Nature Trail
- Stewart Falls
- Sundance Mountaini Resort

Y Mountain Hike

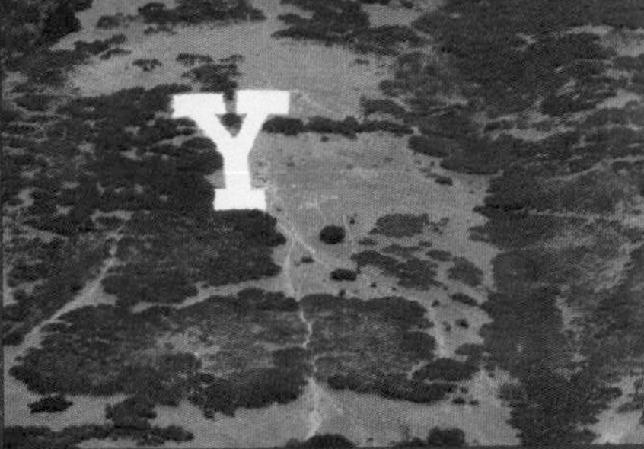

East side of Provo

Hours:
5am-11pm

Distance:
2.4 miles out and back

Time:
2 hours

Suggested Age:
10 and older

Picnic Areas:
There are no picnic areas at the trailhead.

Directions to Trailhead:
From 900 East in Provo, turn east up 820 North. The road will hook left turning into Oakmont Lane. Turn left onto Oak Cliff Drive. Stay right, then turn right onto Terrace Drive. Turn left up the dirt road and park in the upper parking area.

Parking:
Find the parking area by hooking up to the right (south) after you enter the gate. You may pass cars parked in a small parking area. The Y Trail parking lot is higher.

Other locations for hiking or nature walks:

- Antelope Island
- Great Salt Lake Nature Center
- Great Salt Lake Shoreland Preserve
- Red Butte Garden
- Swaner EcoCenter
- Thanksgiving Point Gardens

What to expect...

You are not a true BYU fan until you have made the ultimate trek up to the Y! Located on the mountain behind Brigham Young University, this large block letter is 380 feet high and 180 feet wide. This iconic symbol is made of concrete that is whitewashed on a regular basis. This trail is known to be easy and well-marked.

A large gate with the letter Y marks the entry to the trail. A map of the path is located a short distance up the road. You can take a picture of the map with a cell phone so that you can monitor your progress. The hike consists of 12 switchbacks which are great because kids can count them as they go. After climbing the 10th switchback, instead of going to the right up two more, you can continue going up (left) to arrive at the bottom of the Y. Or you can continue up the last two switch-backs to the top of the Y. Signs discourage hikers from walking on the Y, although plenty of people do it anyway. Just be careful, because it is fairly steep. From the Y you can see beautiful views of Provo, Orem, and Utah Lake. Return the way you came. The hike offers little shade, so try to go during a cooler time of day. There are resting spots along the way.

I recommend this hike for kids age 10 and up, although I read a review online about a 3-year-old who walked the entire way. In my opinion, the steepness of the trail and the length qualify it for older elementary-aged kids. Restrooms are located at the trailhead parking lot. There are no changing tables.

Just Around the Corner...

- BYU Broadcasting
- BYU Museum of Art
- BYU Museum of Paleontology
- BYU Museum of Peoples and Cultures
- Children's Library at Provo City Library
- Comedy Sportz
- FatCats (Provo)
- Monte L. Bean Life Science Museum
- Nickel City Fun Center
- Provo Recreation Center
- Royden G. Derek Planetarium
- Seven Peaks (Provo)

Performing Arts

"The Arts are an essential element of education, just like reading, writing, and arithmetic. . . music, dance, painting, and theater are all keys that unlock profound human understanding and accomplishment"— William Bennett. Every destination in this chapter will give you the opportunity to expose your children to the wonderful world of music, dance and theater. Even though some of these locations may seem more appropriate for adults, look a little closer. You will see that we share how you can enjoy these performances with children. Be sure to also look at the appendix in the back of the book where you will find a list with many of the family-friendly theaters along the Wasatch Front.

Courtesy of Utah Symphony/Utah Opera

Ballet West

Capitol Theater
50 West 200 South
Salt Lake City, 84101
(801) 869-6900
www.balletwest.org

Season:
Runs *November through May*. Shows run for about two weeks on weekdays and weekends including a Saturday matinee.

Tickets:
Prices for a single ticket ranges from $19-$75. Prices change based on seat location, show, and time of purchase.

Purchase tickets through the Ballet West website, over the phone, in person, or on www.arttix.org.

Season Tickets:
There are various choices for grouping tickets. Prices range from $48-$341.

Parking:
Metered parking is available on most streets (free after 6 & on weekends). Suggested paid parking facilities nearby include: 250 South West Temple, 301 South West Temple, or 306 South West Temple.

Food:
Concessions sell snacks and drinks.

Discounts:
Group and student discounts are available.

Social:

What to expect...

Ballet West is a professional ballet company that calls Utah's Capitol Theater home. Established in 1963, Ballet West has entertained audiences for years with a wide variety of both classical and contemporary ballet. The company is made up of 40 members, 11 second company members, and a thriving ballet academy.

Artists of Ballet West in Willam Christensen's "The Nutcracker." Photos by Luke Isley.

Each season runs from November through May with an opening gala and five shows. The shows each run 7 to 10 days, although *The Nutcracker* runs for the entire month of December. The annual presentation of *The Nutcracker* is Ballet West's most popular performance and tickets may be purchased starting in mid-October. Directly following each Saturday matinee of *The Nutcracker* (except Christmas Eve), Ballet West hosts a Sugar Plum Party on stage for children. Children get to meet the Sugar Plum Fairy and other members of the ballet and enjoy some refreshments. Tickets must be purchased separately for these parties for a small price. The Company also a Family Series presentation each season. In years past, they have performed *The Little Mermaid* and *Aladdin*.

Shows usually run about 2 to 2 ½ hours with an intermission. You should arrive 30 minutes before curtain to allow time to get settled. Shows are most appropriate for children ages 8 and older, but they allow parents to decide. Children under 3 will not be permitted to enter. All audience members must have a ticket. Ballet West offers booster seats for younger audience members.

A boutique is set up in the lobby during each performance selling clothing and ballet-themed gifts. Around Christmas they also sell ornaments, gifts, and a large variety of nutcrackers. Ballet West also offers private and group tours of Capitol Theater including the chance to observe a rehearsal. Call 801-869-6917 for more information.

See Appendix 1 for Downtown Destinations close to this area

The Children's Theatre

3605 South State Street
Salt Lake City, 84115
(801) 532-6000
www.uctheatre.org

Season:
October through May. It includes 5 Mainstage shows and 2 Youthstage shows.

Shows:
Shows usually happen on Fridays at 7pm and Saturday afternoons.

Tickets:
$14 for Mainstage Shows and $9 for Youthstage Shows. Purchase tickets on the website or by calling the box office. Tickets can be picked up at will-call before the show.

Parking:
Free parking is available on the north and south sides of the building. There is also free street parking.

Food:
No outside food or drink is allowed. Concessions are sold before the show and during intermission.

Discounts:
Discounted group rates are available for groups of 10 or more. Other promotions are offered through email.

What to expect...

The Children's Theatre is the perfect place to introduce children to the theater. Founded in 1985, the Children's Theatre has been entertaining young audiences for many years. Now, in a new, more permanent location the theater will continue to offer kid-friendly plays for years to come.

Check out *Appendix 7* for the many family-friendly theaters!

The Children's Theatre offers two play experiences. Mainstage plays are performed by adults for the general public. Youthstage plays are performed by youth ages 9-19 for the general public. These shows tell stories that appeal to young audiences. Shows from the past include titles such as *Pippi Longstocking*, *The Hunchback of Notre Dame*, and *Robin Hood*. Each show has two acts that last 30-45 minutes long with a 15 minute intermission.

There is no assigned seating at Children's Theatre shows, so try to arrive about 30 minutes before a show to be sure you get a good seat. The lobby opens 45 minutes prior to show time. Typical shows are recommended for ages 4 and up though some shows may be recommended for older kids. The Children's Theatre advises you not to bring toddlers and babies as they will not be allowed to enter.

The Children's Theatre offers backstage tours that last 25 minutes. Tours must be scheduled in advance. The Theatre also offers a Shakespeare festival during the summer, which is a great introduction to Shakespeare and is perfect for families with short attention spans. Drama classes are offered after school. They also offer summer camps.

Just Around the Corner...

- Fairmont Aquatic Center
- FatCats (SLC)
- Holladay Lions Fitness and Recreation Center
- Murray Aquatic Center
- Redwood Road Drive-In
- The Park Center

Mormon Tabernacle Choir

50 North West Temple Street
Salt Lake City, 84150
(801) 240-4150
www.mormontabernaclechoir.org

Season:
Performances are year-round.

Shows:

Music and the Spoken Word
Sundays: 9:30am-10am;

Rehearsals open to the public
Thursdays: 8pm-9:30pm.

See the website schedule for special performances.

Tickets:
FREE!

Parking:
There is a paid parking garage under the Conference Center (entrance on West Temple along side the Conference Center), or another is located under the Joseph Smith Memorial Building (entrance on South Temple between State and Main Street).

Food:
No food or drink is allowed.

What to expect...

The Mormon Tabernacle Choir is a professional choir well-known internationally. The group is made up of 360 volunteers ranging in age from 25 to 60 years old. The choir has performed all over the world including the inaugurations of five U.S. Presidents, 13 of the World's Fairs, and the 2002 Winter Olympics held in Salt Lake City.

Other locations with Performing Arts in this book:

- Comedy Sportz
- LDS Conference Center
- Hale Center Theater Tour
- Homestead Friday Night Campfires
- Peery's Egyptian Theater Tour
- Theaters Appendix
- Treehouse Children's Museum

The Choir performs on a regular basis on Temple Square. The Tabernacle was built by early pioneers and serves as the choir's primary home. The choir loft sits in front of the large, historic pipe organ which has become synonymous with The Mormon Tabernacle Choir. During the summer months and the entire month of December, the Choir performs in the Conference Center (across the street) to accommodate a larger audience.

Since 1929 the Choir has been broadcasting Music and the Spoken Word, an inspirational program with choral music and a short message. This program reaches millions of people through TV, radio, and the internet. Children as young as 8 years old may attend the live broadcast of this show on Sunday mornings at 9:30am. No tickets are necessary, just show up a half hour before the broadcast begins. Because it is a live recording, children need to be as silent as possible during the 30 minute show. The choir's weekly rehearsals are also free and open to the public, held every Thursday in the Tabernacle.

See Appendix 1 for Downtown Destinations close to this area

The Choir performs a number of special concerts throughout the year including two annual concerts. The Pioneer Day Commemoration Concert is offered two different evenings around Pioneer Day (July 24th). The Christmas Program is the most popular concert given by the Choir. These special events require registration for a lottery system to secure free tickets. Go to the website and click "tickets" to register. Registration is open usually two months prior to the special event.

Utah Symphony Family & Lollipops Concerts

123 West South Temple Street
Salt Lake City, 84101
(801) 533-6683
www.utahsymphony.org

Season:
Season runs from September through May.

Tickets:
Prices change depending on shows and seating. Purchase tickets at Abravanel Hall box office, through the website or by calling (801) 355-2787. Prices are raised the day of performances. Lollipops Concert tickets for children 3 and under are free.

Parking:
Abravanel Hall is located on the corner of South Temple and West Temple. TRAX will drop you off directly in front. Limited street parking is available. Parking for performances is available at the Salt Palace Convention Center or City Creek Center parking garages.

Food:
No outside food or drink is allowed.

Discounts:
Utah K-12 students may receive one free ticket each year for Symphony performances. Season subscriptions are available at a discounted rate. Discounts available for groups of 10 or more.

Social:

What to expect...

Utah Symphony and Utah Opera (USUO) both perform their own seasons of concerts each year. They also work together to provide a series of Family Concerts as an outreach to people of all ages. Unless otherwise noted, concerts are held in Abravanel Hall.

The **Family Concert Series** is a set of three shows presented on Tuesday evenings at 7pm. These last two hours and are recommended for ages 6 and up. Each year concerts include: a showcase of exceptional youth performers, a concert with well-known classical music that kids will recognize (for example Peter and the Wolf), and a Halloween concert that features familiar spooky symphonies and one of Utah's largest costume contests! Audience and orchestra members all participate.

The **Lollipops Concert Series** is a set of three concerts held on Saturday mornings that each last one hour. They are designed for children ages 5-12, but are open to all ages. All children must have a ticket, but children 3 and under are free. These concerts offer pre-concert activities in the lobby including musical games, crafts, activities, and performances. When advertised, the orchestra turns the lobby into a Musical Instrument Petting Zoo, where children can touch and play orchestra instruments.

Children's Opera Showcase is presented every year as a culmination of opera projects created in Utah Elementary Schools. These operas were completely created by students with direction and help from their teacher and composers, sponsored by the Utah Opera. Three original operas are presented in this showcase at the Jeanne Wagner Theatre.

USUO also offers an annual free **concert for individuals with special needs**. They share this concert, knowing that many families cannot come to cultural events because their special needs child acts in distracting ways. Tickets are free, but registration is required. This concert is presented at the Capitol Theater.

Indoor Playspaces

Has your front room ever turned into a soccer field on a cold winter day? How do you keep kids entertained when it is too cold or even too hot to play outside? From bounce houses to trampoline arenas and indoor playgrounds, this chapter is full of fun indoor play places that will keep kids moving and exercising no matter what the weather.

Courtesy of Get Air

Airborne

12674 South Pony Express Rd.
Draper, 84020
(801) 601-8125
www.airbornesports.com

Hours:
Open Monday through Saturday. Hours are seasonal. See website for current schedule.

Admission:
Open Jump (ages 5 and older) *1st hour (M-F):* $9.36, (Sat): $11.23. *Additional hours:* $7.49; *Additional 30 minutes:* $5.61.

Ages 0-2 *1st hour:* $2.00; *Additional Hour:* $1.87;
Ages 3-4 *1st hour:* $6.55; *Additional Hour:* $4.68.

Food:
No outside food or drink is allowed. On-site concessions are available.

Discounts:
Lowered group rates and discounted punch cards are available.

What to expect...

Trampoline enthusiasts won't be disappointed with a jumping session at Airborne Trampoline Arena. Not only does Airborne offer a large square footage of wall-to-wall trampoline jumping, but also a variety of specialized trampoline activities. With high ceilings and sky lights, the arena is bright and open. Open cubbies are available for use and lockers can be rented for fifty cents. There is free WiFi , a small lounge area with leather couches and a TV. Hand sanitizer is plentiful.

Lil' Kids Arena: Airborne's kids arena ranked as our favorite trampoline space for younger kids (8 & under) as this small arena features nine connected trampolines, a zip line, and a foam pit. A TV featuring kid programing provides a nice break when needed. My favorite feature is the 8-foot balance beam that lies across a small foam pit, inviting kids to try to balance their way across.

Dodge Ball Arena: This large area is sectioned off with mesh netting and includes 12 trampolines that angle up the walls on both sides. There is a maximum of 10 players per side. During busy times there is a sign-up sheet for a turn to play.

The Main Arena: This is a huge arena of wall-to-wall trampolines as well as basketball hoops.

The Pit: Two long, Olympic-style trampolines end at a huge foam pit where jumpers can do tricks. There is also a tall platform with a ten foot drop into the foam pit called the Tower. After jumping into the pit, kids can scramble up to catch an instant replay of their jump on a TV monitor.

Air X: This area features four Olympic tramps with another foam pit and TVs on a fifteen second delay that allow you to watch your jump. Jumpers must be 60" to use the platforms in this area.

Zip Line: This 40-foot zip line carries riders over an equally long foam pit. Let go at any time and fall into the soft, foam cubes below. A padded wall at the end of the zip line helps to cushion a landing for anyone who forgets to let go. You must be 54"to ride.

A waiver must be signed before participating, but can printed and completed at home. Don't forget the legal guardian signature. It's good for one year. Kids age 12 and under must be supervised by an adult. There are eight different party rooms available for rental. Both men's and women's restrooms have changing tables.

Just Around the Corner...

- Boondocks (Draper)
- Color Me Mine (Draper)
- Dimple Dell Recreation Center
- Real Salt Lake
- Scheels
- South Jordan Recreation Center

City Creek Dinosaur Play Area

50 South Main Street
Salt Lake City, 84101
(801) 521-2012
www.shopcitycreekcenter.com

Hours:
10am-9pm

Admission:
FREE!

Parking:
The closest parking garage to the food court is in the KeyBank building on 50 South Main Street.

Food:
No food is allowed in play area.

What to expect...

Shopping can take its toll on all of us, but especially kids. The dinosaur play area located in the food court of the east City Creek building is the perfect place to take a break and let the kids work off their energy. The play area was inspired by Utah's prehistoric past. It carries a dinosaur theme with a large colorful mural and many soft sculpted dinosaur figures that make it comfortable and safe for kids to climb on, hang from, crawl through, and slide down. Extra soft padding under the floor makes for soft landings. When we were there, there were approximately 40 kids playing, but it didn't seem overly crowded. The play area is enclosed by 4-foot walls with only one entrance in and out. Shoes must be removed before entering the play area. Soft benches line the walls for comfortable parent supervision The height restriction on the play area is 42" or less. The play area is surrounded by tables and chairs, so you could grab some lunch and then let the kids play.

Restrooms and drinking fountains are located on the exact opposite side of the food court, kitty-corner to the play area. The facilities are exceptional. There is a large family bathroom available with regular and child-sized toilets, as well as a changing table. If you have a nursing baby, the mother's room offers soft couches, a changing table, and sink. The women's restroom also offers a changing table.

Edutainment Play Center

West Valley Family Fitness Center
5415 West 3100 South
West Valley City, 84120
(801) 955-4000
ww.wvc-ut.gov/fitnesscenter

Hours:
Monday-Saturday: 8am-8pm;
Sunday: 9am-12:00am

Admission:
Under 4: Free; *Age 4-11*: $3.75; *Age 12-17*: $4.75;
Age 18-61: $5.50; *Age 62+*: $4.

Parking:
Free parking lot.

Food:
No food, gum, or drink is allowed in the Edutainment Center. A snack bar inside sells drinks, snacks, hot dogs, burgers, and more. The snack bar provides tables, chairs, and high chairs.

Discounts:
West Valley City residents receive a discounted admission.

What to expect...

The West Valley Family Fitness Center houses an exciting indoor play center for kids ages 11 and under. This is a separate amenity from the daycare facility inside the Fitness Center. Rather than a daycare, the Edutainment Play Center is a fun indoor play zone.

Imaginative Play – Children can use small shopping carts and buy play food in a mini Harmons Grocery Store. There is also a child-sized fire house, police station, movie theater, dog house, and tree house.

Active Play – Other choices for play encourage activity and fitness. The center offers a small indoor basketball court, a large climbing/play structure, a Dance Dance Revolution station, and other active gaming. There is also a small track for riding Roller Racers, which are low to the ground, sitting scooters.

Toddler/Baby Zone – This is a large, carpeted area that provides baby and toddler toys. Seating is provided for supervising adults.

Mondays at 4pm the Edutainment Center offers free movies for kids ages 11 and under. The movies are shown inside the small movie room on a wall-mounted television.

Children under age six must be accompanied by an adult 18 years or older. Parents who are accompanying their children in the play center do not need to pay to enter. The Play Center is regularly supervised by staff. Lockers are provided at the entry. Restrooms with changing tables can be accessed near the basketball court. Use of this area is prohibited for children wearing wet swim clothing.

Just Around the Corner...

- Kennecott-Magna Recreation Comple
- Centennial Pool
- West Valley Family Fitness Center

Get Air Sportsplex

1188 Sportsplex Dr
Kaysville, 84037
(801) 499-5247
www.getairsportsplex.com

Hours:
See website for seasonal hours.

Facility may be closed occasionally for parties or corporate events. Check website.

Admission (per hour):
Under 46": $5; *Over 46":* $10; *Non jumpers:* Free.

Parking:
Free parking lot.

Food:
Food and drinks are permitted in a designated area on the soccer side of the complex.

Discounts:
Ten time punch card: $80, 2 for Tuesday, Thankful Thursday

Social:

What to expect...

Get Air Sportsplex is one of Utah's largest trampoline arenas with over 24,000 sq ft. of jumping space. It houses an indoor soccer field as well as the trampoline arena with a 12 ft. wall separating the two. Check website for Mommy and Me hours.

Dodge Ball: The trampolines in this section are surrounded by tall mesh netting that keeps the balls in the play area.

Kid's Area: Designed for kids under 46 inches, this area includes several trampolines, angled trampolines for sliding, and a big foam pit. Young children can play freely with others their size. I think my girls spent 20 minutes just trying to stack foam blocks in the foam pit.

Open Jump: This is an enormous wall-to-wall jumping area with angled trampolines on the walls and raised platforms in the middle.

Foam Pits: These trampolines are great for those who like to do tricks. There are five extra bouncy trampolines, each with a foam pit at the end. A large flat screen TV above each foam pit runs on a five second delay allowing the participant to turn around after their jump into the pit and watch themselves on the instant replay.

Shoes are not allowed. Jumpers must either wear socks or go barefoot. Socks are available for $2. Parents can sit in comfortable leather couches located throughout the arena and enjoy the free WiFi.

The bathrooms with changing tables are located on the soccer side of the sportsplex. There are 4 party rooms available for rental. See website for rates. Save time by filling out your waiver form via computer at home.

Good to know...

My girls, ages two and four, had a blast in the toddler area, but were pretty tired after about 30-40 minutes. This facility does not offer any type of toddler play area with toys, however a large colorful childcare area full of toys is visible through clear plastic walls. Unfortunately, the area is not available for trampoline jumpers. It is a childcare area for members using the other areas of the sportsplex.

Just Around the Corner...

- Boondocks (Kaysville)
- Castle Heights Playground at Nicholls Park
- Cherry Hill
- Great Salt Lake Shorelands Preserve
- Heritage Park
- Krispy Kreme (Layton)
- Layton Surf 'n Swim
- Legacy Electric Park
- Three Little Monkeys

Hang Time Extreme Trampolines

1340 Sandhill Rd.
Orem, 84058
(801) 784-6100
www.getairhangtime.com

Hours :
Open Monday-Saturday. See the website calendar for current hours. Occasionally closed for special events.

Admission:
Open Jump 1 hour $10; *Under 46"*: $6
Open Jump 2 hour $16, *under 46"*: $10

Food:
No outside food or drink is allowed. Concessions sell pizza, nachos, drinks, and candy. There is a large area with tables and chairs for eating.

Discounts:
Click on "Deals" on the website to see current promotions.

Social:

What to expect...

Hangtime Sports is one of Utah's newest and largest trampoline arenas. With over 40,000sq ft. of trampolines, it's guaranteed to satisfy any jumper's appetite.

Open Jump Arena: This is an enormous wall-to-wall jumping area with angled trampolines on the walls and raised platforms in the middle. Children must be at least 46" to play here.

Dodge Ball: This dodge ball arena is unique because it is surrounded by angled trampolines on 3 walls (not just 2). There is usually an attendant supervising the games and helping to keep things fair.

Kids Area/Slam Ball: This area is designated exclusively for kids, less than 46" tall during the day. At night, when there are no young children around, it is used for trampoline basketball.

Arcade: The arcade offers video games and ticket redemption games. You can exchange tickets for prizes at the prize counter.

My family had a great experience at Hang Time. The only thing that was tricky during our visit was because the arena is so large, it was easy to lose track of my kids and difficult to find them immediately.

A waiver must be signed by a legal guardian before you can participate. The waiver can be printed at home or filled out on a computer in the lobby. Lockers can be rented for a small fee. There is a changing table in the women's restroom.

Jake's Archery

765 South Orem Boulevard
Orem, 84058
(801) 225-9202
www.jakesarchery.com

Hours:
Monday-Friday: 10 am-7pm;
Saturday: 10 am-6pm

Admission:
$10 per person; *Groups of 6 or larger:* $7 per person

Parking:
Free parking lot.

Food:
There are vending machines and a few tables available for eating snacks.

Discounts:
Discounts are offered to groups of six or more.

What to expect...

Jake's Archery is primarily a pro shop for hunters and outdoorsmen. A secondary part of their business is an indoor archery range, open to the public during regular business hours. The range allows seven archers to shoot at a time.

The adventure begins as you enter the pro shop, which reveals a spectacular display of animal mounts on every wall. The range fee is paid at the register. You may have to wait a minute until an employee finishes helping store customers. The fee allows you to stay as long as you want, with no time limitation. An employee will take you back to the archery range and set you up with finger and arm guards and a proper size bow and arrows. The employee will give instruction on proper technique and form and help guide you until you are comfortable doing it on your own. The regular targets are 20 yards away, but they have 4-5 moveable targets that can be brought up closer for younger children.

The rule of the range is that you put your bow back on the rack until everyone on the line is done shooting all of their arrows. Then everyone can collect their arrows for the next round.

My boys ages 8 and 10 loved this activity. I saw them improve quite a bit in just a half hour. Although there is no official minimum age requirement, I would strongly suggest that children ages 7 and up would most enjoy the activity. Bringing younger kids can be a safety concern and divide your attention. Kids under 18 must be accompanied by an adult and not just dropped off.

Scout groups are frequent patrons. Reservations are not required, but are recommended for large groups.

Just Around the Corner...

- BYU Broadcasting
- BYU Museum of Art
- BYU Museum of Paleontology
- BYU Museum of Peoples and Cultures
- Creativity Art Studio
- Color Me Mine (Provo)
- FatCats (Provo)
- Hang Time Extreme Trampolines (Orem)
- Krispy Kreme (Orem)
- Monte L. Bean Life Science Museum
- Nickle City
- Orem Owlz
- Provo Beach
- Royden G. Derek Planetarium
- Scera Pool
- Seven Peaks Fun Center (Orem)
- Shops at Riverwoods
- University Mall Tree House Court

Jump Around Utah

1519 South 700 West
Salt Lake City, 84104
(801) 977-9000
www.jumparoundutah.com

Hours:
Vary daily. Check the website for current schedules.

Admission:
Under 1: Free; *Age 1:* $2; *Age 2:* $4; *Ages 3 and up:* $10. Parents are always free.

Parking:
Free parking lot.

Food:
No outside food or drink is allowed. A concessions counter sells drinks, fruit, candy, and snacks.

Discounts:
The best deal is to purchase a $50 punch pass that gives you ten admissions for $5 each.

What to expect...

What makes Jump Around Utah different from other bounce houses is its enormous **jumping pillow**. Located in the center of the play area, the 40 by 25 ft. inflated "pillow" is the first place every child runs to upon entering the play area.

Surrounding the pillow are several different **bounce houses** and slides. Children bounce out of one inflatable, jump on the pillow, and then climb into the next bounce house. A large **climbing structure** with tunnels and slides adds another dimension of fun.

Parents always play free, so you can enjoy all the activities with your kids. If you are just supervising from the seating area, you can enjoy the free WiFi. Socks must be worn at all times and can be purchased for $1. There are cubbies in the lobby for shoes and jackets. Lockers are also available at no charge, just ask for a key at the front desk. A waiver must be signed before children are allowed to play, but once the waiver has been filled out, it is good for all subsequent visits within a year. You can save time by printing the waiver at home and bringing it signed. The inflatables are cleaned daily and hand sanitizer is available at the front desk. There are restrooms located near the front desk with a small changing table. Drinks and snacks can be purchased at the front desk.

Jump Around Utah is one of my favorites because the visibility of the inflatables from the seating area makes it easy to keep tabs on your kids. Family-owned and operated, the customer service is excellent and the atmosphere friendly.

See Appendix 1 for Downtown Destinations close to this area

Jump 'N Bounce

7988 South Welby Park Drive (4550 West)
West Jordan, 84088
(801) 280-7988
www.jumpandbouncefun.com

Hours:
Monday-Thursday: 11am-8pm; *Friday-Saturday:* 10am-9pm

Admission:
Monday-Thursday: $7; *Friday-Saturday:* $9; *Children 2 years and under:* $3; *Non-jumping parent on jumping floor:*$3; *Jumping parents (must jump with kids age 2 and under):* $5; FREE admission for parents supervising from the upper lounge or food court.

Parking:
Free parking lot.

Food:
No outside food or drink is allowed. Concessions sell hotdogs, pizza, popcorn, candy, and drinks. There is a large eating area with booth seating.

Social:

What to expect...

Jump 'N Bounce is a new and clean facility offering 10 inflatables ranging from traditional bounce houses to slides and obstacle courses. Socks must be worn at all times and are available for purchase for $1.50.

Adults can supervise from the eating area or from the parent lounge located on a second floor balcony that overlooks the play area. The parent lounge has couches, a TV, free WiFi, and tables and chairs. Stairs from the upper lounge to the play area provide easy access when needed.

Jump 'N Bounce requires that a waiver must be signed *each* time you visit. The waiver can be downloaded online and filled out at home. Because there are no inflatables exclusively designated for young children, I would recommend ages 5 and up. Children that are four years or younger could get overwhelmed by older jumpers. Of course, if you go during the day when kids are in school, there should be no problem for younger children.

Jump 'N Bounce offers four different themed party rooms and multiple party packages. There is a changing table in the women's restroom.

Just Around the Corner...

- Accessible Playground at Veteran's Memorial Park
- Gardner Village
- Gene Fulmer Recreation Center
- Georgell Doll Shop
- Kearns Oquirrh Fitness Center
- Kennecott Utah Copper Mine
- Tiny Tim's Foundation for Kids
- Urban Park Interactive Fountain
- (West Jordan) Conservation Garden Park
- Wild West Jordan Playground at Veteran's Memorial Park

Jump On It!

7 South 1550 West #200
Lindon, 84042
(801) 785-7499t
www.jumponitparty.com

Hours:
Monday-Friday: 2pm-10pm;
Saturday: 10am-10pm

On Friday and Saturday nights, from 10pm-midnight, jumping is open for those 16 years of age and older.

Admission:
Under 4: Free; Ages 4-8: $4 per hour; Ages 9+: $8 per hour, second hour $5.

Parking:
There is a parking lot on the east side of the building.

Food:
No outside food or drink is allowed. There are drink and snack vending machines.

Discounts:
Jump On It offers a homeschooler discount every Wednesday. They also offer a Family Night special on Mondays ($20 for up to 8 jumpers in an immediate family).

Social:

What to expect...

Jump On It is Utah's original trampoline arena. Since its inception in 2007, it has expanded to include a unique variety of play areas. There is something for all ages.

The X Zone: This area is part of the dodge ball arena and includes some new activities. There are two rope swings and basketball hoops. When not being used for dodge ball, the area is open for play.

Toddler Play Area: This small, colorful play area is great for toddlers who tire before older siblings are done jumping. Kids 4 ft. and under are welcome to play with the toys in this area. My 3-year-old spent more time playing with the toy kitchen and blocks here than she did jumping on the trampolines.

Dodge ball: This mesh-enclosed court includes trampolines that angle up the wall on both sides. There are no restrictions on who can play, but it is definitely not an activity area for young children.

Bounce Houses: Jump on It is the only trampoline arena that also offers bounce houses. There are three different bouncers open to those 4 ft. and under.

Open Jumping Arenas: One arena is designated for children under 4 feet tall. It features a foam pit and many adjoining trampolines with a center platform. The largest arena is designated for those taller than 4 ft. and features angled and wall-to-wall trampolines.

Expert Area: This area features a rock-climbing wall with a foam pit under it, angled trampolines for tricks, and platforms; however only those nine and older with a lot of trampoline experience may enter.

Bungee Trampoline: The jumper, equipped with harness and bungee cord, tries to jump as high as possible with the added surge of the bungee cord springing them upward. Additional $4.

Mommy and Me: Every Wednesday and Thursday from 10-11am for children 5 and under.

Chairs, tables, and free WiFi are available for supervising parents. Both men's and women's restrooms have changing tables. There are three party rooms available for rental; see the website for pricing. A waiver must be signed to play. You can download it from their website at home and bring it in filled out.

Just Around the Corner...

- Lindon Aquatics Center
- Novell Children's Discovery Park

Kangaroo Zoo

3 locations
www.kangaroozoo.net

Hours:
Monday-Thursday: 10am-8pm;
Friday-Saturday: 10am-9pm; *Closed:* Sunday

Admission:
Monday-Thursday *Active Play:* $7.99; *Golf:* $5.99;
Active Play & Golf: $10.99.

Friday and Saturday, each of the above activities costs an additional dollar. Children ages 2 and under are always $5 and can golf for an additional $1; Visa, MasterCard, Discover and cash accepted.

Food:
No outside food or drink is allowed, except for reserved birthday parties. Snacks, drinks and pizza are available to purchase at the concessions counter.

Discounts:
Purchase a ten-visit punch pass for $50 (Active play only). Discounts are often available through their website.

Social: 

What to expect...

Location 1	Location 2	Location 3
395 N Redwood Road North Salt Lake, 84401 (801) 295-1900	513 West 700 South Pleasant Grove, 84602 (801) 785-9999	184 20th Street Ogden, 84401 (801) 622-1000

All three Kangaroo Zoo locations offer bouncing fun with a variety of inflatables and bounce houses. Each location is on average about 15,000 square feet with about 10 inflatables, two of which are designated for children under the age of four. There are inflatable slides of varying heights, obstacle courses, sports-themed game inflatables and regular bounce houses. The Pleasant Grove location also offers a small toddler play area with a soft padded floor and small toys for kids 2 and under. This area is a lifesaver when you have older kids who are still playing, and younger kids who are tired out or afraid of the bouncers.

The Redwood Road location is the only one to offer a glow in the dark indoor mini golf course. The nine-hole course on its own is pricey, but you can add it to your active play pass for just $3. Golf may be played as many times as you would like.

Socks are required at all times, even by adults just supervising and are available to purchase for $2. There is a weight limit of 150 pounds, so most parents cannot play on the inflatables with their children. There are several tables and a few couches located throughout the play area where parents can supervise and enjoy the free Wi-Fi.

All inflatables are cleaned weekly and daily cleaning is done on all door handles, tables, and high traffic surfaces. A family restroom with changing tables is located in the lobby. There are very cute themed party rooms available at all locations.

Lowes Xtreme Air Sports

1111 West 100 South
Provo, 84601
(801) 374-JUMP
www.lowesairsports.com

Hours:
Monday-Saturday: 10am-midnight

Each jump session lasts 1 ½ hours. The first session starts at 10:00am. Jumpers join any session starting on the half hour throughout the day.

Admission:
2 and Under: Free (with another paid admission); *Ages 3-4:* $3; *Ages 5-6:* $5, *Ages 7 and up:* $8

Parking:
Free parking lot.

Food:
The Sky Cafe offers pizza, nachos, drinks and ice cream. Vending machines are also available. Outside food or drink is allowed.

What to expect...

Rather than wall-to-wall trampolines, Lowes offers many individual trampolines scattered between foam pits and raised platforms with lots of ways to do tricks into the various pits. We went here twice because my kids liked it so much.

Unlike other trampoline arenas that start hourly jump times when the patron arrives, Lowes jumping schedule runs for 90-minutes. Sessions start every half hour. Due to the clientele of teenagers and college students, I would avoid nights if you are taking young children.

Trapeze Bars: Participants climb up a platform, take hold of the bar, and swing out over an enormous foam pit. Most just let go and drop into the pit while those more daring do flips. Very popular.

Kids Play Area: Due to safety concerns kids 4 and under are not allowed in other areas of the facility, however there is plenty to keep them busy in this gated area: a small trampoline and two foam pits, a slide, a teeter totter, a climbing structure, and more. Kids 5 and 6 are allowed outside this area if closely supervised by an adult.

Cheer Floor: This is a 40′ by 25′ spring floor that cheerleaders and parkourists love. Padded shapes allow for creative play.

Tumbling Tracks: There are two trampoline tumbling tracks (40ft and 50ft).

Rock Wall: The 25 ft. climbing wall is perched over a large foam pit so there is no need for a harness. In fact, the fun of climbing comes secondary to the fun of letting go and feeling the thrill of a free fall into the big foam pit.

Platform Areas: There is an area in the corner that features tall, raised platforms and super bouncy euro tramps. This area is for more experienced jumpers who can handle the bounce from a high platform, to a tramp, and back up to a high platform or into a foam pit.

Just Around the Corner...

- BYU Broadcasting
- BYU Museum of Art
- BYU Museum of Paleontology
- BYU Museum of Peoples and Cultures
- Children's Library at Provo City Library
- CLAS Ropes Course
- Comedy Sportz
- FatCats (Provo)
- Monte L. Bean Life Science Museum
- Provo Recreation Center
- Provo Towne Centre Play Area
- Royden G. Derek Planetarium
- Seven Peaks (Provo)
- Y Mountain Hike

Provo Towne Centre Play Area

1200 Towne Center Boulevard
Provo, 84601
801-852-2401
www.provotownecenter.com

Hours:
Monday-Saturday: 10am-9pm;
Sunday: 12pm-6pm

Admission:
FREE!

Parking:
Free parking lot. Park near SEARS.

Food:
No food or drink is allowed in the play area.

What to expect...

Shopping with kids just got easier thanks to the kid's play area in The Provo Towne Center Mall. Located on the north end of the first level, directly in front of Sears, the Kid's Play Area invites weary parents and children in for a play break.

The small play area is geared toward toddlers, but my 5-year-old still enjoyed it. A 4-ft. padded wall encloses the play area with only one way in or out. The extra soft padded carpet is designed to look like water, grass, and walking trails. The play area includes soft sculptures, a slide, and interactive wall panels. There are benches along the inside perimeter of the play area for those supervising. A family restroom and drinking fountains are nearby, around the corner by the entrance to JC Penny. Another fun attraction located on the second floor in the food court is a large, brightly lit carousel. Rides are $1.50 each.

There is a Laser Tag arena called Command Deck in a store within 100ft. Information is at commanddeck.com.

Just Around the Corner...

- Children's Library at Provo City Library
- Comedy Sportz
- FatCats (Provo)
- Lowe's Xtreme Air Sports
- Provo Recreation Center
- Seven Peaks (Provo)

Tree House Court

University Mall
575 East University Parkway
Orem, 84097
(801) 224-0694

Hours:
Monday-Saturday: 10am-9pm

Admission:
FREE!

Parking:
Free parking lot. Park on the north side of Sports Authority.

Food:
Outside food and drink is permitted, but not in play area.

What to expect...

The Tree House Court play area in the University Mall is an oasis for parents and children who need a break from shopping. The central feature of the play area is an enormous **tree with a "tree house**." Kids can climb up to the tree house platform and then either slide down or come down the stairs in the hollow of the tree trunk. The large tree trunk has a couple of little entrances and windows. Near the tree house is a large hollowed out log that kids can crawl through, climb on, and jump off.

Other locations with indoor play spaces in this book:

- Discovery Gateway: The Children's Museum of Utah
- The Gale Center of History and Culture
- Provo Recreation Center
- Treehouse Children's Museum

Another major play feature is a large **dinosaur fossil** replica that erupts from the ground in different places. My kids loved climbing and hanging from the vertebrae bones and climbing into the big T-Rex skull. Overhead skylights make the whole play area bright. There are clouds painted on the ceiling and a wonderful fairytale mural on the north wall. Benches are located all around the play area and drinking fountains and restrooms are found along the east wall. There are tables and chairs on the far end of the play area. The only downside to this play area is that because the tree is so large, you can't see your child at all times.

Just Around the Corner...

- BYU Broadcasting
- BYU Museum of Art
- BYU Museum of Paleontology
- BYU Museum of Peoples and Cultures
- Creativity Art Studio
- Color Me Mine (Provo)
- FatCats (Provo)
- Hang Time Extreme Trampolines (Orem)
- Jake's Archery
- Krispy Kreme (Orem)
- Monte L. Bean Life Science Museum
- Nickel City Fun Center
- Orem Owlz
- Provo Beach
- Royden G. Derek Planetarium
- Scera Pool
- Seven Peaks Fun Center (Orem)
- Shops at Riverwoods
- Y Mountain Hike

Hands-On Experiences

How many times have you heard the enthusiastic and hopeful words "I want to help" from your child? Children love to create and use their hands, especially when it is an adult-guided activity. They don't mind having sticky hands, glue on tables, chocolate on their nose, or paint on their clothes; they just want to try it all. This chapter includes destinations with hands-on learning including cooking, painting, building, and more. These were some of our children's favorite places to visit. We hope that you and your children will love them too.

Courtesy of Meilani Smith Kongaika

Color Me Mine

Color Me Mine
5 SLC Locations listed below
www.colormemine.com

Hours (SLC Location):
Monday-Thursday: 10am–8pm;
Friday-Saturday: 10am-9pm; *Sunday:* 11am–5pm

Last studio seating is one hour prior to close. See website for holiday closings. Check hours, prices, and policies for specific locations on the website.

Cost:
Age 12 and under: $6; Age 13 and up: $10. Fee covers paint, glaze, and firing. Pay an additional fee for the cost of your chosen item to paint ($10-$60).

Parking:
Free parking lot.

Food:
Color Me Mine discourages eating while working on projects. If your child needs a little snack after their project is done, you are welcome to eat in the store.

Discounts:
Each location offers a number of themed discounts on specific days of the week or month. See the each location's calendar for details. Entertainment Book.

Social: f

What to expect...

Color Me Mine Salt Lake City is part of a chain of paint-it-yourself ceramics studios. The Salt Lake City store is one of five locations found in Utah. The studio provides a unique, creative experience with a final product that kids can proudly display. Reservations recommended on weekends, school days off, and for large groups.

Upon entering the studio you may peruse shelves full of over 400 ceramic ready-to-paint pieces including plates, platters, cups, mugs, bowls, pots, vases, and figurines (dolphins, fairies, penguins, elephants, etc.). Once you choose your piece, the friendly staff explains how to use the paints (over 50 colors to choose from) and materials including paintbrushes, stencils, sponges, pens and stamps. All paint washes out of clothes. Take as much time as you need. Once your piece is done, just leave the mess on the table. The staff cleans up for you (possibly my favorite part of the experience!).

Payment is made at the main desk when you are done. From there the ceramics are glazed and fired. All materials are non-toxic, lead-free, and food safe. About five days later, the completed project is beautifully done and ready for pick-up.

My three and four-year-old children loved the experience, but needed a little help. They only lasted about 45 minutes. My older children (ages 7 and 10) spent an hour longer than the younger kids and could have spent more time. My children were happy with their final product and all talk about going again.

Creativity Art Studio

1063 South 750 East
Orem, 84097
(801)-788-4284
www.creativityartstudio.com

Hours:
Monday-Thursday: 12pm-9pm;
Friday: 12pm-11pm; *Saturday:* 11am-11pm

Admission:
Studio Fee (covers paint, materials and firing) *Ages 13-up:* $7; *Ages 12-younger:* $4

Price of ceramic piece is separate and depends on the piece you choose.

Parking:
Free parking lot.

Food:
No food or drink allowed in the studio.

What to expect...

What child doesn't enjoy painting? Yet, what mom likes cleaning up the painting mess? Enter Creativity Arts Studio. This is a drop-in ceramic studio that provides all the materials, help, and... all the clean up! Reservations are not required, but encouraged if you are coming with a large group.

The studio is bright and cheery with colorful walls and modern tables and chairs. Shelves of unfinished ceramic pieces that are ready to be painted line the studio. Pick and paint ceramics include things like plates, bowls, mugs, figurines, piggy banks, jewelry boxes, and more. Items range in price from $6-$44, with most items falling within the range of $8-$14.

The paints are easily accessible and clearly labeled with sample chips displaying their finished look after firing. All materials are non-toxic, lead-free, and food safe. Tables are stocked with paintbrushes, colorful paint pallets, paper towels, and water. Art aprons are available to protect clothes from inevitable drips!

Price is based on the item you choose to paint and not the time you spend painting it. You can stay as long as you want and even come back multiple times to work on the same piece with no extra cost. Keep in mind that younger children under age six will finish their projects rather quickly, while older children tend to take more time and care with their painting. You might want to have something ready to entertain younger siblings who finish first.

Projects will be fired and ready for pick-up within a week. Restrooms without changing tables are available.

Just Around the Corner...

- BYU Broadcasting
- BYU Museum of Art
- BYU Museum of Paleontology
- BYU Museum of Peoples and Cultures
- Color Me Mine (Provo)
- FatCats (Provo)
- Hang Time Extreme Trampolines (Orem)
- Jake's Archery
- Krispy Kreme (Orem)
- Monte L. Bean Life Science Museum
- Nickel City Fun Center
- Orem Owlz
- Provo Beach
- Royden G. Derek Planetarium
- Scera Pool
- Seven Peaks Fun Center (Orem)
- Shops at Riverwoods
- University Mall Tree House Court

Harmons Cooking School

3 Locations listed below
www.harmonsgrocery.com/cooking-school/

Hours:
Check monthly calendar on website for a list of kid's classes.

Admission:
Varies, usually between $15- $20 per student.

Parking:
Free parking lot.

Food:
No outside food,everything is provided.

What to expect...

Location 1	Location 2	Location 3
Bangerter Crossing 125 East 13800 South Draper, 84020 (801) 617-0133	**Station Park** 200 North Station Pkwy Farmington, 84025 (801)928-2635	**City Creek** 135 East 100 South Salt Lake City, 84111 (801) 428-0365

Locally-owned and operated, Harmons is a grocery store that prides itself on offering more to the community than just groceries. Check the events calendar at the entrance to your local Harmons and it may surprise you to see how many fun activities they offer every month.

One of the ongoing classes Harmons offers is at their cooking school located within the grocery store. Approximately once a month they offer a cooking class for children. These classes are specifically designed for kids, with recipes that involve basic skills like mixing, measuring, kneading, and pouring. Kids under 12 must have an accompanying adult. Parents may be required to pay and participate in the class, but this policy varies depending upon the class. You may want to inquire ahead of time.

All of Harmons cooking school kitchens are spacious with state of the art equipment, including TV monitors that give an overhead view of the chef's workstation. All the ingredients for the class are ready for you and in between steps, a staff helper does the clean up. Each class usually makes three different recipes.

This was definitely a favorite activity for our family. If possible, I would suggest parents plan on being a helper rather than a student. It was hard for me to keep up with my own cooking while trying to help my two boys. It was one of their top ten activities we participated in for this book. Private classes can be scheduled for families or birthday parties.

Lakeshore Learning

Oakwood Village Shopping Center
5480 South 900 East
Salt Lake City, 84117
(801) 268-2224
www.lakeshorelearning.com

Hours:
Craft hours: *Saturdays:* 11am-3pm

Store hours: *Monday-Friday:* 9am-8pm;
Saturday: 10am-8pm

Admission:
FREE!

Parking:
Free parking lot.

Food:
No food or drink is allowed.

What to expect...

Lakeshore Learning is a teacher supply store with a wide variety of educational resources for both parents and teachers. All of the activities and toys created and sold by Lakeshore Learning are designed to help kids reach developmental milestones while having fun. They also sell a large variety of art and craft supplies.

Every Saturday from 11am to 3pm Lakeshore Learning offers a free craft activity with all the supplies provided. Check their website to see what the offered craft is for the week. Crafts are geared toward kids ages 10 and under. Kids are invited to step up to the table and create their project with the instruction of an employee and the supervision of an adult. My kids took about 15 minutes to complete their craft. When we were there, they made masks, which they decorated with tissue paper, beads, feathers, and more. Employees were very kind and helpful.

The outing for the craft activity can also include time to play and discover the toys in the store. There are lots of demonstration toys available for kids to try. The little kids found a bucket holding plastic fish that could be caught with magnetic fishing poles. The big kids could not be pulled away from an Interactive Wipe Board, or Smartboard, that featured touch screen learning games in all subjects and for all ages. The far end of the store, where the preschool items are found, has a small child-size table, a wooden play kitchen with food and dishes, puzzles, books, and magnet boards. Restrooms with changing tables are available.

Just Around the Corner...

- Holladay Lions Fitness and Recreation Center
- Jungle Jim's Playland
- Mountview Park
- Wheeler Historic Farm

Lowes Build and Grow Clinics

Multiple locations throughout Utah
www.lowesbuildandgrow.com

Hours:
10am every other Saturday year-round. In December, clinics are offered every Saturday. See the website for the current schedule.

Cost:
FREE!

Parking:
Free parking lot.

Social: f

What to expect...

Lowe's Home Improvement stores offer free building clinics every other Saturday year-round. Each participating child is provided with a wooden project kit, an apron, goggles, and a patch unique to the project. During the clinic, children build things like flower boxes, birdhouses, trucks, games, and other wooden creations using basic tools like hammers and nails. Many of the projects have stickers to apply for a finished look.

I attended a clinic with two of my children at our local Lowe's store. They loved being able to use the kid-sized hammers and wear their own aprons. I had to help my five-year old quite a bit with his project, but he felt happy with the final product. The staff was friendly and helpful and even provided us with an extra kit when we bent too many nails. Projects take about 20 to 40 minutes to put together.

You must register for classes through the website. Enrollment opens typically a few weeks before each date. You will be required to create an account before completing your registration. Spaces tend to fill quickly, especially for popular projects. You should receive a reminder email about your clinic a few days before the date. If your store is full, you can show up half way through the class (10:30am) to see if there were any no shows.

Parents must fill out a waiver form before children can participate in building projects. Kids can bring back their apron and goggles each time or receive new ones if needed. Each patch is unique to the project completed and can stick directly onto the aprons.

The Home Depot Kids Workshops

Multiple Locations throughout Utah
www.homedepot.com

Hours:
First Saturday of every month from 9am-12pm.

You may show up any time during these hours to do your project.

Cost:
FREE!

Parking:
Free parking lot.

What to expect...

Every Home Depot store offers free Kids Workshops on the first Saturday of the month. These workshops provide a kit, a project pin, and a kid-sized Home Depot apron for each participating child. During the classes children build the kits, which make things like toolboxes, wooden trucks, and birdhouses, using basic tools like hammers, nails, screwdrivers and glue. Some projects require painting as well.

Parents do all of the helping and support for each child. Once the project is completed, children receive a pin (different kind of pin for each activity) and a certificate. Many children we observed had obviously been there multiple times based on the number of pins on their apron. Returning children are encouraged to bring these back each time, but if a child's apron is getting old and worn they are happy to provide another.

Classes are geared towards children ages 5-12 with an accompanying adult although I observed children there who were younger than five. Parents are encouraged to use their judgment in deciding if a project is right for a younger child and each parent must sign a waiver form before allowing their child/children to begin.

Online registration is recommended, but not required. You can also just show up during the activity hours. There are over 22 Home Depot locations throughout Utah. Go to the website and click on "Store Finder" to locate the store nearest you. Find out the type of project offered for the month through the website.

Amusement Parks & Fun Centers

Amusement parks and fun centers are always a favorite with kids. Thrilling rides, laser tag, mini golf, and rock climbing walls are all things that can't be experienced at home. Although you have to pay to play, there are many affordable options along the Wasatch Front. Buying an all-day pass is always the best deal. There are discounts offered for one place or another almost constantly on sites like Groupon, KSL Deals, and City Deals. Lagoon is our only true amusement park in the state, but there are many different fun centers that offer the same fun on a smaller scale and for a smaller price.

Courtesy of FatCats

Boondocks Food & Fun

2 locations
www.boondocks.com

Hours:
Sunday-Thursday: 10am- 10pm (until 11pm in summer);
Friday-Saturday: 10am-midnight;
Closed: Thanksgiving (Kaysville is open), and Christmas

Admission:
Unlimited Fun (60" and above): $25.95;
Junior Unlimited Fun (under 60"): $19.95;

Many different combo passes are available. Attractions can be purchased individually.

Parking:
Free parking lot.

Food:
No outside food or drink is allowed. A snack bar and The Back Porch Grill restaurant offer many types of food on-site.

Discounts:
Entertainment Book.

What to expect...

Location 1
525 South Desert Drive
Kaysville, 84037
(801) 660-6800

Location 2
75 E Southfork Dr.
Draper, 84020
(801) 838-9800

Boondocks Food and Fun offers both indoor and outdoor activities. Attractions can be purchased individually or as part of a package.

Boondocks Food and Fun is well-maintained and clean. Their ticket redemption process is very slick with TV monitors displaying the amount of points each child has left to spend on prizes. The unlimited fun pass is the best deal if you are planning on staying for several hours. All restrooms have changing tables.

Kiddie Cove is an enormous play area for kids under 48 inches. It features a four-story climbing structure where kids can climb, crawl, swing, slide, jump, and play. Benches are located within the play area for supervising adults.

The **Arcade** features traditional video games, ticket redemption games, as well as games like skee ball, basketball, and air hockey.

The Kaysville Boondocks uses a Fun Card system. These are plastic debit cards that are loaded with the amount you choose to put on it. Every attraction and arcade game at Boondocks is able to read the Fun Card and will automatically deduct the appropriate amount from the card. Cards can be registered at the main desk, so if lost, no one else can use it.

Mini Golf offers two outdoor 18-hole courses. Both courses are stroller friendly.

Bumper Boats must have a driver at least 44 inches and passengers must be at least 36 inches.

Bowling lanes have available ball ramps and automatic bumpers. Kaysville Only.

Laser Tag covers a 2 story play area. Must be 40 inches to play.

Rookie Track is designed for young drivers at least 48" tall.

Go-Karts must have a driver at least 58" and passengers must be at least 40".

Batting cages offer slow and fast softball and hardball cages with speeds ranging from 40-60 miles per hour. Use of helmets and bats is complimentary.

Roller Ball (miniature bowling) is great for any age, especially younger children. Kaysville Only.

Maxflight Simulator is an indoor full motion fighter jet simulator. If you don't like flying you can choose between mild to wild simulated roller coaster rides. (This attraction is exclusive to the Draper location)

XD Theater 4D is a theater with 4D motion simulation which means, it's a 3D movie with a chair that moves. There are four different adventures to choose from. (This attraction is exclusive to the Draper location).

Classic Fun Center

3 locations
www.classicfuncenter.com

Hours:
Sandy and Layton hours are the same while Orem hours are different. Check the Orem website for specific hours.

Monday-Thursday: 10am-9pm;
Friday: 10am-10pm; *Saturday:* Noon-10pm

Admission:
There are many different options and combinations for admission. See website for daily deals and specials.

Parking:
Free parking lot.

Food:
No outside food or drink is allowed. Concessions are available at all three locations.

Discounts:
Best deal: Mom's club Monday-Thursday from 10am-4pm. Admission includes bouncing, skating, 1 rental, climbing structure, and 10 tokens for just $7.50 a kid! Entertainment Book.

What to expect...

Location 1
9151 South 255 West
Sandy, 84070
(801)568-9781

Location 2
867 North 1200 West
Layton, 84041
(801) 544-3451

Location 3
250 South State Street
Orem, 84058
(801) 224-4197

Classic Fun Center is an indoor recreation facility with a wide range of activities appropriate for various aged children. Although each Classic Fun Center is independently owned and operated, all three of them offer most of the same activities. We visited the Sandy and Orem locations.

Bring in your own rollerblades, kick scooters or push trikes to ride in the roller skating rink. Scooters are available to rent for $3. Using the roller skating rink is an especially good deal on Thursdays when skating is only $2. There are several different activity options and pass combinations available. Below is a list of activities with a special note if they are only offered at one specific location.

The **skating** rink can be used for skating, blading or scooters. Comfortable seating surrounds the rink. Music and lighting add to the fun atmosphere.

The amazing **play structure** at the Sandy location is two stories tall with over 10,000 square feet of climbing, slides, bungee bouncing, zip lines and even a ball pit.

There are several inflatables and **bounce houses**, one of which is designated for kids four and under. The inflatables in Sandy are impressive.

The **Blast Zone** is unique to the Sandy location. It is an enclosed play area with over 5000 foam balls, air powered ball blasters, canons, targets, an exploding ball fountain and a huge slide. There is a kiddie area within Blast Zone for younger children. You pay for 30 minutes of play.

3-D Laser Tag has an age requirement of seven years old and up. Only the Sandy location offers 3-D, the others offer traditional laser tag.

Skate Road is another unique feature offered at Classic Fun in Sandy. Skate Road is a "track" for skating and scooters that circles around the bounce house play area. It is painted to look like a road and has ramps and jumps for the more experienced skaters.

The **Dimecade** is a small arcade with video games and ticket redemption games.

Time Freak is unique to the Orem location. It is a fun attraction that challenges players to push buttons as they light up. The more buttons you push before time runs out, the higher your score. My boys LOVED this game.

The **Rock Wall** in Layton is recommended for ages 6 and up.

Mini Bowling in Layton is easy for all ages because it uses smaller bowling balls and shorter lanes.

Fastkart Speedway

2840 South Wadman Drive
Ogden, 84401
(801) 547-9199
www.fastkartspeedway.com

Hours:
Monday-Thursday: 4pm-10pm;
Friday-Saturday: 11am-11pm; *Sunday:* 12pm-6pm

Admission:
First-time racing license: $5
See website for various race prices.

Parking:
Free parking lot.

Food:
Outside food and drink permitted. There are vending machines, tables and chairs in the lobby.

Only the Ogden Location offers kid size go-carts.

What to expect...

The go-karts at Fastkart speedway are not the typical ones found in most fun centers. These heavy-duty kid-sized go-karts can reach a speed of 25 mph while the adult sized go-karts reach a blazing speed of 35 mph. The indoor racetrack is open all year and is the only one to offer child-sized go-karts. My boys were unbelievably excited about this activity. I'm kind of a stick in the mud about high adventure type activities (i.e. not the fun parent). I had my reservations, but this was both a fun and safe activity.

The experience starts with a short safety film that all participants must watch in order to receive their license to race. The film explains the rules of racing and specific safety concerns. My 9-year-old got a little nervous as he watched the video because he was afraid he would forget everything. I thought he was going to back-out, but the guy running the racetrack was wonderful as he encouraged him and patiently helped him understand that really all he needed to remember was how to stop and start. All racers must wear a helmet, which is provided. Part of the $5 license fee pays for a head sock that must be worn under the helmet for sanitary reasons. The head sock is yours to keep and can be used on subsequent visits. The license is good for visits within a year.

The warehouse is light and airy with large doors open to keep the gas fumes down. **Dress warmly in the winter.** There is just one track that all racers use, so groups must wait for the group ahead of them to complete their racing before they are allowed to get suited up. It can be a long wait if you come on a busy night. The best time to go with kids is when they open at 4 until about 6 or 6:30pm. After that, the older crowd starts coming in and the wait time will be longer. We requested that only our kids race in their heat, because we didn't want them racing with adults. That is a great option for kids under 12. After the race, the front desk will hand each racer a print-out detailing each participants lap times. There is one party room available. See website for pricing.

Just Around the Corner...

- Birdsong Trail
- Coleman's Motor-VU Drive-In
- Color Me Mine (Ogden)
- FatCats (Ogden)
- Fort Buenaventura
- Ogden Dinosaur Park and Museum
- Ogden Nature Center
- Ogden Raptors
- Ogden River Parkway
- Ott Planetarium
- Union Station
- Peery's Egyptian Theater
- Riverdale Park
- Treehouse Children's Museum

Courtesy of Fastkart Speedway

FatCats

3 locations
www.fatcatsfun.com

Hours:
Ogden Location *Sunday-Thursday:* 10am-12am; *Friday-Saturday:* 10am-1am

*Hours vary at each location and can change seasonally.

Pricing:
See pricing below.

Parking:
Street and garage parking at Ogden location.

Food:
Ogden offers Strikers Grill and Costa Vida. Salt Lake City offers Pizza Factory. Provo offers Costa Vida.

Discounts:
Free bowling games for the Junior Jazz. Join the birthday club for discounts. Entertainment Book.

Social:

What to expect...

Location 1
2261 Kiesel Avenue
Ogden, 84401
(801)627-4386

Location 2
3739 South 900 East
Salt Lake City, 84106
(801)262-9890

Location 3
1200 N. University Ave.
Provo, 84604
(801)373-1863

FatCats is a bowling fun center with three locations in the state of Utah. Each varies in hours, attractions and pricing.

Ogden Attractions Include:

Thunder Alley Bowling: Bowling prices vary based on special offers, day of the week, and time of day. Thunder Alley provides glow-in-the-dark bowling, music, dining at your lane, updated technology, automatic scoring, and automatic bumpers.

Pirate Glow Golf Adventure: ($1.99 for kids, $2.99 for adults) This is offered at the Ogden and Salt Lake City locations. It is a 9-hole, pirate-themed, glow-in-the-dark mini-golf game. Rental shoes available.

Bumper Cars: ($1.99) Only offered at the Ogden location. One person is allowed per car. The minimum height to ride is 44" and the maximum weight is 275 pounds.

Arcade: FatCats offers a wide variety of games that use a token and ticket system. Exchange tickets for prizes.

Kid Zone: (FREE!) An enclosed room with a small play structure. Kids 8 and younger.

Billiards: ($5-$8 per hour) A separate room with multiple billiard tables.

FatCats is known for having a clean environment and delicious food options. Inside FatCats Ogden you can access two complete restaurants: Costa Vida and Pizza Factory. Other food options are available at the Striker Grill where food can be ordered and brought to your bowling lane. Champzz sports bar serves alcoholic beverages and is offered inside both Ogden and Salt Lake locations. The bar in Ogden is a completely enclosed room. Restrooms with changing tables can be found near the Pizza Factory.

Hollywood Connection

3217 Decker Lake Drive
West Valley City, 84119
(801) 973-4386
www.hollywoodconnectionslc.com

Hours:
See website for current hours.

Admission: Unlimited Wristband
Sunday-Thursday: $12.95; *Friday:* $12.95, $19.95 after 5pm; *Saturday:* $12.95, after 1pm $19.95;
Kids 3 and under: Free with paying adult.
Rides can be purchased individually, but the best deal is to purchase the unlimited wristband.

Parking:
Free parking lot.

Food:
No outside food or drink is allowed. Concessions are available as well as the Lieutenant's Diner that serves a wide selection of food including things like burgers, shakes, and ice cream.

Discounts:
Entertainment Book and check the website for promotions.

Social: 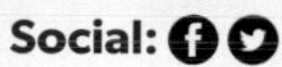

What to expect...

The Hollywood Connection offers a variety of indoor activities. You could easily spend between 3 to 5 hours here the unlimited wristband.

Mini Amusement Rides: There are 5 little amusement park rides including: Dragon Coaster, Krazy Kars, Balloon Tower, Crazy Bus, and the Carousel. The coaster has a height requirement of 43 inches. Children ages 3 and under must ride with an adult. These rides are mostly for younger children.

Climbing Structure: This play structure features a ball pit, tunnels, slides, and lookout points. Key info: height restriction of 45 inches tall or less and shoes are not allowed.

Mini Golf: The indoor golf course at Hollywood Connection is the best course that I have visited. Most indoor golf courses are somewhat dark, but this course has high ceilings and floor to ceiling windows that allow natural light to fill the room. As a result, the golf course is bright, open and cheery. Golf balls must be picked up at the main ticket counter and clubs are found at the caddy shack at the entrance to the golf course. It is possible to take a stroller, but not recommended.

Roller Skating: During the day and early evening, there is plenty of space for little ones to safely skate. Nights (especially weekends) tend to be crowded with teenagers and adults and would not be the best time to skate with young children. Skate walkers are available for those who can't quite skate by themselves and parents can skate and push a stroller. The price to skate includes the use of regular roller skates. Rollerblades are available for an extra $2.

Tron Laser Tag: This is one activity not included in the unlimited wristband, but can be added on. There is no official age requirement, but kids must be able to wear the laser pack. Usually ages 4 and up can play.

Arcade: The arcade is a mix of video games and ticket redemption games. Games are run on tokens.

Avoid Friday and Saturday nights, as it is a very popular place for teenagers. If you are thinking of risking it anyway, don't say I didn't warn you... Restrooms are located just past the ticket counter and café. Party rooms are available for rental. Hollywood Connection adjoins Carmike Cinema 16 Movie Theater.

Just Around the Corner...

- Hale Center Theatre
- LDS Humanitarian Center
- Redwood Road Drive-In
- Taylorsville Community Swimming Pool
- Utah Grizzlies
- Valley Fair Mall

Jack and Jill Lanes

2 locations
www.jackandjilllanes.com

Hours:
Monday-Thursday: 9am-10pm; *Friday-Saturday:* 9am-12:30am; *Sunday:* 9am-10pm (A.F. Location only)

Pricing:
See pricing below.

Food:
Each location has a cafe that serves breakfast, lunch, and dinner in a small diner setting. Lehi also sells pizza. You may order food and eat at your bowling lane.

Parking:
Free parking lot.

Discounts:
They offer discounted packages, daily deals as well as summer passes.

What to expect...

Location 1
113 South 600 East
Lehi, 84043
(801)766-1699

Location 2
105 South 700 East
American Fork, 84003
(801) 756-6097

Jack and Jill Lanes is a family-friendly bowling fun center. There are two locations, both in Utah County. Each offers a similar variety of options for family fun. We visited the Lehi location.

Bowling ($3.50-$4.75) – All 22 bowling lanes are updated and accessible. Shoe rental costs $2.50. Prices change based on time of day and day of the week. You may also pay per hour.

VIP Room ($4.75-$6) – This room offers 10 lanes at a slightly higher price. Many people use this room for parties or family gatherings. You may also pay for bowling per hour.

Laser Tag ($6-$7) – Laser tag can be accessed through the arcade. It is best if you play in a group. There is no age limit; use your judgment. Jack and Jill Lanes offers bounce back games for $4.

Arcade (.25-$3) – The arcade is a large room with a variety of redemption and video games. The average cost is 50 cents. There are a handful of games for young children, and many others including: basketball shoot, skee ball, Deal or No Deal, and more. Redeem tickets for prizes at the prize counter.

Restrooms with changing tables can be accessed near the cafe (Lehi location).

Jungle Jim's Playland

739 East Fort Union Boulevard
Midvale, 84047
(801) 568-1111
www.junglejimsutah.com

Hours:
Monday-Thursday: 11am-9pm;
Friday: 11am-10pm; *Saturday:* 10am-10am

Admission:
All day wristband: $9; Under age 2: $6; Single ride tickets: $1.50 each

Parking:
Free parking lot.

Food:
No outside food or drink is allowed. Concessions sell nachos, hot dogs, pizza, drinks, and other snacks.

Discounts:
Entertainment Book.

What to expect...

Jungle Jim's Playland is an indoor fun center that is geared towards kids 10 and under. It is the perfect place to have a small indoor amusement park experience. Plan to spend 2-3 hours there.

Rides: There are seven different mini amusement park rides. Adults can ride with kids for free, although a few rides aren't big enough to accommodate adults. Attendants are usually supervising a couple of rides at a time, so if no one is at the ride you want, just stand in line and wait and an attendant will come. Lines and wait time are usually not long at all. Rides include: a Carousel, Bumper Cars, Jungle Patrol Jeeps, Swings, Flying Jets, a Roller Coaster, and Spinning Tops.

Play Structure: This has no specific height restriction. Shoes must be removed and stored in available cubbies. It features slides, tunnels and lookout points.

Arcade: The arcade has regular arcade games and ticket redemption games. Some of the games are getting pretty old and will malfunction. Just let an employee know, and they will help get the game going again or refund your coins.

Playhouse: Located in the back near the party area is a miniature house. It has some toys inside and a slide.

There are a number of picnic tables available for use near the arcade. There is also a very large area of tables available only to those hosting a birthday party. See the website for party pricing. Restrooms with changing tables are available.

Just Around the Corner...

- Cottonwood Heights Recreation Center
- Lakeshore Learning
- Mountview Park
- Seven Peaks Fun Center
- Wheeler Historic Farm

Lagoon

375 N. Lagoon Drive
Farmington, 84025
(801) 451-8100
www.lagoonpark.com

Hours:
Open *April-October*. Hours and days change seasonally. See the website for a current schedule.

Admission:
Under age 3: $29.95; *4 years-50 inches tall:* $40.95; *51 inches tall-64 years:* $45.95; *Age 65+:* $40.95
Prices may change seasonally.

Children 2 years of age and younger may enter the Park and Lagoon-A-Beach at no charge, but to participate in any rides, a Toddler Single Day Passport or Individual Ride Tickets are required. Individual Ride Tickets are sold 2 for $1.00. Rides vary between 4-10 tickets per ride.

Season Pass:
Season Passports are available. See the website for pricing.

Parking:
Parking is $9 per vehicle and $12 for oversized vehicles, campers, trailers, etc.

Preferred parking is available on a limited basis for $16 (2 small lots closest to park entrance). Credit cards are accepted for parking payment.

Food:
There are many concession stands throughout the park, all of which accept credit cards. On the north end of the park you can find Arby's and Subway restaurants. You may bring in your own food and drink. Picnic tables and pavilions are located in many areas of the park.

Discounts:
On the website, click "Admissions" then "Special Offers" for up-to-date discounts. Lagoon offers Bounceback tickets on specific days each season. On these days, you can pay a small fee to come back for another full day of fun. You can purchase Lagoon passes and vouchers through Costco and Deseret Book.

What to expect...

Lagoon is the largest amusement park in the mountain west with over 50 rides and attractions. Covering over 100 acres, there are a wide variety of activities for all ages. Included in the price of a Single Day Passport is admittance to Pioneer Village, Lagoon-A-Beach Water Park, and almost every ride in the park (X-Venture Zone attractions cost extra).

Rides: There are over 45 rides, including several roller coasters, the Sky Ride, the Rocket, water rides in Pioneer Village, and many more. Each ride has specific height requirements. See the website.

Kiddieland: This area offers over 15 rides designed for toddlers and young children. Some of the rides include boats, cars, helicopters, and a small roller coaster. Lines in Kiddieland are usually shorter. Benches are positioned throughout the area, many under shady trees. Right next to Kiddieland is the beautiful 120 year-old wooden carousel with the original hand carved animals. There are several other rides throughout the park that would also be suitable for young children when accompanied by an adult.

Lagoon-A-Beach: This is a 6 acre water park within Lagoon that contains several exciting big slides for older children. There is an area called Castaway Island that is dedicated to young children. It has small slides and a shallow play area. You can rent tubes to use in the Lazy River for $3. Because the water in

Lagoon-A-Beach is heated by the sun, it is still pretty chilly through the first part of June. Lockers are available and bathroom/changing rooms are located at the entrance of Lagoon-A-Beach.

Interactive Fountain: This water feature provides a fun water experience without the crowds of Lagoon-A-Beach. Located near the park entrance, the fountain area features over 129 nozzles spraying water at random. Changing into swimming suits is recommended unless you don't mind being wet the rest of the day.

Pioneer Village: This village is a reconstruction of a western community in the 1800s. It includes 42 authentic 19th century buildings, stores and artifacts all furnished as they might have been in the past. Children can tour the old one-room schoolhouse, clock shop, millinery shop, hardware store, cobbler shop, doll museum, and much more. It is on the east end of the park with a screening of large trees serving as a buffer from the park noise and rides. There are shaded grassy areas and picnic tables available for eating or just relaxing for a while.

X-Venture Zone Attractions: These rides are located at the north end of the park and include the Catapult, Skycoaster, and Double Thunder Raceway. These rides carry an additional cost.

Games: Traditional carnival games are scattered throughout the park. Games must be paid for with cash.

Entertainment Shows: Shows are free and take place throughout the day on the Carousel Stage.

Frightmares: Every fall Lagoon transforms into FRIGHTMARES! This Halloween celebration includes most of Lagoon's rides, four Haunted Houses, and two walk-thrus just for kids. There's lots of freaky entertainment for the whole family!

Plan on spending about 8-10 hours in the park. Restrooms are located all throughout the park with changing tables in every bathroom. Strollers can be rented for $9 and wagons can be rented for $12 and $14. Small and large lockers can be rented for $5 and $12 with a $2 refund when the key is returned.

Just Around the Corner...

- Castle Heights Playground at Nicholls Park
- Cherry Hill
- Robert N. Hasenyager Great Salt Lake Nature Center
- S&S Shortline Train Park
- Three Little Monkeys (Kaysville)

Nickel City Fun Center

1515 South State St.
Orem, 84097
(801) 802-8555
www.nickelcityorem.com

Hours:
Monday-Thursday: 1pm-11pm; *Friday:* 1pm-Midnight; *Saturday:* 11am-Midnight; *Closed:* Sunday

Pricing:
There is a $2.25 entrance fee for everyone age 3 and over. All games run on nickels (between 1-8). Laser tag is $4 for the first game and $3 for additional games.

Food:
No outside food or drink is allowed. City Pizzeria provides a variety of freshly made pizzas, drinks, and treats in the lobby of the arcade.

Parking:
Free parking lot.

Discounts:
Admission fee discounts are available with party packages. Visit their Facebook page for occasional deals.

Social:

What to expect...

Nickel City is an arcade with over 100 games that all operate on nickels. Games dispense tickets that are easily redeemed for a variety of prizes. The arcade and restaurant are bright, clean, and pleasant.

Games and rides that are friendly to young children include: skee ball, basketball shoot, popcorn game (try to catch as many moving balls as possible in a net), spin 'n' win, spider stompin' (children stomp on buttons that light up), air hockey, a three-horse carousel, and many other games that only require a push of a button (and a little bit of luck). The arcade also contains many games more appropriate for teens and adults including laser tag and a number of shooting games with guns.

After visiting multiple arcades with my children, this is one of my favorites. All of the other arcades have the same games, but cost more money. We gave each child two dollars in nickels that lasted us about 45 minutes to an hour of play. In other arcades, five dollars lasted less time. Also, other arcades use a card system that is less appealing for younger children. It is much easier for children to keep track of nickels/tokens and tickets rather than the swipe of a card. There is also much more satisfaction for children in receiving the tickets as a reward after playing.

Bathrooms are located in the back of the arcade with changing tables in both men's and women's.

Just Around the Corner...

- BYU Broadcasting
- BYU Museum of Art
- BYU Museum of Paleontology
- BYU Museum of Peoples and Cultures
- Creativity Art Studio
- Color Me Mine (Provo)
- FatCats (Provo)
- Hang Time Extreme Trampolines (Orem)
- Jake's Archery
- Krispy Kreme (Orem)
- Monte L. Bean Life Science Museum
- Orem Owlz
- Provo Beach
- Royden G. Derek Planetarium
- Scera Pool
- Seven Peaks Fun Center (Orem)
- Shops at Riverwoods
- University Mall Tree House Court
- Y Mountain Hike

Cherry Hill Courtesy of Rachel Clarke

Provo Beach

4801 N University Avenue
Provo, 84604
(801) 224-5001
www.provobeach.com

Hours:
Monday-Thursday: 11am-10pm;
Friday: 11am-11pm; *Closed:* Sundays

Admission:
Free to enter, but pay to play. Prices vary with each activity. You may also purchase an annual pass. See details online.

Parking:
Free parking anywhere in The Shops at Riverwoods.

Food:
The Pier Cafe offers snacks and meals. Ike's Creamery serves ice cream, malts, shakes, and more.

Discounts:
Check social websites for occasional discounts, typically around holidays.

Social:

What to expect...

Located on the west end of The Shops at Riverwoods, Provo Beach is a large complex full of attractions and entertainment for the whole family. Everything runs on a card swiping system. You can load a card with as much money as desired and enjoy the attractions of your choice. Choices include:

Toddler Town ($1) – Ages four and under. It is an enclosed play area with a tube slide, climbing structure, and movable soft gym. It is cleaned daily.

Kid's Mega Playground ($4) – Ages four and up. Socks are required. This is a huge indoor playscape with five levels including a tall corkscrew slide. Surveillance video is shown on a screen in the parents lobby. Parents enter for free.

Carnival Games – The games use a "ticketless" system. Cards are swiped at each game and etickets are automatically loaded to the card. Exchange etickets for prizes.

Ropes Course ($8) – Children must be 48 inches tall. No flip-flops or open-toed shoes are allowed. We observed children as young as 7 years old climbing this course. The Ropes Course hangs 32 feet off the ground. Participants are securely harnessed and move from platform to platform over tight ropes and swaying rope bridges.

Sunset Lanes Bowling ($3-$5, $2.50 Shoe rental), **Boardwalk Carousel** ($1)

Indoor Flow Rider ($20/Hour per person) – First time riders must sign a waiver. The minimum height for surfing is 52 inches tall and boogie boarding is 42 inches tall. Minimum of 5 people, or payment of equal value required. The Flow Rider is an indoor wave machine that pumps 30,000 gallons of water per minute. Call ahead for open surf hours or to reserve a time.

Miniature Croquet ($6 Adults, $4 Under 12 years) – Play on the world's first Miniature Croquet Course. This course is a colorful and fun way to experience the game of croquet.

Pinewood Derby ($80/hour to rent the space) – Race your cars on an 8 lane electronic track. Bring your own car or buy a kit ($5-$10 plus $3 shop fee). Groups of 5 or more must contact an events coordinator before racing. This is a one-stop location for everything to do with pinewood derby racing. A custom shop is available for those who want to build their own car on the premises.

Lazer Frenzy ($2.50) – This is not laser tag; it is a race through a maze of lasers. There are different game options and levels of difficulty.

Beach Cruisers (rental costs vary) – Bikes are available seasonally for rental between March and October. Rent a Tandem Cruiser, Single Cruiser, Kid Cruiser, or Kid Carrier Bike Trailer. See website for hours. Bikes can be rented by the hour, or for the day.

During the summer months, you can let the kids splash and play in a floor fountain out in front of the main entrance. All restrooms have changing tables.

Suggestion:
Feed your child and feed the hungry in Africa at the same time! Malawi's Pizza is a great restaurant directly in front of Provo Beach. For every meal you buy, they provide a nutritious meal to a child in Malawi, Africa. Malawi's Pizza serves pizza, pasta, salad, and dessert pizza all made with fresh ingredients.

Just Around the Corner...

- BYU Broadcasting
- BYU Museum of Art
- BYU Museum of Paleontology
- BYU Museum of Peoples and Cultures
- Creativity Art Studio
- Color Me Mine (Provo)
- FatCats (Provo)
- Hang Time Extreme Trampolines (Orem)
- Jake's Archery
- Krispy Kreme (Orem)
- Monte L. Bean Life Science Museum
- Nickel City Fun Center
- Orem Owlz
- Scera Pool
- Seven Peaks Fun Center (Orem)
- Shops at Riverwoods
- University Mall Tree House Court

Seven Peaks Fun Center

3 locations

Hours:

Winter Schedule *Monday-Thursday:* 2-10pm; *Friday:* 2pm-12am; *Saturday:* 10am-12am

Admission:

Attractions can be purchased individually or as part of a package. There are many different passes available starting at $12. The basic unlimited all day pass costs about $20.

Parking:

Free parking garage in Lehi and parking lots in Orem and Sandy.

Food:

No outside food or drink allowed. There is a dining area with concessions that sells pizza, hamburgers, fries, and other snacks.

What to expect...

Location 1
1320 N. 300 W.
Lehi 84043
(801) 766-4386
www.sevenpeaks.com

Location 2
168 South 1200 West
Orem, 84058
(801) 224-6000
www.sevenpeaks.com

Location 3
7984 South 1300 East
Sandy, 84047
(801) 734-8077
www.sevenpeaks.com

Seven Peaks Fun Centers feature indoor and outdoor activities that appeal to all ages. There are three locations along the Wasatch front. We chose to visit the **Lehi** location because it is the only one that offers amusement park rides. All three locations have indoor attractions that are available year round. Orem and Sandy locations each offer different activities. See below for details on those locations.

Indoor

Mini Golf has two courses, one indoor featuring nine holes of black light golf, and one outdoor with 18 holes. Pick up your golf ball at the laser tag counter.

Play Park is a climbing structure for young children under 48 inches. Parents can supervise from soft benches in the Play Park area.

Rollerball has four lanes and a height requirement of at least 30 inches.

Arcade Games include video games and ticket redemption games. My boys really liked Laser Frenzy, which challenges the player to maneuver their body through laser beams without touching any of them.

Rock Climbing has 13 available climbing stations on a 32ft. wall and is supervised by an employee. It uses an auto-belay device, which makes coming down easier and the wait shorter. Kids must be at least 36" tall to participate.

Laser Tag runs every 30 minutes all day with each game lasting about 20 minutes. This is a popular activity, so you may want to put your name on a waiting list when you first arrive. Kids must be at least 40 inches tall to participate.

Outdoor

Mini Golf has two courses, one outdoor (18 holes) and indoor, featuring nine holes of black light golf. Pick up your golf ball at the laser tag counter.

Go-Karts have a height requirement of 36 inches tall to ride and 60 inches to drive. Only a few go-karts can be run at a time, so expect to wait in line.

Bumper Boats have a height requirement of 36 inches to ride and 48 inches to drive. Only four or five boats run at a time, so expect to wait in line.

Amusement Park Rides all have a height requirement of 36 inches. There are several different miniature amusement park rides to choose from.

A drinking fountain and restrooms with changing tables are located near the ticket redemption counter.

Seven Peaks Fun Center Orem offers batting cages, go-karts, an XD theater, indoor and outdoor mini golf, and an arcade.

Seven Peaks Fun Center Sandy offers bowling and is currently under construction to add laser tag, indoor mini golf, and an arcade.

Toad's Fun Zone

1690 West 400 North
Ogden, 84404
(801) 392-4653
www.toadsfz.com

Hours:
See website for current hours.

Pricing:
There are multiple package options depending on what you want to do. See below for more information.

Parking:
Free parking lot.

Food:
Outside food or drink is not allowed. A small restaurant in the main building sells pizza, salad, chicken, drinks, and more.

Discounts:
See their website for current deals and promotions or simply ask about them at the front desk. The best deal is the Annual Pass. You may also also find deals on Facebook, Twitter and sites like Living social and KSL.

Social:

What to expect...

Toad's Fun Zone is an exciting fun center set in a very clean and family-friendly environment. Any of the following attractions can be bundled together for a lowered rate.

Arcade ($0.25-$3 per game) – More than 70 video and arcade games. Most games cost 50 cents. Almost all games use a card swiping system that returns tickets as a reward. We put $5 on a card for each child which lasted them about 20 minutes. Exchange Tickets for prizes.

Miniature Golf ($6 a round) – Toad's offers three 18-hole mini golf courses, one indoor and two outdoor. The courses are clean, well-maintained and stroller-friendly.

Mini Grand Prix (Drivers: $6; Riders: $3) – Toad's offers an outdoor go-kart race track. Drivers must be 58 inches tall and riders at least 48 inches tall.

Laser Tag ($6) – Play unlimited for $14.95 every Tuesday. Laser Tag is housed in a 4,300 square foot, two-story arena. The whole experience lasts about 20-25 minutes including time for instruction, getting suited up, and playing for about 7-10 minutes. There is no age or height requirement.

Batting Cages ($2-$16) – The batting cages offer fast or slow pitch softball and baseball.

Climbing Wall ($6) – Each person gets three climbs. This is only open on Saturdays.

Toad's provides multiple party rooms that can be used with the purchase of a birthday package. Restrooms with changing tables are located in the arcade. Lockers are available for $1 near the restrooms.

Just Around the Corner...

- Cold Springs Trout Farm
- Harrisville City Park
- Ogden Nature Center

Splash Pads & Fountains

Splash pads are a great way to stay cool and have fun in the summer without the dangers that come with swimming pools. Parents can sit back and relax as children play and splash freely. We are lucky to have so many splash pads available to us along the Wasatch Front. Some offer more spraying toys than others, and some consist only of ground fountains. Choose the one that looks right for your kids. All splash pads and fountains are well-maintained and monitored regularly by local health departments. They are generally open from Memorial Day through Labor Day.

Be sure to dress children in swimsuits with lots of sunscreen (unless rules require clothing). Most of these splash areas are perfect places for picnicking. You might also want to bring your own shade umbrella. There is often a playground situated nearby. These parks are great because children end up playing back and forth between the playground and splash pad.

Below is a list of general rules that apply to most splash pads/fountains in Utah. The majority have rules posted on-site. Be sure to check and adhere to the rules specific to your location.

Courtesy of Meilani Smith Kongaika

- Infants must wear swim diapers.
- Adult supervision is required for children younger than 14 (ages change based on location).
- Use splash pad at your own risk.
- No skateboards, rollerblades, bicycles, scooters etc. allowed on splash pad.
- No animals allowed on splash pad.
- No food or drink allowed on splash pad.
- No running or rough play allowed.
- No glass containers allowed.
- Do not climb or hang on equipment.
- Be courteous to younger patrons.
- Diapers must be changed in restrooms and not near the splash pad.
- Do not use the splash pad if you have a communicable illness, open lesion, or diarrhea.
- Do not drink splash pad water.

Creekside Park

100 South 600 East
Alpine, 84004
(801) 756-6347
www.alpinecity.org

Hours:
Daily from 10am-8pm (Memorial Day-Labor Day)

Admission:
FREE!

Parking:
Free parking lot. Splash pad is on the east side of the park.

Picnic Areas:
There is a large pavilion and a lot of lawn area to spread out a blanket.

What to expect...

My favorite splash pad is found at Creekside Park in Alpine. This is a large city park that also offers several playground areas, swings, basketball courts, and tennis courts. In addition to a really fun splash pad play area, it also offers three shade canopies with picnic tables underneath. In my opinion, if it's hot enough to be at a splash pad, it's hot enough to need some serious shade for those supervising! Granted, the pavilions might be occupied, so bring along an umbrella just in case.

The circular splash pad is enclosed by a fence with just two openings to enter or exit. Several benches are stationed around the outside of the splash pad, which allow close supervision. The splash pad features buckets that dump water, mushroom fountains, two water guns, a spinning flower that sprays water, and short spurting ground fountains that are perfect for little ones. All activities randomly turn off at different times for about 30 seconds and then start up again. If the water turns off completely, push the yellow sensor button on the green pole to start the water again.

Restrooms and a drinking fountain are adjacent to the splash pad. There are no changing tables available. A large picnic pavilion is also very close to the splash pad and the playground area.

Just Around the Corner...

- Highland Town Center Splash Pad
- Manila Creek Pond

Engage Fountain at City Creek

50 South Main Street
Salt Lake City, 84101
(801) 521-2012
www.shopcitycreekcenter.com

Hours:
Monday-Thursday: 10am-9pm;
Friday-Saturday: 10am-10pm; *Closed:* Sundays

Admission:
FREE!

Parking:
There is a large paid parking garage with many entrance points.

Food:
Tables and chairs surround the area. There are plenty of fast food choices and restaurants at the mall.

What to expect...

One of three fountains at City Creek Center was created just for children. It is located in front of Nordstrom in a large plaza. Children are allowed to play in this ground fountain, but are required to wear clothing and shoes. Swimming suits and sunbathing are not allowed.

Fountain shows set to music happen every hour during regular business hours. The City Creek Fountains were built by the same company that built the Bellagio Fountains in Las Vegas. Water, light, music, and fire are combined to create a beautiful display. I highly recommend watching one of these shows at night. The fountains run year round.

To find the restrooms, look for the elevators located behind the fountain. Once upstairs, follow signs to the restrooms, which are located halfway down the large walkway. There are child-sized toilets in the family bathroom as well as changing tables. Comfortable, private areas for nursing are also available. If you would like to access the fountains quickly, park near the Nordstrom store in the underground parking (from State Street, go west onto 100 South, go in the second entrance to the parking garage).

See Appendix 1 for Downtown Destinations close to this area

Site 106

The Gateway

Splash Pads & Fountains

400 West 100 South
Salt Lake City, 84101
(801) 456-2000
www.shopthegateway.com

Hours:
Monday-Saturday: 10am-9pm; *Sunday:* noon-6pm
There are extended hours through the summer and on holidays.

Admission:
FREE!

Parking:
The Summer and Winter Parking Garages can be accessed from 100 South, 200 South, and 400 West. The first hour of parking is free. Validations are available in stores with purchase. Free parking on Sundays. There is also parking available on the surface lot just north of South Temple and the parking garage off 500 West behind Old Navy.

Food:
There is a food court with many fast food choices and individual restaurants throughout the mall.

Social:

What to expect...

The Gateway is a large open-air shopping center set in downtown Salt Lake City. It offers 130 stores and restaurants, movie theaters, and a large ground fountain. The Gateway also houses the Discovery Gateway: The Children's Museum of Utah and Clark Planetarium. Build-A-Bear Workshop is also a favorite stop for my children.

The Olympic Legacy Plaza is a circular, open court at street level on the northeast end of the Gateway. During regular business hours, water spouts up from the plaza surface, creating a large floor fountain. The music and water come on every 30 minutes. In-ground lights add another exciting element to the fountains at night. This is a very popular location for young children, especially in the summer. Many families come prepared with swimsuits and towels, others let their children cool off in their clothes. Seating for parents surrounds the plaza. Our children love playing in these fountains. We often pair a trip to the Discovery Gateway with a visit to the fountains.

Annual Events

Chalk Art Festival – June. Over two days, 125 artists come together to paint the streets of the Gateway with beautiful chalk art. Over 20,000 people turn out every year to see the amazing artwork. One area of the street is reserved just for children to draw with chalk.

See Appendix 1 for Downtown Destinations close to this area

St. Patrick's Day Parade – This is a family friendly parade that draws thousands of people to view floats, dancers and marchers travel down the center of the Gateway. A party takes place following the parade with Irish food, dancing and live music.

Harrisville City Park

1350 North Highway 89
Harrisville, 84404
(801)940-6716
www.cityofharrisville.com

Hours:
Monday-Saturday: 10am-8pm

Admission:
FREE!

Parking:
Free parking lot.

Picnic Areas:
Three covered picnic areas and grass surround the splash pad.

What to expect...

Harrisville City Park offers a fun and colorful splash pad surrounded by a fence. Features include a big dumping bucket, ground fountains, three tall spouts, a fountain post, a showering spray, and a controllable water cannon. You can place your hand over the post to turn water on when it stops. Picnic tables with shade structures conveniently surround the splash pad but you can also bring your own shade. Additionally, the park houses a baseball field. Restrooms can be found next to the splash pad, including a family bathroom with a changing table.

Just Around the Corner...

- Cold Springs Trout Farm
- Toad's Fun Zone

Heritage Park

250 North Fairfield Road
Kaysville, 84037
(801) 544-1788
www.kaysvillerec.com

Hours:
Monday-Saturday: 10am-8pm

Admission:
FREE!

Parking:
Free parking lot.

Picnic Areas:
There is grassy area at the park as well as a pavilion.

What to expect...

Heritage Park is home to a large new splash pad. Features include a spray tunnel, three dumping buckets, three leaf spraying structures, three water cannons, and ground fountains. You can press your hand on top of the post to start the water when it stops. There is a large shade structure next to the splash pad but you may want to bring your own umbrella in case that spot is taken. There are also benches and grassy areas for supervising adults. A large pavilion is located nearby. Restrooms are situated next to the splash pad.

Just Around the Corner...

- Boondocks (Kaysville)
- Castle Heights Playground at Nicholls Park
- Cherry Hill
- Get Air Sportsplex
- Layton Surf 'n Swim
- Three Little Monkeys (Kaysville)

Highland Town Center Splash Pad

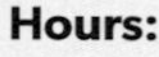

Hours:
Monday-Saturday: 10am-dusk

Admission:
FREE!

Parking:
Free parking lot.

Picnic Areas:
A large open lawn near the water is ideal for spreading out a towel or picnic. Bring your own shade.

5400 West Civic Center Drive
Highland, 84003
(801) 756-5751
www.highlandcity.org

What to expect...

The Highland Splash Pad is different than any other along the Wasatch Front. Located in a large plaza, the play area features a large ground fountain and a wading area designed to look like a stream. Be aware that the water completely turns off at ten minutes to the hour and then starts back up on the hour.

The Stream: The water originates from a rock waterfall and then flows under a grated bridge to a streambed. The depth of the water is about 2 inches and the current is gentle. The sides of the streambed have a gentle slope, making it easy for young children to get in and out. Several large rocks sit in the water, perfect for kids to climb. Some of the rocks house a spurting fountain.

Ground Fountain: The ground fountain is about 20 yards away in the center of the plaza. This is not a delicate, gentle fountain. The fountain has 57 spray nozzles, each sending up powerful surges of water. Older children especially enjoy this area. The fountain goes on and off, leaving kids anticipating the next eruption.

There are lots of benches along the sides of the stream, but there is no shade as the trees are still small. If you plan to be there awhile, bring your own umbrella. Restrooms are located near the fountain.

Just Around the Corner...

- Cabela's
- Children's Discovery Garden at Thanksgiving Point
- Creekside Park
- Farm Country at Thanksgiving Point
- Hangtime Extreme Trampolines (Lehi)
- Holdman Studios
- Museum of Ancient Life
- Seven Peaks Fun Center (Lehi)
- Thanksgiving Point Gardens
- Timpanogos Caves

Legacy Park

1120 W. 1100 N.
North Salt Lake, 84054
(801) 335-8683
www.nslcity.org/facilities.aspx

Hours:
Monday-Saturday: 10am-8pm;
Sundays: 12pm-6pm

Admission:
FREE!

Parking:
Free parking lot.

Picnic Areas:
A grassy area and a large pavilion with barbeques sit next to the splash pad.

What to expect...

The splash pad at Legacy Park is a large ground fountain, perfect for young children. Geysers and fountains spout up gently from the ground in all directions. There is a playground nearby, on the other side of the restrooms. Children tend to play back and forth between the two areas. A low brick wall surrounds part of the splash pad where parents can sit and monitor their children. This is a newer park, so there is not a lot of shade. Showers line the outside wall of the restrooms facing the splash pad. Visitors are encouraged to rinse in these showers before play. The park offers two changing rooms, two family restrooms with changing tables, and men's and women's restrooms all in the same building next to the splash pad.

The water turns off automatically if winds exceed 20 miles per hour. They also turn off regularly throughout the day. Simply press the button on top of the post on the East side of the splash pad to start the fountain.

Finding this park can be a little confusing. Online maps call the park Foxboro North Regional Park, but North Salt Lake City calls it Legacy Park. Get off on the 2600 South exit and head west. Go to the left at the T in the road and then continue west until you drive right into the Foxboro housing development.

Just Around the Corner...

- Kangaroo Zoo

Mountview Park

1651 East Fort Union Boulevard
Salt Lake City, 84121
(801) 943-3160
www.cottonwoodheights.com

Hours:
9am-8pm daily

Admission:
FREE!

Parking:
Free parking lot.

Picnic Areas:
There is a large pavilion and two picnic tables near the splash pad as well as grassy areas for picnics.

What to expect...

The splash pad at Mountview Park is worth a visit. It features a spray tunnel, dumping buckets, two spray cannons, and a unique frog spray toy. Benches and large rocks surround the splash area for supervising adults. If the water is not spraying during regular hours, press the button on the post to start the water.

The splash pad is situated right next to a large and exciting playground. Children tend to play back and forth between the two areas. One unique feature of the adjoining playground is an electronic game play structure. Children choose from a list of games outlined on a posted sign, and then have to tap parts of the equipment that light up. Another great playground, geared more towards toddlers, is also nearby. The park is new, so there is very little shade from trees. Both men's and women's restrooms have changing tables.

Just Around the Corner...

- Cottonwood Heights Recreation Center
- Jungle Jim's
- Lakeshore Learning
- Seven Peaks Fun Center (SLC)
- Wheeler Historic Farm

Nature Park (South Ogden Nature Park)

East 5850 South
South Ogden, 84405
(801) 622-2700
www.southogdencity.com

Hours:
10am-8pm daily

Admission:
FREE!

Parking:
Free parking lot.

Picnic Areas:
Picnic in the nearby pavilion or on the grass.

What to expect...

Nature Park has a small splash pad located near two playgrounds and a pavilion. The splash pad features spray toys, water cannons, and dumping buckets. You can press the button on top of the post to turn the water on during working hours.

Restrooms are right next to the splash pad, but do not have changing tables. Be aware that Nature Park is situated deep inside a community. We had to take quite a few twists and turns to reach the park. The liste address does not come up correctly on online maps. I suggest putting in "South Ogden Nature Park" and that will take you to the right place. The park is located across the large parking log of the Ogden Athletic Club. Be aware that you may have to pay a fee on a toll road as well.

Just Around the Corner...

- Coleman's Motor-VU Drive-in
- Hill Aerospace Museum
- Ogden's Union Station
- P.Ott Planetarium
- Riverdale Park
- Treehouse Children's Museum

Nolan Park

7862 North Tinamous
Eagle Mountain, 84005
(801) 789-6679
www.emcity.org

Hours:
9am-9pm daily

Admission:
FREE!

Parking:
Free parking along the tree-lined street.

Picnic Areas:
There is a lot of lawn area for spreading out a blanket. Bring your own shade.

What to expect...

This splash pad might not be as flashy as others, but it still provides a lot of fun water play. There are overhead faucets that drizzle water like a shower and rotating dumping buckets. Spurting fountains from the ground come on and off in intervals, leaving the kids waiting and excited for the next eruption.

There is no shade and there are no benches available near the splash pad, so bring your own umbrella and camping chair or blanket to set up on the grass. There is a large playground a long way up the hill from the splash pad and not close enough for kids to play back and forth between the two.

Restrooms and a drinking fountain are adjacent to the splash pad. No changing tables are available.

Just Around the Corner...

- Airborne
- J.L. Sorenson Recreation Center
- South Jordan Recreation Center
- Western Springs Park

Old Farm Splash Park

13680 S. 3250 West
Riverton, 84065
(801) 208-3101
www.recreation.rivertoncity.com

Hours:
10am-8pm daily

Admission:
FREE!

Parking:
Free parking lot.

Picnic Areas:
There is a pavilion next to the splash pad and lots of grass.

What to expect...

Old Farm Splash Park features a large farm-themed splash pad. The splash pad includes a tractor that sprays water with wheels that can turn and a steering wheel, a tall water tank, two movable spraying canons, and ground spouts on a soft non-slip surface. The play surface has four different buttons that turn on the water. The color of the button turns on the coinciding colored spouts. This is one of my favorite splash pads. My children loved the themed toys and really enjoyed controlling the water by pressing the various buttons.

The adjoining playground is also farm-themed. It looks like a tractor and a barn. There isn't much shade, so I would bring your own umbrella. There are a few benches for supervising parents. The restrooms do not have changing tables. The park also features a baseball field and a fishing pond located across the parking lot.

Just Around the Corner...

- Airborne
- J.L. Sorenson Recreation Center
- South Jordan Recreation Center
- Western Springs Park

Pioneer Park

500 West Center Street
Provo 84601
(801) 852-6600
www.provo.org

Hours:
Monday-Saturday: 10am-8pm

Admission:
FREE!

Parking:
Street parking surrounds the park.

Picnic Areas:
A large pavilion with picnic tables sits near the fountain.

What to expect...

A beautiful ground fountain opened in Spring 2013 at Provo's Pioneer Park. The floor of the splash area looks like a large wagon wheel. The design highlights the different peoples who have lived in Provo throughout history. It includes artwork that recognizes Mormon pioneers, Native Americans, trappers and Spanish explorers. Gentle spouts of water spray up from the ground making it especially suitable for young children. Seating conveniently surrounds the fountain for supervising adults. There is also a great playground within the park.

Just Around the Corner...

- BYU Broadcasting
- BYU Museum of Art
- BYU Museum of Paleontology
- BYU Museum of Peoples and Cultures
- Children's Library at Provo City Library
- CLAS Ropes Course
- FatCats (Provo)
- Lowe's Xtreme Air Sports
- Monte L. Bean Life Science Museum
- Provo Recreation Center
- Provo Towne Centre Play Area
- Royden G. Derek Planetarium
- Seven Peaks (Provo)
- Y Mountain Hike

Riverdale Park

4300 South Parker Drive
Riverdale, 84405
(801) 621-6084
www.riverdalecity.com

Hours:
Monday: 10am-8pm; *Tuesday:* 10am-7pm; *Wednesday:* 12pm-8am; *Thursday-Sunday:* 10am-7pm

Admission:
FREE!

Parking:
Free parking lot. Please do not park in front of the Fire Department.

Picnic Areas:
There are plenty of shady areas for picnics as well as many pavilions in the park.

What to expect...

This colorful splash pad is located just beyond the Riverdale Fire Station in Riverdale Park. It has a variety of bright spray toys and water dumping features, and is surrounded by a fence. Set in an inviting park with lots of big cottonwood trees for shade, it is the perfect location for a picnic. There are also three separate playgrounds and swings in the surrounding area.

Restrooms are located next to the splash pad but do not have changing tables. This splash pad and surrounding park can attract large crowds. If the parking lot is full, the city asks that you park at the nearby Community Center and not at the Fire Department.

Just Around the Corner...

- Birdsong Trail
- Coleman's Motor-VU Drive-In
- Color Me Mine (Ogden)
- FastKart Speedway (Ogden)
- FatCats (Ogden)
- Fort Buenaventura
- Hill Aerospace Museum
- Ogden Dinosaur Park and Museum
- Ogden Nature Center
- Ogden Raptors
- Ogden River Parkway
- Ogden's Union Station
- Ott Planetarium
- Peery's Egyptian Theater
- Treehouse Children's Museum

Rosecrest Park

14070 South Rosecrest Road (5600 W.)
Herriman, 84096
(801) 446-5323
www.herrimancity.org

Hours:
9am-8pm daily

Admission:
FREE!

Parking:
Free parking lot.

Picnic Areas:
Two small pavilions and grassy areas next to the splash pad.

What to expect...

Rosecrest Park offers a large splash pad surrounded by a fence. Features include a set of small dumping buckets, a spouting coconut tree, a spray tunnel that looks like a rainbow, and other ground spraying geysers. This splash pad has two posts with buttons that control the water spouts. It is set on a non-slip, hard surface. A nice playground sits right next to the splash pad. Children tend to play between the two areas. Park benches are situated inside the fenced area for supervising adults. The women's restroom provides a small toddler toilet, but there are no changing tables.

Just Around the Corner...

- Blackridge Reservoir
- J.L. Sorenson Recreation Center
- Umbria Splash Park
- Western Springs Park

Shops at Riverwoods

4801 North University Avenue,
Suite 480
Provo, 84604
www.shopsatriverwoods.com

Hours:
Monday-Saturday: 10am-9pm

Admission:
FREE!

Parking:
Free parking lot.

Food:
There are many fast food choices as well as restaurants. Provo Beach, in front of the splash pad, sells snacks and kid-friendly food.

What to expect...

The Shops at Riverwoods offers two splashing areas for children. Many children come wearing their suits, prepared to get wet, while others decide to play in what they are wearing. The first is a small ground fountain that sits between Provo Beach and Malawi's Pizza. The other ground fountain is smaller and appears to attract fewer visitors. It is located just down the way, near Tucanos Restaurant. There are no grassy areas surrounding the floor fountains, but there are a few benches for supervising parents.

Just Around the Corner...

- BYU Broadcasting
- BYU Museum of Art
- BYU Museum of Paleontology
- BYU Museum of Peoples and Cultures
- Creativity Art Studio
- Color Me Mine (Provo)
- FatCats (Provo)
- Hang Time Extreme Trampolines (Orem)
- Jake's Archery
- Krispy Kreme (Orem)
- Monte L. Bean Life Science Museum
- Nickel City Fun Center
- Orem Owlz
- Provo Beach
- Royden G. Derek Planetarium
- Scera Pool
- Seven Peaks Fun Center (Orem)
- University Mall Tree House Court

Umbria Splash Park

12790 South Brundisi Way (5230 W.)
Herriman, 84096
(801) 446-5323
www.herrimancity.org

Hours:
9am-8pm daily

Admission:
FREE!

Parking:
Free parking lot.

Picnic Areas:
Grassy areas, a picnic table, and a pavilion surround the area.

What to expect...

This is a large splash pad surrounded by a fence. Features include a spouting coconut tree, tall spraying toys, and ground geysers. The toys spray water in cycles around the play area; when one goes off, another comes on. There are two different posts with buttons that allow children to start the water. This splash pad features a non-slip surface. A playground is connected to the splash pad.

This splash pad is found in the middle of a little neighborhood. This makes for smaller crowds compared to the nearby Rosecrest Park splash pad. Restrooms do not have changing tables.

Other locations with splash pads in this book:

- Clearfield Aquatics Center
- Kearns Oquirrh Recreation Center
- Lagoon
- Lehi Legacy Recreation Center
- Liberty Park
- Kennecott-Magna Aquatics Complex
- Red Butte Garden
- Roy Aquatics Center
- South Davis Recreation Center
- Scera Pool
- This Is The Place Heritage Park
- Thanksgiving Point Children's Garden

Just Around the Corner...

- Blackridge Reservoir
- J.L. Sorenson Recreation Center
- Rosecrest Park
- Western Springs Park

Valley Fair Mall

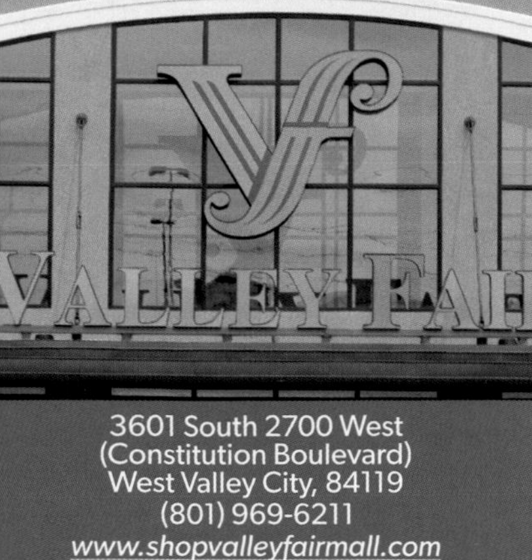

3601 South 2700 West
(Constitution Boulevard)
West Valley City, 84119
(801) 969-6211
www.shopvalleyfairmall.com

Hours:
Monday-Saturday: 10am-9pm; *Sunday:* 12am-6pm

Admission:
FREE!

Parking:
Free parking lot.

Food:
There are plenty of fast food restaurants.

What to expect...

Valley Fair Mall has a beautiful ground fountain in an outdoor plaza. Geysers shoot up from the plaza floor and from the surrounding wall, all in rhythm to music playing from speakers above you. At night, lights are added to this attraction. Children may play in these fountains dressed in swimwear. This plaza area feels very secure and friendly for families. In fact, while we were there, I noticed mall security checking on the area. Benches and small amphitheater seating are positioned around the fountain for supervising adults. The plaza is located on the West side of the mall in an outdoor shopping area, near The Children's Place.

Just Around the Corner...

- Centennial Pool
- Edutainment Play Center
- Hale Center Theatre
- Hollywood Connection
- LDS Humanitarian Center
- Redwood Road Drive-In
- Taylorsville Community Swimming Pool
- Utah Grizzlies
- West Valley Family Fitness Center

Western Springs Park

4570 West Goshute Drive
Riverton, 84096
(801) 208-3101
www.recreation.rivertoncity.com

Hours:
10am-8pm daily

Admission:
FREE!

Parking: Free parking lot.

Picnic Areas: There are picnic benches, grassy areas, and a pavilion.

What to expect...

The Western Springs Park splash pad has a spray tunnel, two water cannons, and some ground spouts. Press the button on the top of the post to start the water spraying. This is a nice place for children to cool off, but just past the edge of the splash pad is a steep grassy hill. This hill is used for sledding in the winter. A fence does not surround the splash pad, so it may be necessary to watch children more closely. There isn't much shade so you may want to bring an umbrella. A nice playground is connected to the splash pad. Children tend to play between the two areas. Restrooms do not have changing tables.

Just Around the Corner...

- Blackridge Reservoir
- J.L. Sorenson Recreation Center
- Old Farm Splash Park
- Rosecrest Park
- Umbria Splash Park

Willow Pond Park

6059 South Murray Parkway Avenue
(1080 West)
Murray, 84123
(801) 264-2614
www.murray.utah.gov

Hours:
Dawn to dusk

Admission:
FREE!

Parking:
Free parking lot. The only way to enter the park is at the north end from Murray Parkway Ave.

Picnic Areas:
There are lots of grassy areas for picnic blankets and there are some picnic tables in a courtyard near the wading stream.

What to expect...

Willow Pond Park offers a couple of different water play options for kids. The first is a small ground fountain that sprays water up at varying times. It's much more modest in size and excitement than some others, but is still fun on a hot day.

The second water option is a shallow man-made stream that is perfect for wading or floating a small boat. The gentle water current makes its way through the streambed to a second wading area. My kids were magnetized to both wading areas most of the time we were there.

The park also offers three play structures, a baseball diamond, and basketball courts. There are not any large trees in the park, so shade is slim. I suggest bringing your own shade. There is also a large pond for fishing. Those under 12 can fish without a license. Restrooms are right next to the wading area. The only way to enter the park is at the north end from Murray Parkway Ave.

Just Around the Corner...

- Accessible Playground at Veteran's Memorial Park
- Gene Fullmer Recreation Center
- Murray Aquatics Center
- Taylorsville Community Swimming Pool
- The Park Center
- Tiny Tim's Foundation for Kids
- (West Jordan) Conservation Garden Park
- Wild West Jordan Playground at Veteran's Memorial Park

Indoor Swimming

The Wasatch Front is home to a large number of recreation centers with indoor pools. We have highlighted some of the best in this chapter. In the winter, indoor swimming allows for warm play despite the cold. In the summer, indoor swimming can be a great way to avoid sun exposure especially for young kids. Each pool has a unique design with features that make swimming with your children a memorable and fun experience.

All pools in the state of Utah require children age 3 and younger (or if they are not yet potty trained) to wear a swim diaper as well as plastic pants. Most pools sell both items from their front desk. Other rules tend to vary. See each specific location for rules like minimum height requirements for slides, age requirements for swimming alone, life jacket and floatation device policies, and so on. Most pool facilities ask that parents do not bring children of the opposite sex into locker rooms and encourage you to use family bathrooms instead.

Photo by Paul Richer, Richer Images

Clearfield Aquatic Center (also outdoor)

825 South State Street
Clearfield, 84015
(801) 525-2640
www.clearfieldcity.org

Hours:
Hours vary daily and seasonally. Visit the website to see the current schedule. *Closed:* Christmas and Easter.

Admission:
Under 4: $1; *Age 4-17:* $3; *Age 18-59:* $5.50; *Age 60+:* $3

Parking:
Free parking lot which is shared with the high school.

Food:
No outside food or drink is allowed in the indoor pool area, though it is permitted in the outdoor pool area. Tables and chairs are available on the outside deck. There are vending machines that sell a variety of drinks, candy and snacks.

Discounts:
There is a 15 punch pass available at a discounted price. Entertainment Book.

What to expect...

Clearfield Aquatic Center is a beautiful facility located next to North Davis Junior High School. It houses two indoor pools and an outdoor pool with a splash pad.

Indoor Pools

Leisure Pool and Play Structure – The leisure pool features zero-depth (beach) entry with an in-water play structure that sits in 1½ ft. of water. Features include spraying water, turning wheels, a tube slide, and dumping buckets. This area of the pool is roped off to keep young children inside the shallow waters.

Current Channel and Bubble Couch – Part of the leisure pool includes a small, circular current channel or "lazy river." In the middle of the current channel is a bubble couch.

Water Slide – The water slide is two stories high. Lap riding is permitted.

Lap Pool – A 6-lane lap pool sits next to the leisure pool and is open for swimming during open plunge. Depths range from 3½ to 12ft. There is a one meter diving board.

Outdoor Pool and Splash Pad

Wading Pool – This small, heated wading pool is only 2-foot deep and is a local hot spot for young families to picnic and swim. It is open from Memorial Day to Labor Day and can be used with admission to the indoor pool. It is perfect for babies and toddlers.

Splash Pad – Spraying fountains, a spray tunnel, ground fountains, and water cannons.

Sitting or Lounge Areas – There is seating surrounding the indoor pool. The outdoor pool has a grassy area and picnic tables.

Locker Rooms – Family bathrooms have a changing station. Lockers are available but you must bring your own lock. Mandatory safety breaks occur at the top of every hour.

Annual Events

Egg Dive – Saturday before Easter. Kids dive for eggs, and exchange for prizes.

Boonanza – October. Indoor carnival with food, booths, prizes, and a unique experience in the pool on canoes with floating pumpkins. Free to enter. Pay per activity.

Breakfast with Santa – December. Pictures, breakfast with Santa, and free swim.

Just Around the Corner...

- Great Salt Lake Shorelands Preserve
- Hill Aerospace Museum
- Krispy Kreme (Layton)
- Layton Surf 'n Swim
- Legacy Electric Park

Dimple Dell Recreation Center Pool

10670 South 1000 East
Sandy, 84094
(385) 468-3355
www.recreation.slco.org/dimpledell/

Hours:
Hours vary daily and seasonally. See the website for a current schedule.
Tot Time (kids 5 and under): *Monday-Friday:* 11am-noon

Admission:
Under 3: $2; *Ages 3-15:* $4; *Ages 16-59:* $5.50; *Ages 60+:* $4.50; *Tot Time Admission:* $1.50 children 5 and under, $2.50 for adults

Parking:
Free parking lot.

Food:
No food or drink is allowed on the pool deck.

What to expect...

Leisure Pool and Play Structure – It features a zero-depth (beach) entrance, going down to 3 ft. deep. The play structure has a twisty slide and lots of spraying fountains.

Lazy river and Bubble Couch – The small horseshoe-shaped lazy river is 3½ ft. deep. A bubble couch is tucked into the arch of the lazy river. It is a bench surrounded by jets that create lots of bubbles.

Water Slide – You must be 6 years old and the recommended height is 44" tall to slide.

Sitting and Lounge Areas – Benches are located around the perimeter of the pool.

Locker Rooms – Men's and women's locker rooms have free lockers; just bring your own lock. There are two family changing rooms; ask a lifeguard for access. No inflatables are allowed in the pool. Life jackets may be worn and are available free of cost on a limited basis.

There is a special **Tot Time** for kids 5 and under and their parents. The price is discounted and the leisure pool is less daunting without bigger kids.

Other activities offered at the recreation center include: a rock climbing wall, ping-pong, and a small indoor and outdoor track.

Just Around the Corner...

- Airborne
- Classic Fun Center (SLC)
- Color Me Mine (Draper)
- Gale Center of History and Culture
- Real Salt Lake
- Scheels
- Seven Peaks Fun Center (SLC)

Fairmont Aquatic Center

1044 East Sugarmont Drive
(2225 South)
Salt Lake City, 84106
(385) 468-1540
www.recreation.slco.org/fairmont

Hours:
Hours vary daily and seasonally.
Visit the website to see the current schedule.

Admission:
Ages 15 and younger: $2, Adults 16-59: $3.50, Seniors:$2

Parking:
Free parking lot.

Food:
No outside food or drink is allowed in the pool area. In the summer, food is allowed in a small outdoor area right off the pool. Vending machines are located in the lobby. Fairmont Park, which is in front of the Aquatic Center, is a great place for a picnic.

Discounts:
Group discounts available

What to expect...

Fairmont Aquatic Center is a beautiful facility operated by Salt Lake County Parks and Recreation. It is located on the edge of the large and inviting Fairmont Park.

Leisure Pool – The leisure pool features zero-depth (beach) entry. The floor surface is soft, perfect for babies and young children to play comfortably. Depths range from zero to 3½ ft. Water toys include a large fountains, a pipe works structure with interactive play/spray features, and five big dumping buckets. There are also ground fountains along the edge of the pool.

Current Channel and Vortex – This small, circular "lazy river" is a great area to swim and feel pushed along by the water. The vortex spins water in a circular motion.

Water Slide – A two-story water slide. Lap riding is not allowed. Minimum of 48" and 6 years old to ride.

Lap Pool – Although the lap pool sits close to the leisure pool it is never open for free swim. It is used for swimming lessons, exercise, school groups, and other courses. A curtain separates the two pools.

Sitting or Lounge Areas – There are a few sitting areas around the outside of the pool. During the summer months there is a small grassy area out the back door with seating.

Locker Rooms – Locker rooms and two family bathrooms with changing tables are located just off of the pool deck. Lockers are available but you must bring your own lock or rent one from the front desk.

All children five and younger must be accompanied in the water within arm's reach by someone 14 or older. Floatation devices are not allowed except for Coast Guard approved life jackets which are available for use. Just ask a lifeguard for assistance.

Just Around the Corner...

- Color Me Mine (SLC)
- FatCats (SLC)
- Liberty Park
- Salt Lake Bees
- The King's English
- Tracy Aviary

Gene Fullmer Recreation Center

8015 South 2200 West
West Jordan, 84088
(385) 468-1951
www.recreation.slco.org

Hours:
Hours vary daily and seasonally.
Visit the website to see the current schedule.

Admission:
Under 3: $2; *Age 3-15:* $4.00; *Age 16- 59:* $5.50; *Age 60+:* $4.50. Cash, checks, Mastercard, and Visa accepted.

Parking:
Free parking lot.

Food:
No outside food or drink is allowed in the pool area.

Discounts:
Group discounts are available. Please call pool coordinator in advance to get approval.

What to expect...

Gene Fullmer Recreation Center is operated by Salt Lake County Parks and Recreation. It houses two indoor pools, a fitness area, an aerobics center, an indoor walking/ jogging track and a gym. West Jordan Pool is located across the parking lot. It offers outdoor swimming in the summer months.

Leisure Pool and Play Structure – Depths range from 1-3½ ft. The floor surface is soft with a large one-step entry. The play structure features a tunnel, a slide, and spraying toys.

Current Channel and Bubble Couch – Part of the leisure pool includes a small, circular current channel or "lazy river." In the middle of the current channel is a bubble couch.

Water Slide – There is a 30-foot twisty water slide. Recommended height for riding the slide is 48 inches tall. Lap riding is not allowed.

Lap Pool – The lap pool is open during most hours of public swim. Depths range from 4 to 9 ft.

Sitting or Lounge Areas – Limited bench seating surrounds the pool.

Locker Rooms – Lockers require your own lock. You can purchase a padlock at the front desk. One family bathroom with a changing table is available; a key from the front desk is required. Ages 5 and under must have an adult in the water with them. Ages 6-9 must have a supervising adult present in the pool area at all times.

Just Around the Corner...

- Accessible Playground at Veteran's Memorial Park
- Classic Fun Center (SLC)
- Gale Center of History and Culture
- Gardner Village
- Georgell Doll Shop
- Jump 'N Bounce
- South Jordan Recreation Center
- Tiny Tim's Foundation for Kids
- (West Jordan) Conservation Garden Park
- Wild West Jordan Playground at Veteran's Memorial Park

Holladay Lions Fitness and Recreation Center

1661 East Murray-Holladay Road
Holladay, 84117
(385) 468-1700
www.recreation.slco.org/HolladayLions

Hours:
Open Plunge *Monday-Thursday:* 12pm-8:30pm; *Friday:* 12pm-7:30pm; *Saturday:* 11:30am-6pm; *Sunday:* 10am-2:30pm

See website for holiday hours and closings.

Admission:
Under 3: $2; *Age 3-15:* $4; *Age 16-59:* $5.50; *Seniors 60+:* $4.50.

Parking:
Free parking lot.

Food:
No outside food or drink is allowed.

What to expect...

Holladay-Lions Recreation Center is a large facility operated by Salt Lake County Parks and Recreation. It offers an indoor leisure/lap pool in a spacious setting.

Leisure Pool and Play Structure – Depths range from 6 inches to 3½ ft. throughout the pool. The play structure includes a tube slide, spraying water features, and three dumping buckets nearby.

Lazy River & Bubble Couch – Part of the leisure pool includes a large, rectangular lazy river. On the inside of the lazy river is a bubble couch.

Water Slide – Children must be at least 48 inches tall to ride the large 3-story slide.

Lap Pool – Only swimmers age 15 or older are allowed to swim in this area. It is connected to the leisure pool by a small channel.

Seating and Lounge Areas – Limited bench and chairs surround the pool.

Locker Rooms – Besides the locker rooms, there are two family changing room. Lockers are available, but you must bring your own lock. You can also purchase locks from the front desk.

Flotation devices are not allowed in the pool except coast guard approved life jackets. There are life jackets on deck available for use. Children age 5 and under must have an accompanying adult (14 or older) in the water with them at arm's reach.

The Holladay Lions facility also has a fitness area, an aerobics center, a gym, and an indoor track.

Just Around the Corner...

- FatCats (SLC)
- Lakeshore Learning
- Murray Aquatics Center
- The Children's Theatre
- The Park Center
- Wheeler Historic Farm

J.L. Sorenson Recreation Center

5350 West Herriman Main Street
Herriman, 84096
(385) 468-1340
www.recreation.slco.org/jlsorenson

Hours:
Splash and Swim *Monday-Saturday:* 12pm-8:30pm; *Sunday;* 11am-2:30pm;
Closed: Easter, Independence Day, Thanksgiving, and Christmas

Facility hours may change on other holidays.

Admission:
Under 3: $2; *Age 3-15:* $4; *Age 16-59:* $5.50; *Age 60+:* $4.50

Parking:
Free parking lot.

Food:
No outside food or drink is allowed.

What to expect...

J.L. Sorenson Recreation Center is operated by Salt Lake County Parks and Recreation. It houses both a leisure and lap pool in addition to a top-notch workout facility.

Leisure Pool and Play Structure – The leisure pool features zero-depth (beach) entry with depths ranging from zero to 3½ ft. The floor surface is soft; perfect for young children and babies to play on. The play structure is one of the best I have seen. It includes five slides and spraying and dumping toys. There is also a clown fish slide for ages 3 to 6 and the Lily Pad Crossing, a rope climbing/hanging area.

Lazy River and Cyclone Pool – The lazy river is a fun swimming experience as you let the water push you along a circular channel. The cyclone pool swirls water in a circular motion and sits in the middle of the lazy river.

Water Slide – The large twisty slide is three-stories high. Lap riding is not allowed.

Lap Pool – The lap pool has a high and low dive and ranges in depths from 3½ to 13ft.

Sitting or Lounge Areas – Some bench seating surrounds the pool.

Locker Rooms – Four family bathrooms with changing tables are available in addition to the locker rooms. Lockers are available, but you need to bring your own lock.

Flotation devices are not allowed in the pool except for Coast Guard approved life jackets. Kids ages 6-9 must be supervised by someone age 14 or older. Kids 5 and under must have a supervising chaperone age 14 and older in the water at all times. The front desk sells locks, swim diapers, and plastic pants.

Annual Events

Egg Dive – Easter

Triathlons – Winter and Summer

New Year's Eve Party

Just Around the Corner...

- Blackridge Reservoir
- Old Farm Splash Park
- Rosecrest Park
- Umbria Splash Park
- Western Springs Park

Lehi Legacy Recreation Center (also outdoor)

123 North Center Street
Lehi, 84043
(801) 768-7124
www.lehi-ut.gov/discovery/legacy-center

Hours:
Hours change daily and seasonally.
See the website for a current schedule.

Admission:
Under 4: FREE!; *Ages 4-11:* $3; *Ages 12-17:* $4; *Ages 18-59:* $5; *Ages 60+:* $3

Parking:
Free parking lot.

Food:
No food or drink is allowed in the indoor pool area. Food is permitted near the outside splash pad. A food stand is located in the lobby.

What to expect...

This pool was my personal favorite of all the indoor pools and is a great place for kids of all ages. One interesting thing about this pool is that it has a retractable ceiling and walls that open in the summer months. When the large glass paneled doors are opened up, people can go back and forth easily between the outdoor splash pad and the indoor pool area.

Leisure Pool – This play area has a zero-depth (beach) entrance that goes down to 3½ feet. The leisure pool features a Hawaiian-themed play structure with a huge dumping bucket suspended above. It slowly fills with water and eventually tips over, dumping hundreds of gallons of water on those waiting below. There is no warning sound, but the buckets dumps about every 3 minutes and it's pretty obvious when it's about to go over.

Baby Wading Pool Area – This is for kids ages 5 and under and their parents. The whole area is about 8 inches deep and features a double slide and suspended baby bungee chairs which gently bounce up and down with a baby's movements.

Lazy River – This small horseshoe-shaped lazy river is 3½ feet deep. The lazy river connects to the outdoor play area during summer months.

Bubble Couch and Vortex – The Bubble Couch is an underwater bench with lots of jets. The Vortex is a water current that goes around like a whirlpool.

Big Water Slide – You must be able to touch the bottom at the end of the slide or be able to swim to ride the big water slide. No life jackets are allowed on the slide. Lap riders are permitted.

Outdoor Splash Pad – The splash pad has spurting fountains and water cannons.

Lounge areas and Seating – There are chairs lining the walls of the indoor pool area and lots of lounge chairs around the outside splash pad.

Locker Rooms – Changing tables are located in both men's and women's locker rooms. Lockers are available; just bring your own lock. There are also two family changing rooms located on the deck of the indoor pool. A small life guard station on the pool deck has a little shop offering items like swim diapers, goggles, nose clips, swim suits, etc. No inflatables are permitted. Life jackets are allowed and available for use at no cost on a limited basis.

Other activities available at the recreation center include a climbing wall, indoor track, and basketball.

Just Around the Corner...

- American Fork Fitness Center
- Jack and Jill Lanes
- John Hutchings Museum of Natural History
- Neptune Park
- Seven Peaks Fun Center (Lehi)

Northwest Recreation Center

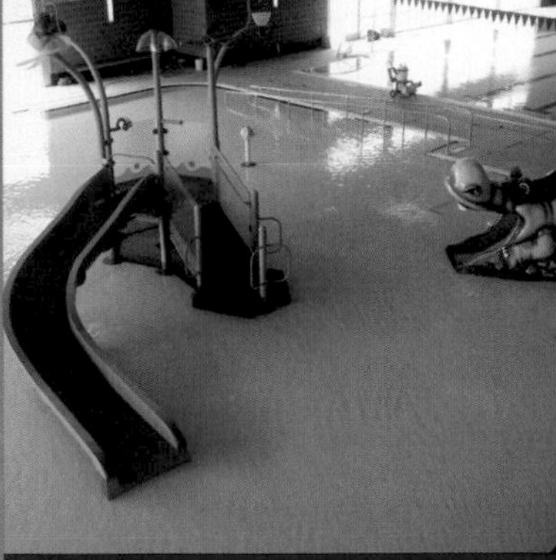

1255 Clark Avenue (300 North)
Salt Lake City, 84116
(385) 468-1305
www.recreation.slco.northwest

Hours:

Monday-Thursday: 3pm-8:30pm; *Friday:* 1pm-7:30pm; *Saturday:* 12pm-6:30pm; *Sunday:* 10:30am-2pm;

Parent/Tot Time (for kids not in school yet)

Monday-Thursday: 10am-3pm; *Friday:* 10am-1pm

Hours change seasonally. See website.

Admission:

Under 3: $2; *Age 3-15:* $3; *Age 16-59:* $4.50; *Age 60+:* $3.50

Food:

No outside food or drink is allowed. Vending machines sell drinks and snacks in the lobby.

Discounts:

The Recreation Center offers 30-day, 90-day, and annual passes (individuals or families).

Social:

What to expect...

Northwest Recreation Center is operated by Salt Lake County Parks and Recreation. It is a beautiful and well-maintained facility. The indoor pool offers fun for all ages.

Leisure Pool and Play Structure – The leisure pool features a zero-depth (beach) entry, a hippo toddler slide, and an in-water play structure featuring spray toys and a longer child-sized slide. There are also ground fountains and spraying fish toys. Depths reach 3 feet in this area.

Current Channel & Vortex – The current channel is a long lazy river. Water swirls like a whirlpool in the vortex. Both areas are 3 ½ ft. deep.

Water Slide – The large, twisty water slide is two-stories high. Children must be at least 48 inches tall to ride. Lap riders are not allowed.

Lap Pool – The lap pool is always open during free swim. It provides two lanes that run as permanent lap lanes. This pool is also used for swimming competitions. Depths range from 3½ to 9 feet deep.

Sitting and Lounge Areas – There is a lot of spectator seating along one side, above the lap pool. There are also a few benches around the outside of the pool.

Locker Rooms – Locker rooms and family bathrooms with changing tables are available. Lockers are available, but you need to bring your own lock. Children 9 years and under must be accompanied by an adult. An adult must be in the water and within arm's reach of children ages 5 and under. Floatation devices of any kind are prohibited except for coast guard approved life jackets.

See Appendix 1 for Downtown Destinations close to this area

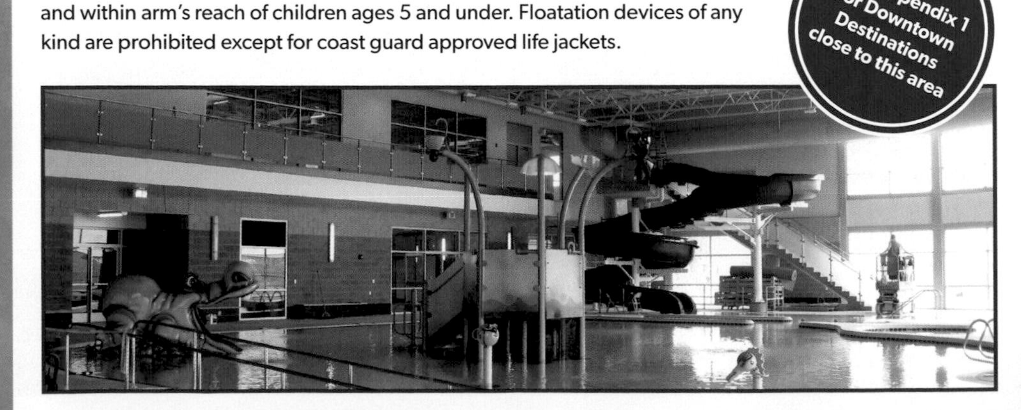

The Park Center

202 Murray Park Avenue
Murray City, 84107
(801) 284-4200
www.murray.utah.gov

Hours:
Hours vary daily and seasonally. See website for the current Open Plunge schedule.

Admission:
Under 1: Free; *Age 1-12:* $3; *Age 13-17:* $4; *Age 18-59:* $6; *Age 60+:* $5

Parking:
Free parking lot.

Food:
No food or drink is permitted.

Discounts:
Discounted pricing is available for residents. Multi-visit cards and season passes are available.

Social: 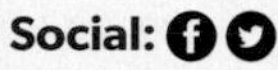

What to expect...

The Park Center Leisure Pool is located in beautiful Murray City Park.

Leisure Pool Play Structure – The leisure pool has a zero-depth (beach) entry. There is a play structure with a twisty slide, crawling tunnel, spraying toys, and dumping buckets.

Lazy River & Bubble Couches – Water pushes swimmers along a channel. The bubble couches are a great area to sit and relax in the pool.

Water Slide – 8 yrs. and older can ride the two-story water slide. Lap riding is permitted.

Lap Pool – The lap pool is connected by a doorway and is sometimes open for free swim. The pool depth is 9ft.

Sitting and Lounge Areas – Benches are available.

Locker Rooms – Besides the ocker rooms, there is one family bathroom. Lockers are available but you must bring your own lock.

Children under six years must be accompanied by an adult in the water. Children age 8 and under must have an adult 18 or older supervising them. Coast guard approved life jackets are the only accepted floatation devices. A large basket of approved life-jackets sits on deck for swimmers to use.

The Park Center offers a variety of facilities including three basketball courts, three volleyball courts, a three lane indoor track, and games like pool and foosball.

Just Around the Corner...

- Holladay Lions Fitness and Recreation Center
- Lakeshore Learning
- Murray Aquatics Center
- Wheeler Historic Farm

Provo Recreation Center (also outdoor)

320 West 500 North
Provo 84601
(801) 852-6600
www.provo.org

Hours:
Hours change seasonally.
Visit the website to see a current schedule.

Admission:
Under 3: Free; *Age 3-17:* $4; *Age 18-59:* $5; *Age 60+:* $4

Parking:
Free parking lot.

Food:
A cafe inside the rec center sells hot dogs, nachos, and other kinds of snacks.

Discounts:
Residents receive discounted pricing. The recreation center offers 3 month, 6 month and annual memberships.

Social:

What to expect...

After visiting swimming pools all along the Wasatch Front, this one seems to have it all. The Provo Recreation Center newly opened in Spring 2013. It is a beautiful facility that offers many ammenities including appealing options for both indoor and outdoor swimming.

Indoor Pools

Leisure Pool and Play Structure – The leisure pool features zero-depth (beach) entry and a play structure with slides, dumping buckets and spraying toys.

Lazy River and Programming Pool – This long lazy river pushes swimmers through the channel into a whirlpool as well as a bubbling channel. A small three-lane pool is also available for swimming and playing basketball.

Water Slide – There are two big indoor, stand alone water slides. Only single riders are allowed.

Teen Pool – This is a 12ft 6in deep pool equiped with a rock wall and a diving platform.

Competition Pool – There is a separate pool used for swim competitions and lap swimming.

Indoor Swimming located in the Outdoor Swimming chapter of this book:

- Cottonwood Heights Rec Center
- Kearns Oquirrh Park Fitness Center
- Layton Surf 'N Swim

Outdoor Pool

From Memorial Day to Labor Day the outdoor pool (Veteran's Memorial Pool) is available for swimmers at no additional cost. There are two options for entry: the main entrance to the recreation center or the outdoor kiosk that allows entrance straight into the outdoor pool gates.

Leisure Pool and Play Structure – The outdoor leisure pool also features zero-depth (beach) entry and a play strucutre with slides and spraying fountains and toys.

Water Slides – There are two large water slides that end in a small splash pool.

Recreation Pool – Another large outdoor pool outdoors with depths from 5-5½ ft.

Sitting and Lounge Areas – There are plenty of seating options indoors and outdoors.

Locker Rooms – Men's and women's locker rooms are provided. There is also a unique family locker room lounge where multiple family bathrooms/changing rooms are made available. Lockers are provided but you must bring your own lock. Locks and swim diapers can be purchased at the front desk. Floaties are not allowed in the pools.

Go One Step Further

Don't miss the exciting two-level **indoor playground** inside the Provo Recreation Center. It is available to anyone for free! This would be a great spot for indoor play in the winter months.

Just Around the Corner...

- BYU Broadcasting
- BYU Museum of Art
- BYU Museum of Paleontology
- BYU Museum of Peoples and Cultures
- Children's Library at Provo City Library
- CLAS Ropes Course
- Comedy Sportz
- FatCats (Provo)
- Lowe's Xtreme Air Sports
- Monte L. Bean Life Science Museum
- Provo Towne Centre Play Area
- Seven Peaks (Provo)
- Y Mountain Hike

South Davis Recreation Center (also outdoor)

550 North 200 West
Bountiful, 84010
(801) 298-6220
www.southdavisrecreation.com

Hours:
Hours change seasonally.
Visit the website to see a current schedule.

Admission:
Under 4: Free; *Age 4-11:* $3; *Age 12-17:* $3.50; *Age 18-59:* $5; *Age 60+:* $3.50.

Parking:
Free parking lot.

Food:
No outside food or drink is allowed. Concessions are available. Tables, chairs, and vending machines are located in the front lobby.

Discounts:
Residents receive discounted memberships. A 25-punch pass is available. Entertainment Book.

Social:

What to expect...

South Davis Recreation Center is a large complex that offers a wide variety of activities. It houses multiple pools both indoors and outdoors. The front desk sells swim diapers for a small fee. Children under 9 years old must be accompanied by an adult in the water at all times.

Indoor Pools

Leisure Pool and Play Structure – The leisure pool features zero-depth (beach) entry down to 2 ½ ft. The play structure has three slides, dumping buckets, and spraying toys.

Lazy River – A long lazy river winds around one corner of the leisure pool.

Water Slide – There is a two-story twisty water slide. Lap riders are permitted.

Lap Pool – This pool is connected to the other leisure pool by a small channel and is always open for free swim. Depths range from 3½ ft. to 4½ ft.

Competition Pool – Located across the hall is a large lap pool which is open for diving during "open plunge" hours. There are three diving boards. On Wednesdays, the lap pool also provides an inflatable obstacle course called the Wibit.

Outdoor Pool

From Memorial Day to Labor Day, the outdoor pool is available for swimmers at no additional cost. It can be accessed through doors that open from the indoor leisure pool.

Leisure Pool - This pool features a large pirate ship with two slides, a crawling tunnel, and spraying water. It has a zero-depth (beach) entry.

Splash Pad – This large splash pad offers water cannons and colorful spraying features.

Sitting and Lounge Areas – Bench seating surrounds the leisure pool indoors. The lap pool features a large spectator area. Lounge chairs and picnic tables are available outside.

Locker Rooms – Besides the locker rooms, there are two large family bathrooms. Lockers are provided, but you must bring your own lock. You can purchase or rent locks from the front desk.

Annual Events

Egg Dive – Egg-gathering fiesta in the leisure pool on Saturdays before Easter. Prizes for all.

Kids Triathalon – This is held twice a year: May & Labor Day.

Spooktacular – October. The rec. center turns into a Halloween carnival. Wear costumes to win prizes.

Swimming with Santa – December

Dogapalooza – The outdoor pool goes to the dogs just before the outdoor pool closes for the fall.

South Jordan Recreation Center

10866 South Redwood Road
South Jordan
(801) 253-5236
www.sjc.utah.gov/recreation

Hours:
See website for current schedule.

Admission:
Under age 4: Free; *Ages 4-17:* $3; *Ages 18-59:* $5; *Ages 60+:* $3

Parking:
Free parking lot.

Food:
Outside food and drink is permitted, but only in the outdoor sun deck area where there is a pavilion with picnic tables.

Discounts:
Entertainment Book.

What to expect...

Leisure Pool – It has a zero-depth (beach) entrance going down to 3 feet. There is a cute crocodile slide, a mushroom fountain, spurting fountains, and wheels that release water.

Lazy River – The small lazy river is 3½ feet deep.

Water Slide – The water slide has a height requirement of 48 inches. Lap riding is not allowed.

Baby Wading Pool – Babies have their own pool that is just 1½ feet deep. It features suspended baby bungee chairs.

Sitting or Lounge Area – There is limited seating around the perimeter of the pool.

Locker Rooms – There are two family changing rooms available as well as locker rooms. No inflatables or water wings are allowed in the pool but swim noodles are permitted. Life jackets are available free of charge on a limited basis.

Other activities offered at the recreation center include: basketball, indoor soccer, and an indoor track.

Just Around the Corner...

- Accessible Playground at Veteran's Memorial Park
- Airborne
- Classic Fun Center (SLC)
- Color Me Mine (Draper)
- Gardner Village
- Gene Fullmer Recreation Center
- Georgell Doll Shop
- Old Farm Splash Park
- Real Salt Lake
- Scheels
- Tiny Tim's Foundation for Kids
- Urban Park Interactive Fountain
- (West Jordan) Conservation Garden Park
- Wild West Jordan Playground

West Valley Family Fitness Center

5415 West 3100 South
West Valley City, 84120
(801) 955-4000
www.wvc-ut.gov/fitnesscenter

Hours:
Monday-Friday: 11:30am-9pm; *Saturday:* 11:30am-8pm; *Sunday:* 1pm-4pm

*The slide opens at 5pm in the winter (except on holidays) and 11:30am in the summer.

Admission:
Age 3 and under: Free; *Age 4-11:* $3.75; *Age 12-17:* $4.75; *Age 18-61:* $5.50; *Age 62+:* $4

Parking:
Free parking lot.

Food:
There is a snack bar inside the fitness center with tables, chairs, and high chairs

Discounts:
West Valley City residents receive discounted admission.

What to expect...

West Valley Family Fitness Center is a 96,000 square-foot facility next to the Acord Ice Center that offers many amenities which include a spacious indoor pool, basketball and racquetball courts, an indoor track, an exercise room, a large climbing wall, dance and aerobic rooms, a weight room and a one-of a kind indoor play room called the Edu-tainment Center.

Leisure Pool – The leisure pool features zero-depth (beach) entry going down to 3ft. 4 in. There is a large spraying structure with turning wheels, spraying fountains that line the edge of the pool, large dumping buckets, and a toddler slide that looks like a duck.

Lazy River – A channel of water that pushes swimmers along a current.

Water Slide – Children must be 42 inches tall to ride the three-story twisty slide.

Lap Pool – The lap pool sits next to the leisure pool. Depths range from 4 to 9½ ft.

Sitting and Lounge Areas – There is some bench seating around the pool.

Locker Rooms – There are locker rooms and family changing rooms with diaper changing stations.

Children 8 years old and under must have a supervising adult in the water with them at all times.

Annual Events

Egg Dive – Around Easter, children dive for eggs and receive prizes.

Dog Days of Summer – End of the summer. Bring your dog for a swim before the pool is cleaned.

Just Around the Corner...

- Centennial Pool
- Edutainment Play Center
- Kennecott-Magna Aquatics Complex

Outdoor Swimming

Splash and play with your children in one of the many outdoor pools, reservoirs, or water parks all at your fingertips along the Wasatch Front. There are so many options for swimming in the hot summer months. Outdoor locations generally run from Memorial Day through Labor Day.

All pools in the state of Utah require children ages 3 and younger (or if they are not yet potty trained) to wear a swim diaper as well as plastic pants. Most pools sell both items from their front desk. Other rules tend to vary. Many facilities ask that parents do not bring children of the opposite sex into the locker rooms and encourage you to use family bathrooms instead. All of the pools and water parks run weather-dependent and must close for lightning storms or rain.

Be sure to bring sunscreen, towels, and portable shade (where possible). And don't forget to take potty breaks with young kids.

Courtesy of Seven Peaks

Water Design Inc.

*A special thank you to Water Design Inc. for allowing us to use so many of their pictures. This company is responsible for building a large number of the awesome splash pads and pools highlighted in this book.

American Fork Fitness Center Leisure Pool

454 North Center Street
American Fork, 84003
(801) 763-3080
www.afcity.org

Hours:
Hours vary daily and seasonally.
See the website for a current schedule.

Admission:
Under 4: Free; *Age 4-17:* $4; *Age 18+:* $4.50;
Senior Citizens: $3

Parking:
There is a free parking lot to the north of the building and a lower parking lot to the south of the building. The pool can be accessed from either the front entrance or the back entry from the lower parking lot.

Food:
You may bring your own food and drink. Concessions are available.

What to expect...

American Fork Fitness Center has a large outdoor pool facility. The leisure pool closes during the winter, but the lap pool is covered with an insulating bubble.

Leisure Pool and Play Structure – The leisure pool has a zero-depth (beach) entrance that goes down to 3½ ft. The play structure has a slide and a couple of spray toys.

Water Slide – Children must be at least 40 inches tall to slide. Lap riding is not allowed.

Lazy River – The lazy river is 3½ ft. deep. Inflatables are not allowed.

Lap Pool – The large lap pool combines with a shallow zero-entrance pool area. There is a toddler slide on the shallow end.

Sitting or Lounge areas – There is very little shade, so bring your own umbrella. There are many lounge chairs available for use.

Locker Rooms – Besides the men's and women's locker rooms, there are two family changing rooms. Ask a lifeguard for the code. Lockers are available but you need to bring your own lock. Swim noodles and life jackets are available at no cost on a first-come basis.

Other activities offered at the recreation center include: racquetball, aerobics, an indoor track, gymnastics, and basketball.

Just Around the Corner...

- Creekside Park
- Highland Town Center Splash Pad
- Jack and Jill Lanes
- Manila Creek Pond

Blackridge Reservoir

15000 S. Ashland Ridge Dr. (5390 W.)
Herriman, Utah 84096
(801) 254-7667
www.herriman.org

Hours:
Season runs April 15 through October 15:
7:30am-9pm daily

Admission:
FREE!

Picnic Areas:
Concessions stands may be available. Bring a cooler or snacks and eat them on the beach. No glass or alcohol is allowed.

Parking:
Free parking lot.

What to expect...

You may be surprised to know that there is a beach in Herriman. Blackridge Reservoir, located on the upper west side of Herriman City, gives Utahans a place to enjoy swimming, splashing at the water's edge, digging in the sand, and basking in the sunshine. The Reservoir is fairly small, but well worth a visit. The sand is a little grainier than beach sand but still works well for digging and sand play. The shallow area is marked by white floating buoys. There are no lifeguards on duty, so keep a close eye on your children. I recommend bringing pop-up shade, hats, sand toys, floaties, sunscreen, snacks, and drinking water.

Motorized boats are not allowed in the water. There is a launching area for paddle boats. Animals are not allowed on the beach or in the water. There is also a playground on site.

Just Around the Corner...

- J.L. Sorenson Recreation Center
- Rosecrest Park
- Umbria Splash Park
- Western Springs Park

Centennial Pool

5355 West 3100 South
West Valley City, 84120
(801) 840-2338
www.acordice.slco.org

Hours:
Season runs Memorial Day through Labor Day
Monday-Saturday: 11am-7pm;
Sunday/Holidays: 11am-5pm
Hours can vary at the beginning and the end of the season.

Admission:
Under 3: $2; *Age 3-15:* $2.75; *Age 16-59:* $3.25;
Age 60+: $2.25

Summer Pass:
Season passes (3 months) as well as 30-day passes are available at the front office. Season passes range in price from $50 to $65 per person.

Parking:
Free parking lot.

Food:
Concessions sells snacks, ice cream, hot dogs, and more.

Discounts:
Discounted group rates are available.

What to expect...

The Centennial Pool is an outdoor swimming facility operated by Salt Lake County Parks and Recreation. It is located inside Centennial Park across the street from the Acord Ice Center and the West Valley City Family Fitness Center.

Leisure Pool and Play Structure – The very large leisure pool ranges from zero-depth (beach) entry to 4 ft. deep. Ground fountains spray from the zero-entry area. There is a play structure with a tube slide, a tunnel and spraying toys.

Water Slide – You must 6 years old to ride the slide. Lap riding is not allowed.

Lap Pool – The lap pool sits right next to the leisure pool and is open for free swim. It ranges in depths from 5ft to 9ft.

Sitting or Lounge Areas – The pool deck is has large umbrellas, chairs, picnic tables, and pavilions.

Locker Rooms – Family restrooms with diaper changing stations are available; ask for a key at the front desk. There are also locker rooms. Lockers are available, but you must bring your own lock.

Everyone entering the facility must pay the daily rate (even if you do not intend to swim). Children 5 years and under must be accompanied by an adult in the water within arm's reach. Children ages 6-9 must be accompanied by an individual 14 or older. Flotation devices are prohibited except for Coast Guard approved life jackets. The concessions counter also sells beach balls, goggles, and pool toys.

Just Around the Corner...

- Edutainment Play Center
- Valley Fair Mall
- West Valley Family Fitness Center

Cherry Hill

1325 South Main Street
Kaysville, UT 84037
801-451-5379
www.cherry-hill.com

Summer Hours:
Monday-Saturday: 10:30am-8:30pm; *Closed:* Sundays.

The water park has limited days and hours in May and September. Check website for details.

Admission:
Activities can be purchased separately or as part of a package. See website for pricing.

Parking:
Free parking lot. Limited parking is available near the entrance. Follow the small paved road to a large parking lot behind the water park.

Food:
Outside food and drink is permitted. Concessions are available, which include; The Pie Pantry, Grant's Pizza, and The Pirates Grill.

Discounts:
Discounted entry after 4pm and 6:30pm. Group rates available.

What to expect...

Cherry Hill is a family fun center that offers a variety of outdoor activities. 'Relaxing and low key' describes the vibe of the park. It doesn't offer as many large slides as other waterparks, but it is our favorite because of the family-friendly atmosphere.

The Water Park is the most popular attraction at Cherry Hill. Young children especially enjoy the **Pirate's Cove** activity pool with a zero depth (beach) entrance and 40 ft. pirate ship. The shallow water and spurting fountains provide just the right amount of fun and safety for little ones. For the more adventurous, **Cardiac Canyon River Run** is a wild tube ride down waterfalls and swirling whirlpools. The waterpark also features two large twisting tube waterslides called the **Double Dragons**. Small children can ride down on a parent's lap. There are also two regular swimming pools. One of our family's favorite activities is to float the 4 ft. deep **lazy river** which stretches around a large grassy lounge area. Tubes are included in the price of entry, but you may also bring in your own inflatables. There is a shaded lawn area near the pools with plenty of lounge chairs where you can spread out your towels and have a picnic. Large pavilions are available for rent. There are no family changing rooms. Lockers are available for a $3 rental.

Other great activities at Cherry Hill

- Mini Golf: 18 hole, No strollers recommended.
- Batting Cages: slow/fast pitch & includes equipment.
- Hamster Haven: tunnels, ropes, slides. 54" height restriction.
- Rock Climbing Wall: 30 ft. tall, four stations, varying levels.
- Aeroball: one-on-one trampoline basketball.
- Camping: 180 sites, 700 trees. See website for into.

Just Around the Corner...

- Boondocks (Kaysville)
- Castle Heights Playground at Nicholls Park
- Get Air Sportsplex
- Heritage Park
- Lagoon
- Layton Surf 'n Swim
- S&S Shortline Train Park
- Three Little Monkeys (Kaysville)

Cottonwood Heights Rec Center (also indoor)

7500 South 2700 East
Cottonwood Heights, 84121
(801) 943-3160
www.cottonwoodheights.com

Hours:
Hours vary by pool and by day. See the website.

Admission:
Under 3: Free; *Ages 3-17:* $4.50; *Ages 18-61:* $5.50; *Ages 62+:* $4.50

Parking:
Free parking lot.

Food:
No food or drink is allowed indoors, but is permitted in the outdoor pool area. Concessions are available.

What to expect...

The Cottonwood Heights Recreation Center is a large complex that offers many different pools and swimming options. There are 3 indoor pools and an indoor splash pool for children, but the main bulk of swimming activities are outside. During the summer, entrance to the pool is accessed through an outdoor kiosk near the parking lot.

Indoor Pools

Leisure Pool and Play Structure – This play area features a zero-depth (beach) entry down to 3 ft. deep. The play structure has a twisty slide, spurting fountains, and a small tunnel. There are also mushroom fountains and a cute frog slide.

Indoor Specialty Pool – Always kept at a warm 87 degrees, this pool is handicap accessible with a ramp and a zero-depth (beach) entrance. Anyone can play in the warm pool. Check the website for specific open plunge hours.

Indoor Diving Pool and Racing Pool – Check the website for open plunge hours.

Outdoor Pools

Outdoor Leisure Pool – This area has a zero-depth (beach) entrance gradually going down to 5-6 ft. The area features spurting fountains and a small slide.

Water Slide – There are two big water slides with a height requirement of 48 inches. Lap riders are not permitted.

Three Tier Diving Platform – There are three platforms of varying heights, as well as springboard diving boards. Children must be eight years old to use the platforms.

Olympic Size Swimming Pool – This large pool is 6 ft. deep with lots of open area for swimming.

Seating and Lounge Areas – There are lots of chairs, lounge chairs, and tables available. Bring your own shade umbrella. There are some large shade pavilions close to the leisure pool.

Locker Rooms – Men and women's locker rooms have free lockers; just bring your own lock. There are two family changing rooms available. Inflatables and life jackets are permitted.

Just Around the Corner...

- Classic Fun Center
- Jungle Jim's Playland
- Lakeshore Learning
- Mountview Park
- Seven Peaks Fun Center (SLC)
- Wheeler Historic Farm

Kearns Oquirrh Park Fitness Center (also indoor)

5624 South Cougar Lane (4800 W.)
Kearns, 84118
(801) 966-5555
www.kopfc.com

Hours:
The outdoor season is Memorial Day weekend through Labor Day weekend, although the enclosed 50 meter pool is open year round. Hours change seasonally. See the website for a current schedule.

Admission: Rates vary by season.
Winter:Under 3: Free; *Ages 3-17:* $3.75; *Ages 18-59:* $4.25; *Ages 65+:* $3.75

Summer:Under 3: Free; *Ages 3-17:* $4.75; *Ages 18-59:* $5.50; *Ages 65+:* $4.75

Parking:
Free parking lot.

Food:
Outside food is permitted in the outdoor pool area. Concessions are available.

What to expect...

Indoor Pools

Leisure Pool – Depth of 1½ ft. to 3½ ft. It features spraying fountains.

Lazy river – The small lazy river is 3½ ft. deep.

Water Slide – Children must be 48 inches tall to slide. Lap riders are not permitted.

Competition Pool – This pool is located in a separate indoor area with large doors that open to the outdoors. All but two lanes are used for open plunge. On the weekends, the Wibit, an inflatable obstacle course that floats on the water, is set up in this pool. Wibit Weekends are extremely popular. Children must be 6 years old to play on it and ages 6-8 must be accompanied by a person age 13 or older.

Locker Rooms – The indoor locker rooms offer keyed lockers for a 50-cent rental. Non-keyed lockers are available at no cost; just bring your own lock. There are six family changing rooms available for use just outside the locker rooms.

Outdoor Pools

Leisure Pool and Play Structure – We voted this the best outdoor leisure pool. It has a zero-depth (beach) entrance down to about 18 inches and features a large play structure with lots of spraying nozzles and fountains. There are three slides to choose from, all perfect for young kids to ride alone. The most exciting feature of the play area is an enormous overhead bucket that slowly fills up with 1,000 gallons of water and eventually tips, dumping water on those waiting below. There is an alarm that sounds 10 seconds before it is going to dump so those who want to move away can do so.

Second Leisure Pool – It has a zero-depth (beach) entry that goes down to 4½ ft. and a play structure that features slides and spraying water.

Dive Pool – This pool offers 3 varying height diving platforms and two high and two low springboards.

Seating and Lounge Areas – There are many shade umbrellas, chairs, and lounge chairs, but on busy days they might all be taken, so bring your own shade umbrella and blanket for the grass.

Additional Tips...

Inflatables and noodles are allowed. A limited number of life jackets are available for free. Restrooms are on the outdoor pool deck. There are also 4 private changing rooms, one of which has a changing table. Other activities offered at the rec center include: Basketball and tennis.

Just Around the Corner...

- Jump 'N Bounce
- Taylorsville Community Swimming Pool

Kennecott-Magna Aquatics Complex

3270 South 8400 West
Magna, 84044
(801) 468-1835
www.recreation.slco.org/magna

Hours:
Season runs Memorial Day through Labor Day. Hours vary. See website.

Admission:
Under 3: $2; *Age 3-15:* $2.75; *Age 16-59:* $3.25; *Age 60+:* $2.25.

Parking:
Free parking lot.

Food:
No outside food or drink is allowed. The concessions counter, located on the pool deck, sells snacks and drinks.

What to expect...

The Kennecott-Magna Aquatics Complex is a large outdoor pool located across the parking lot from the Magna Fitness and Recreation Center. This facility is operated by Salt Lake County Parks and Recreation. It features a large splash pad and a spacious pool that is roped off into different sections.

Leisure Pool – The leisure pool features a roped-off bay that is perfect for babies and toddlers. It has a zero-depth (beach) entry that progresses to depths of 3 feet. There is another roped-off section that is 4 ft. deep. On the opposite end of the pool two low diving boards hang over depths of 13 feet.

Tube Slides – Two playground-sized tube slides are recommended for strong swimmers only.

Splash Pad – Just past the pool is a large splash pad. There is a rainbow spray tunnel, dumping buckets, water cannons, ground fountains, and spray toys. The area is surrounded by park benches.

Sitting and Lounge Areas – The pool has picnic benches, lounge chairs and benches for seating. You may also bring your own shade and sit on the grass.

Locker Rooms – The Complex does not offer family bathrooms though it does provide locker rooms. Lockers are available, but you must bring your own lock.

Everyone entering the facility must pay. Floatation devices are prohibited except for Coast Guard approved life jackets. Kids 5 and under must have a supervising adult in the water at arm's length at all times. Children ages 6-9 must have a supervising person 14 years or older on deck. The front desk sells swim diapers and plastic pants.

Just Around the Corner...

- Centennial Pool
- Edutainment Play Center
- West Valley Family Fitness Center

Layton Surf 'N Swim (also indoor)

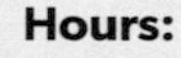

465 North Wasatch Drive
Layton, Utah 84041
(801) 336-3939
www.laytoncity.org

Hours:
Hours vary. See the website for current hours.

Admission:
Winter *Children under 3:* Free; *Age 4 and up:* $3.50
Summer *Children under 3:* Free; *Age 4 and up:* $4.50

Parking:
Free parking lot.

Food:
Outside food and drink is allowed on the outside perimeter of the pool deck and the grassy picnic area.

Discounts:
During the winter months, Layton Surf N' Swim offers discounted Monday Family Night (5 people for $10), Wednesday Dollar Nights ($1 per person) and group rates. They also offer a 20 Punch Pass for $60. During the summer, they offer a 20 punch pass for $80. Entertainment Book.

What to expect...

Layton Surf 'N Swim is a city-owned swimming facility offering two different pool experiences.

The biggest and most popular pool is The Wave Pool measuring 75ft by 165ft. It features a zero depth (beach) entrance. The waves simulate the waves of an ocean but do not run continuously. Two alarms sound before the waves start to provide enough time to get out if you prefer. The waves last 10 minutes and are followed by 20 minutes of calm. Those who brave the waves in the deep end are required to be on a tube the entire time (one person per tube). Tubes are available for rent at the front desk. From 12-3pm every day the facility offers "open plunge" when the waves are turned off.

There are lounge chairs surrounding the pool and a grassy area with picnic tables, benches, and a moderate amount of shade. There is also a sand volleyball court and a children's playground. The wave pool is open all year because in the winter (Labor Day to Memorial Day) it is covered with an enormous inflatable dome called a "bubble," which insulates the pool from the outside elements.

There is a second pool located outside that is open only during the summer. It is a small traditional style pool with depths ranging from 2-10 feet.

Both locker rooms have changing tables and coin-operated lockers. There is one family bathroom available. Swim diapers can be purchased at the front desk for $8 and can be reused and washed.

The snack bar located off the lobby offers hot dogs, nachos, ice cream etc. Tubes cost $3 to rent, but you get $1 back when the tube is returned.

Just Around the Corner...

- Cherry Hill
- Clearfield Aquatic Center
- Get Air Sportsplex
- Great Salt Lake Shorelands Preserve
- Heritage Park
- Krispy Kreme (Layton)
- Legacy Electric Park

Lindon Aquatic Center

60 West 60 North
Lindon, 84042
(801) 610-4160
www.lindoncity.org/aquatics-center.htm

Hours:

Season runs Memorial Day through Labor Day.

Open Plunge: *Monday:* 12:30- 8:30pm; *Tuesday-Thursday:*12:30-8pm; *Friday:* 12:30-6pm; *Saturday:* 11am-6pm

Hours may vary at the beginning and end of the season.

Admission:

Under 4: Free; *Age 4-17:* $4; *Age 18-54:* $5; *Age 55+:* $3; *Flow Rider:* $10

Parking:

Free parking lot on the south side of the building. You can also use overflow parking across the street.

Food:

No outside food or drink is allowed. Concessions are available.

Discounts:

$1 discount for Lindon residents. Family Night Monday (6pm-8:45pm): $15.

What to expect...

Lindon Outdoor Aquatics Center offers a fun, music-filled atmosphere with many swim/play options. Children under the age of 9 must be accompanied in the facility by an adult and children under 6 must have the adult in the water with them. Life jackets are available at no cost on a first-come basis.

Leisure Pool and Pirate Play Structure – This features a zero-depth (beach) entry down to 3 ft. The ship has a long wide slide.

Baby Wading Pool – The baby wading pool is15 inches deep throughout with a subdued waterfall on one side.

Lazy River – This is said to be the longest and fastest lazy river at a public pool facility in Utah. Child-size inner tubes and swim noodles are allowed in the lazy river. Watch out for the waterfalls and dumping buckets!

Water Slide – The big water slide has a height requirement of at least 48 inches. Life vests can be worn down the slide and lap riding is permitted.

Lap Pool – Depths range from 3½ ft to 9 ft.

Flowrider – The flow rider simulates an ocean wave and allows participants the chance to try out surfing or boogie boarding. This is the only outdoor Flowrider in Utah. You must be at least 52" to stand up on the boogie board and 42" to lie on a boogie board. Participants must be able to swim and must complete a waiver. A parent's signature is required for riders under 18.

Sitting or Lounge Areas – Chairs, lounge chairs, and canopies are available on a first-come basis. You can bring your own camp chairs, umbrella, or shade structure.

Locker Rooms – Lockers are available, but you must bring your own lock. There are two family changing rooms.

Just Around the Corner...

- Jump On It
- Novell Children's Discovery Park

Manila Creek Pond

900 West 3300 North
Pleasant Grove, 84062
(801) 785-7275
www.plgrove.org

Hours:
Dawn to dusk

Admission:
FREE!

Parking:
Free parking lot.

Picnic Areas:
There are no tables, but there is plenty of room to spread out a blanket on the beach or grass.

What to expect...

Manila Creek Pond was created and officially opened in 2011. The man-made pond is a delightful surprise nestled within a residential neighborhood and a place I will definitely visit again. The southwest side of the pond is designated as a shallow swimming/wading area perfect for young children. Floating buoys section off the designated swimming area from the rest of the pond. The deepest area is about 3-4 ft. near the buoy line and swimming is not permitted past the buoy line.

Kids 8 and under would most enjoy the swimming area as older kids might get bored quickly because of the shallow waters and limited play area. We loved our time there, especially my little girls. Many visitors pull their beach chair or umbrella right up to the waterline to be close to toddlers. Bring an umbrella if you want shade. When we were there they were in the process of installing a couple of water spigots to wash sandy feet off before getting into the car.

Fishing is a popular activity in the other areas of the pond. Kids 12 and under don't need a license. Each of my kids caught a fish fairly quickly, which means there wasn't much complaining about waiting. There is a fish cleaning station near the restrooms. There are no changing tables in the restrooms.

Don't confuse this pond with Manila Park, which is located about a mile away. Without the exact address, my GPS sent us to Manila Park instead of Manila Pond.

Just Around the Corner...

- American Fork Fitness Center
- Battle Creek Falls Hike
- Creekside Park
- Highland Town Center Splash Pad
- Jack and Jill Lanes

Murray Aquatics Center

5109 South Murray Park Road
Murray, 84107
(801) 290-4190
www.murray.utah.gov

Hours:
Season runs Memorial Day through Labor Day.

Monday-Thursday: 11am-8pm; *Friday:* 11am-6pm; *Saturday & Sunday:* 10am-6pm

Hours can vary at the beginning and end of the season.

Admission:
Under 1 year: Free; *Age 1-3:* $1; *Age 4-17:* $3; *Age 18-54:* $3:50; *Age 55+:* $3

Summer Pass:
$200 per family ($150 for residents).

Parking:
Free parking lot.

Food:
Concessions sell candy and snacks.

Discounts:
Residents receive discounted pricing. Discounted punch passes (10 visits) are also available

What to expect...

Murray Aquatics Center is located in the middle of the large and inviting Murray City Park. The facility offers both a leisure pool and a lap pool.

Leisure Pool – The leisure pool has a large zero-depth (beach) entry bay as well as a ramped entry with a handrail. A mushroom and a teacup fountain spray water in this area.

Water Slide – The 4-story water slide is for riders ages 8 and up. Lap riding is permitted.

Lap Pool – The lap pool has two 3-meter diving boards and 4 lanes for lap swimming.

Sitting and Lounge Areas – There are chairs, a grassy area and picnic tables.

Locker Rooms – Bathrooms do not have changing stalls.

Mandatory safety breaks are held the last 10 minutes of every hour. Floatation devices are not allowed in the pool. Only Coast Guard approved life jackets are allowed.

Go one step further. . .Visit Murray City Park

Murray City Park is a beautiful, shady park with Little Cottonwood Creek running right through it. Amenities include a baseball diamond, soccer and softball fields, playgrounds, an amphitheater, picturesque bridges, a gazebo, an arboretum, and multiple pavilions.

Just Around the Corner...

- Holladay-Lions Recreation Center
- Lakeshore Learning
- The Park Center
- Wheeler Hisoric Farm

Pineview Reservoir

Uinta-Wasatch-Cache National Forest
1st Street
Huntsville, 84317
(801) 625-5306

Hours:
Season runs May 1 through September 20.

8am-10pm daily

Admission:
$13 per car. Cash and checks ONLY. Pay at the checkpoint.

Parking:
There is a large parking lot at the first bay. More parking spaces are available near picnic areas down the road along Cemetery Point.

Picnic Areas:
Picnic areas with tables, grills, and plenty of shade are found along Cemetery Point.

What to expect...

Pineview Reservoir is managed under the U.S. Forest Service. It offers a variety of water recreation, including boating, swimming, fishing, windsurfing, and playing in the sand. The Reservoir has three beaches: Cemetery Point, Anderson Cove, and Middle Inlet Beach. Our family visited the popular beach along Cemetery Point, called Bluff Swim Beach. We have missed the beach since we moved to Utah from Hawaii and this place has the relaxed, sunny, playful atmosphere that we've been wanting.

The beach changes in size over the season. The Reservoir is higher in the spring, with less sandy beach, and lower at the end of the summer. Motorized boats may dock on parts of the beach but do not pose a hazard. Bring something for shade like an umbrella or pop-up tent. Also, consider bringing sun screen, sand toys, camping/beach chairs, floatation toys, hats, and sunglasses.

For those interested in trying out a boating experience, there is an on-site boat rental company at the Cemetery Point Marina. Rules at the beach prohibit glass containers, alcohol, and dogs. Restrooms line the picnic areas but there are no changing tables. Each small restroom building has a spigot for spraying sand off of your legs and feet.

To find Cemetery Point, enter Ogden Canyon and follow signs to Huntsville. Turn west onto Main Street (follow signs for the marina) and drive straight until you reach the fee station. Pay the entrance fee, then drive forward and park in front of your chosen beach spot. Be sure to bring cash or your check book, otherwise you will have to turn around and go back to the nearest gas station for cash.

Just Around the Corner...

- Powder Mountain
- Snowbasin
- Wolf Mountain Resort

Roy City Aquatic Center

2977 West 5200 South
Roy, 84067
(801) 774-8590
www.royutah.org

Hours:
Season runs Memorial Day through Labor Day.
Monday: 11am-8pm; Tuesday-Sunday: 11am-6pm

Hours can vary at the beginning and end of the season.

Admission:
Under 4: Free; *4-7 years:* $4.50;
8 years and older: $5.50; *65 and older:* $4.50.

Parking:
Free parking lot.

Food:
Concessions sell pizza, hot dogs, ice cream, and other snacks. Outside food is permitted in the Aquatic Center.

Discounts:
Resident and non-resident discounted 10-punch passes are available. Group rates are also available. Family Day Mondays offers a flat rate for the entire family.

What to expect...

The Roy City Aquatic Center is a large outdoor pool facility. It is a fantastic place for young kids because of the large swimming areas, low depths, and the variety of activities.

Toddler Pool and Splash Pad – This small pool is the perfect spot for babies and toddlers to play. It has a zero-depth (beach) entry that grows to 1½ ft. A small splash pad with a few spray toys sits at the edge of the pool. There is also a **frog slide** for toddlers.

Leisure Pool and Play Structure – A playground with a slide, water cannons and a tunnel sits in this enormous pool. Depths range from zero-depth (beach) entry to 3½.

Water Slides – There are two 3-story-high slides. Children must be at least 48 inches tall to ride alone. One slide allows lap riders.

Lap Pool – Depths range from 3½ to 13 ft. There is a low and a high diving board.

Sitting and Lounge Areas – There are chairs, lounge chairs, picnic tables, grassy areas, and shade structures.

Locker Rooms – Both restrooms have coin-operated lockers. A family restroom with a changing station is available upon request. Ask for a key at the front office.

The entrance window sells swim diapers, plastic pants, and goggles. Rules require that children 8 and younger be accompanied by an adult 18 or older.

Just Around the Corner...

- Coleman's Motor-VU Drive-In
- Hill Aerospace Museum

Scera Pool

701 South State Street
Orem, 84059
(801) 724-3751
www.oremrecreation.com

Hours:
Season runs Memorial Day through Labor Day.
Monday-Thursday: 12:30pm-7pm;
Friday-Saturday: 12:30pm-6pm

Admission:
Under 1: Free; *Age 1-3:*$1.50; *Age 4-13:* $5; *Age 14-54:* $6; *Age 55+:* $5

*All spectators are required to pay the entrance fee. All major credit cards and personal checks are accepted.

Parking:
Free parking lot.

Food:
No outside food or drink is allowed. Concessions sell snacks, hot dogs, pizza, and drinks.

Discounts:
Discounted punch passes are available for 10, 25, or 50 visits. After 6pm, Tuesday-Thursday pay half price. Families pay one fee for the whole family on Monday nights.

What to expect...

The Scera Pool is a large outdoor pool facility located on State Street inside the shady Scera Park.

Leisure Pool – This is a large pool with depths that range from zero-depth (beach) entry to 3 ft. Toy features include a small slide, tumble buckets, a raindrop waterfall, and water rings. There is plenty of open space to swim away from spray/fountain features if you don't want to get splashed.

Current Channel and Bubble Couch – This is a small lazy river paired with a bubble couch.

Water Slides – There are two water slides. Children must be 48 inches or taller to ride alone. Children under the height requirement are allowed as lap riders as long as the lap rider wears a life jacket.

Lap Pool – The lap pool ranges in depth from 4 to 9 ft. There are two low diving boards.

Splash Pad – The large splash pad has numerous spray features including ground fountains, coconut tree fountains, a spray tunnel, water cannons, and more.

Sitting and Lounge Areas – Picnic tables, lounge chairs, and grassy areas with shade are available.

Locker Rooms – There are two family bathrooms with changing tables. Men's and women's locker rooms have coin-operated lockers.

Children 9 and under must be accompanied in the water by someone 14 and older. The front office/window sells life jackets (also rental), goggles, nose clips, floaties, and sunscreen.

Just Around the Corner...

- BYU Broadcasting
- BYU Museum of Art
- BYU Museum of Paleontology
- BYU Museum of Peoples and Cultures
- Creativity Art Studio
- Color Me Mine (Provo)
- FatCats (Provo)
- Hang Time Extreme Trampolines (Orem)
- Jake's Archery
- Krispy Kreme (Orem)
- Monte L. Bean Life Science Museum
- Nickel City Fun Center
- Orem Owlz
- Provo Beach
- Royden G. Derek Planetarium
- Seven Peaks Fun Center (Orem)
- Shops at Riverwoods
- University Mall Tree House Court

Seven Peaks

2 locations
www.sevenpeaks.com

Hours:

Season runs from Memorial Day through Labor Day.
Monday-Saturday: noon-8pm

Season pass holders can enter the park earlier.

Admission:

Under 4 and Seniors: Free; *Under 48 inches:* $19.95; *48 inches and up:* $24.95; *After 4pm:* $15.95; *After 6pm:* $9.95. *Spectator:* may enter for $7.95 (must pay full admission price then receive partial refund when exiting). All major credit cards accepted.

Annual Pass:

Check website for the current price of the **Pass of all Passes.**

Parking:

Both locations charge $7 for all-day parking and $4 after 4pm.

Food:

No outside food or drink is allowed. Cafés and grills inside the park offer everything from pizza to burgers, salads, and ice-cream.

Discounts:

For the best deal, purchase the Pass of All Passes which includes a season pass to the two Seven Peaks Waterparks and many, many other venues in Utah. The **Pass of All Passes** can be purchased on various popular websites such as CityDeals, Groupon, KSL, etc. The waterpark also offers family packages.

What to expect...

Location 1
1330 East 300 North
Provo, 84606
(801) 373-8777

Location 2
1200 West 1700 South
Salt Lake City, 84104
(801) 972-3300

Seven Peaks Provo

The original Seven Peaks in Utah County is the largest waterpark in all of Utah and offers over two dozen attractions.

Rocky Mountain Beach is a wave pool that periodically creates swells up to four feet high.

Canyon River is a lazy river measuring a quarter mile long.

Adventure Bay features a zero-depth entry, an interactive jungle gym that sprays water in all directions, a kiddy slide, a crawling tunnel, a tire-swing, and more.

The Tadpole Pond includes two 24 inch depth pools, kiddy slides, mushroom fountains, waterfalls, and floating animals.

Tyke's Peak offers two covered water slides for younger children. Parents may accompany children on these slides.

Cascade Falls is a great place to swim or just sit under warm waterfalls.

Lily Pad Walk tests your balance across the pool.

Water Slides include fast-paced tube slides, racing slides, double, triple, and single inner tube rides, a vortex slide, a half-pipe style boomerang, and more!

Seven Peaks Salt Lake City

These 17 acres of water attractions for all ages used to be known as Raging Waters. My family spent many days there and loved it.

Tidal Beach is a 500,000 gallon wave pool. Waves start periodically creating swells 3 feet high.

Amazon River is a large lazy river and is a great spot to float on an inner tube and relax. The river floats around a large **splash pad**.

Dinosaur Bay includes two children's pools. These offer low depths, short, wide slides, and a tunnel. Kids can test their balance as they try to cross the water on lily pads.

Monsoon Lagoon has a rope swing and wide slides that go into shallow water.

Water Slides include short slides with a five-foot drop at the end, single, double, and triple inner tube slides, fast slides on sleds that send you skimming across the water, and other thrilling water slides!

Arrive early to secure shady spots. Coast Guard approved children's flotation devices are permitted. Arm floaties are allowed when accompanied with a life jacket, which are available at no cost. Rentals of tubes, lockers for additional fees.

Interesting fact

The name "Seven Peaks" comes from the following seven major peaks that surround Utah Valley (with elevation):

1. **Mount Nebo** – 11,928 ft.
2. **Mount Timpanogos** – 11,750 ft.
3. **Lone Peak** – 11,253 ft.
4. **Provo Peak** – 11,068 ft.
5. **Cascade Mountain** – 10,908 ft.
6. **Santaquin Peak** – 10,687 ft.
7. **Spanish Fork Peak** – 10,192 ft.

Taylorsville Community Swimming Pool

4948 South 2700 West
Taylorsville, 84118
(801) 965-1732
www.recreation.slco.org/taylorsville

Hours:
Season runs Memorial Day weekend through mid-August.

Monday-Saturday: 12:05pm-7:55pm;
Sunday: 12:05pm-5pm

Admission:
Under 3: $2 (includes swim diaper); *Age 3-15:* $3; *Age 16-59:* $3.50; *Age 60+:* $2.50

Summer Pass:
Ages 3-15: $55; *Ages 16-59:* $70; *Ages 60+:* $50; *Family Pass:* $130 (immediate family members in the same household).

Food:
Concessions sell a variety of snacks and drinks.

Parking:
Free parking lot.

Discounts:
Discounted monthly passes are available.

What to expect...

Taylorsville Community Swimming Pool is operated by Salt Lake County Parks and Recreation. This outdoor pool is located right next to the Taylorsville Recreation Center.

Outdoor Swimming located in the Indoor Swimming Chapter:

- Clearfield Aquatic Center
- Lehi Legacy Recreation Center
- Provo Recreation Center
- South Davis Recreation Center

Leisure Pool – The leisure pool features a zero-depth (beach) entry and reaches to a depth of 3½ ft. There is a set of dumping buckets, a mushroom and teacup fountain, and ground fountains that spray along the outer edge of the pool.

Water Slide – There is a two-story, twisty water slide. No lap riders are allowed.

Lap pool – The large lap pool is connected to the other swimming areas by a channel of water. It reaches depths of 13 feet and has a high and a low dive.

Seating and Lounge Areas – There are several large umbrellas for shade and a few picnic tables.

Locker Rooms – Locker rooms and family bathrooms with changing tables are available. Lockers are available, but you must bring your own lock.

Children under 10 must be accompanied by an adult age 18 and older. No floatation devices are allowed in the water except for Coast Guard approved life vests. The facility offers swimming lessons for children as young as 6 months old during the summer.

The Taylorsville Recreation Center sits next to the pool facility. It includes and indoor rock wall, indoor and outdoor batting cages, fitness room, aerobics room, gymnasium, and a multi-purpose court.

Just Around the Corner...

- Hale Center Theatre
- Hollywood Connection
- Kearns Oquirrh Fitness Center
- Redwood Road Drive-In
- Utah Grizzlies
- Valley Fair Mall

Story Time & Libraries

Reading and story time help develop many skills important to kindergarten readiness like socialization, vocabulary, listening, language development, and cognitive reasoning. Although reading aloud is beneficial for all ages, this chapter focuses on story hours for children ages six and under because it's never too early to start reading to your baby. Some of our favorite memories of mothering involve time-spent reading with our children as babies and toddlers.

Every library along the Wasatch Front offers a story hour. In this chapter you will find a complete listing of local libraries though we highlight two libraries that are particularly exciting for young children. Both the Provo and Salt Lake Libraries have large areas designated entirely as a children's library and each offer an amazing variety of free activities. Both are worth a special trip. There are also a number of businesses that provide story hours for free. We share these with you as well so that you can take advantage of all the opportunities around for reading and learning with your child.

Courtesy of Provo Public Library

Public Libraries

1. **American Fork Library** – www.afcity.org 64 South100 East, American Fork, Utah 84003
2. **Davis County Library System** www.co.davis.ut.us/library
   - ***Bountiful*** – 725 South Main Street, Bountiful, Utah 84010
   - ***Centerville*** – 45 South 400 West, Centerville, Utah 84014
   - ***Clearfield*** – 562 South 1000 East, Clearfield, Utah 84015
   - ***Farmington*** – 133 South Main Street, Farmington, Utah 84025
   - ***Kaysville*** – 44 North Main, Kaysville, Utah 84037
   - ***Layton*** – 155 North Wasatch Drive, Layton, Utah 84041
   - ***Syracuse*** – 1875 South 2000 West, Syracuse, Utah 84075
3. **Eagle Mountain Library** – www.eaglemountaincity.org 1650 East Stagecoach Run, Eagle Mountain, Utah 84005
4. **Lehi City Library** – www.lehi-ut.gov/discover/library 120 North Center Street, Lehi, Utah 84043
5. **Murray City Library** – www.murraylibrary.org 166 East 5300 South Murray, Utah 84107
6. **Orem City Library** – www.lib.orem.org 58 North State Street, Orem, Utah 84057
7. **Pleasant Grove Library** – www.library.plgrove.org 30 East Center Street, Pleasant Grove, Utah 84062
8. **Provo City Library** – www.provolibrary.com 550 North University Avenue, Provo, Utah 84601
9. **Salt Lake City Public Library System** www.slcpl.org
   - ***Anderson-Foothill*** – 1135 South 2100 East, Salt Lake City, Utah 84108
   - ***Chapman*** – 577 South 900 West, Salt Lake City, Utah 84104
   - ***Corinne and Jack Sweet*** – 455 F Street (9th Avenue), Salt Lake City, Utah 84103
   - ***Day-Riverside*** – 1575 West 1000 North, Salt Lake City, Utah 84116

- ***Main Library*** – 210 East 400 South, Salt Lake City, Utah 84111
- ***Sprague*** – 2131 South 1100 East, Salt Lake City, Utah 84106

10. **Salt Lake County Library System** www.slcolibrary.org

- ***Alta Reading Room*** - 2nd Floor of the Alta Community Center
- ***Bingham Creek*** – 4834 West 9000 South, West Jordan, Utah 84081
- ***Columbus*** – 2530 South 500 East, South Salt Lake City, Utah 84106
- ***Draper*** – 1136 East Pioneer Road (124th South), Draper, Utah 84020
- ***Herriman*** – 5380 West Herriman Main Street, Herriman, Utah 84096
- ***Holladay*** – 2150 East Murray-Holladay Road (4730 South), Salt Lake City, Utah 84117
- ***Hunter*** – 4740 West 4100 South, West Valley City, Utah 84120
- ***Kearns*** – 5350 South 4220 West, Kearns, Utah 84118
- ***Magna*** – 2675 South 8950 West, Magna, Utah 84044
- ***Midvale (Ruth Vine Tyler)*** – 8041 South Wood Street (55 West), Midvale, Utah 84047
- ***Millcreek*** – 2266 East Evergreen Avenue, Millcreek, Utah 84109
- ***Riverton*** – 12877 South 1830 West Road, Riberton, Utah 84065
- ***Salt Lake City*** (Calvin S. Smith) – 810 East 3300 South, Salt Lake City, Utah 84106
- ***Salt Lake City (Whitmore)*** – 2198 East Fort Union Boulevard, Salt Lake City, Utah 84121
- ***Sandy*** – 10100 South Petunia Way (1450 East), Sandy, Utah 84092
- ***South Jordan*** – 10673 South Redwood road (1700 West), South Jordan, Utah 84095
- ***Taylorsville*** – 4870 South 2700 West, Salt Lake City, Utah 84118
- ***West Jordan*** – 8030 South 1825 West, West Jordan, Utah 84088
- ***West Valley*** – 2880 West 3650 South, West Valley City, Utah 84119

11. **Weber County Library System** www.weber.pl.lib.ut.us

- ***Huntsville (Ogden Valley Branch)*** – 131 South 7400 East, Huntsville, Utah 84317
- ***North Ogden*** – 475 East 2600 North, North Ogden, Utah 84414
- ***Ogden (Main Library)*** – 2464 Jefferson Avenue, Ogden, Utah 84401
- ***Pleasant Valley*** – 5568 South Adams Avenue, Washington Terrace, Utah 84405
- ***Roy*** – 1950 West 4800 South, Roy, Utah 84067

Barnes & Noble Story Time

Check the website for information about story time nearest you.
www.barnesandnoble.com

What to expect...

Most Barnes & Noble Bookstores along the Wasatch Front offer a weekly story time. Days and times of the week vary by location. To find out specifics for your store, go to their website and click "Stores and Events."

Story time most often takes place in the children's book area of the store. Some stores have a more elaborate story area than others. The Barnes & Noble in Sugarhouse features a children's story area with a large mural and a tree that appears to come out of the wall. Child-size benches surround the storytelling chair. Story time lasts about 20-30 minutes. After the reading, there is usually some sort of small activity or craft.

Barnes & Noble also offers a monthly online story time where famous authors read their own books aloud. On a day when you aren't up for going out or maybe have sick kids, this would be a great option. You can also join the Barnes & Noble kid's club and be invited to participate in free monthly activities.

At the publication of this book, all but three of the nine stores along the Wasatch Front offer story time.

Children's Library at the Provo City Library

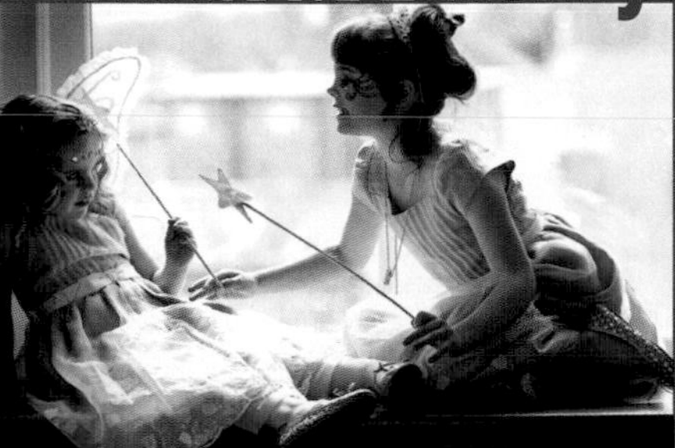

550 North University Avenue
Provo, 84601
(801) 852-6650
www.provolibrary.com

Hours:
Monday – Friday: 9am – 9pm;
Saturday: 9am – 6pm; *Closed:* Sunday

See their website for holiday hours and closings.

Admission:
FREE!

Parking:
There are two free parking lots around the building.

Food:
No food or drink is allowed in the library.

Social:

What to expect...

The children's library, located in the west wing of the beautiful and historic Provo Library, attracts curious children with its low shelves topped with stuffed animals and book characters. Children light up when entering the Story Time Castle's "Secret Passage." Other areas of interest include a sunken stage called the Storytelling Circle, comfortable couches for reading, low tables and chairs, a computer station, a large row of low bucket-shelves full of board books, and a large collection of Spanish children's books.

The Children's Library is best known for its special events, programs, and entertaining story hours. Check the website for story times geared for a variety of ages on a weekly basis. Book Babies is for ages 0-12 months and presents age-appropriate songs, stories, and finger plays. Toddler Time is for ages 1-2 while Preschool Time is for ages 3-5. Both Toddler Time and Preschool Time present puppet shows, stories, songs, finger plays, and a coloring sheet to take home. Children must attend Preschool Time alone inside the special Story Time room and must be registered 10 minutes prior to the start. Other regular events include Monday Night at the Library (a family activity night), Spanish Story Time, Library Kids Jr. and Library Kids Sr. (weekly craft classes), as well as Mother/Daughter, Mother/Son Book Club.

Restrooms with diaper changing stations are next to the librarian's desk. Coat hooks and cubbies are available at the front entrance.

Annual Events

Fairy Tea Party – March. Children dress as fairies and enjoy ballet dancers, a promenade in front of the Fairy King, and a fairy feast. Tickets must be purchased ahead of time.

Big Guy Little Guy – March. A father-and-son activity including lunch. Purchase tickets ahead of time.

Children's Book Festival – May. Multiple events and activities for families.

Summer Reading Program – This is an incentive program to encourage children to read every day during the summer. Story hours called Canopy Capers are offered outdoors once a week in the summer.

Just Around the Corner...

- BYU Broadcasting
- BYU Museum of Art
- BYU Museum of Paleontology
- BYU Museum of Peoples and Cultures
- CLAS Ropes Course
- Comedy Sportz
- FatCats (Provo)
- Lowe's Xtreme Air Sports
- Monte L. Bean Life Science Museum
- Provo Recreation Center
- Provo Towne Centre Play Area
- Royden G. Derek Planetarium
- Seven Peaks (Provo)
- Y Mountain Hike

Salt Lake City Public Library

210 East 400 South
Salt Lake City, UT 84111
(801) 524-8200
www.slpl.org

Hours:
Monday-Thursday: 9am-9pm
Friday-Saturday: 9am-6pm
Sunday: 1pm-5pm

Admission:
FREE! Salt Lake County residents get a free library card. Those living outside Salt Lake County may purchase a card for $80 per year, $20 for three months, or $10 for one month."

Parking:
There is metered parking around the library block. There is also a lower parking garage off of 400 South.

Food:
There are some appropriate areas for food, while other areas are food free. Food vendors may be on location as well.

What to expect...

The Salt Lake City Public Library is one of the most unique buildings in downtown Salt Lake. Completed and opened to the public in 2003, the library administration explained, "The new building embodies the idea that a library is more than a repository of books and computers — it reflects and engages the city's imagination and aspirations." I found that to be true. This library will exceed your expectations.

The entrance, called the Urban Room, offers multiple shops and cafes. Access the **Children's Library** by taking the elevators down the the lower level. The entire floor holds a large collection of books, magazines, and DVDs on low shelves. Glass cases display fun exhibits that change throughout the year. When we were there, my kids enjoyed an "I Spy" display and a Littlest Pet Shop display. There is comfortable seating throughout the library, including child-sized chairs, couches, and tables. Computers are available for searching titles and for other serious work, while another small niche of computers are available for children 12 and under to play educational computer games.

A unique part of the Children's Library is the two alcoves along the South wall called the Attic and the Crystal Cave. **The Attic** actually looks like an attic from the inside and offers places to explore, climb, and sit comfortably to read. **Crystal Cave** looks like an icy cave. My children gravitated immediately to these thoughtfully-designed places that spark the imagination and make reading an inviting experience.

The Children's Library offers many recurring events such as: story hours for babies and preschoolers, family story nights, family-friendly movies as well as craft activities. See the website for a current schedule of events, or ask the children's librarian for current programming information.

Restrooms with changing tables are found in the Children's Library lobby. Within the Children's Library, bathrooms have toddler-sized toilets and stools by the sinks. A Baby Care room with a sink, diaper pail, changing table, and chair for nursing is located behind the computer station.

Annual Events

LEGO-Mania – February. Children bring lego creations to be displayed for a month.

Valentine Making – February

Puppetry Festival – March. Puppeteers from around the nation perform in the library over two days. All-day activities and displays.

Summer Reading Program- Musicians, puppeteers, animal wranglers, and other performers come to the library.

Stuffed Animal Sleepover – Leave your stuffed animal overnight at the library. Come back the next day to see a slideshow of your stuffed animal's adventures in the library.

Haunted Library – October. Kids come dressed in costume to the library and participate in fun, not-too-spooky activities, crafts, and trick-or-treating.

Gingerbread Jamboree – December. Read cookie-themed books and decorate a gingerbread cookie.

The King's English Story Time

Story Time Hours:
Thursday, Friday, and Saturday: 11am

Admission:
FREE!

Parking:
Free parking lot and on the street.

Food:
Food and drink is allowed in the bookstore.

1511 South 1500 East
Salt Lake City, 84105
(801) 484-9100
www.kingsenglish.com

What to expect...

The King's English bookshop is a local favorite and has all of the qualities customers want from an independent bookstore. The charm of the bookshop begins with the tall shelves full of books in every room and hallway. As you wander through one room into the next, you'll find nooks and crannies with comfortable reading chairs.

All of the staff are extremely knowledgeable and ready to give book suggestions if needed. The Children's Room is one of the largest in the building and features colorful stacks of books and delightful displays.

Story Time at the King's English is offered three days a week, with a different storyteller each day. I was there on a Thursday and enjoyed the best story time experience I have ever had with long-time reader Rob Eckman. I'm sure other readers are of equal ability. During the warm months, story time is held on the back patio of the shop under the shade of trees. Story time lasts about 20-30 minutes or for as long as the kids are engaged. During the cold months, story time is held in the Children's Book Room.

Friday Fun is also offered one Friday a month at 4pm for kids ages 3-8. A special story time featuring a specific book is followed by an activity and a craft. There is a $5 fee and a reservation is required.

Just Around the Corner...

- Color Me Mine (SLC)
- Fairmont Aquatic Center
- FatCats (SLC)
- Fort Douglas Military Museum
- Liberty Park
- Natural History Museum of Utah
- Salt Lake Bees
- This Is The Place Heritage Park
- Tracy Aviary
- Utah Museum of Fine Art
- Utah's Hogle Zoo

Three Little Monkeys

Story Time Hours:
Wednesdays: 10:30am and 11:30am

Admission:
FREE!

Parking:
Free parking lot.

Food:
No food or drink is allowed.

Social:

2 locations
www.3littlemonkeys.com

What to expect...

Location 1
Fruit Heights
285 South Mountain Road
Fruit Heights, UT 84037
(801) 444-1470

Location 2
Bountiful
470 South Main Street
Bountiful, UT 84010
(801) 296-TOYS (8697)

Three Little Monkeys specializes in novelty toys and games that help children learn while having fun. They know that play time encourages the development of many attributes like: logical thought, critical thinking, language development, motor and sensory skills, problem solving, and positive socialization. Another important part of learning and development comes from reading. Three Little Monkeys sells a selection of the best and all-time favorite children's books.

Every Wednesday, both locations offer story time. The 30-minute story time is geared towards kids ages 2-5 and is comprised of songs, finger play, stories, and always ends with a small craft. In the Bountiful location, story time is held in a special area with brightly painted walls in the back of the store. Child-sized tables and chairs are used for the craft at the end.

After story time and the craft are over, kids can play with a variety of display toys like puzzles, hand puppets, mini shopping carts, play sized tables with doll houses, a magnetic dartboard and toy cars.

There are several paid classes offered at Three Little Monkeys. See the website for specifics. Restrooms are available.

Other Story Time Hours in this Book:

- **Discovery Gateway: The Children's Museum of Utah**
  The Discovery Gateway offers **Time for Tots**. This is a 30-minute, nationally-recognized literacy program for kids 18 months to 3 years old. You must sign up at the Information Desk to reserve a spot. Classes are held on Tuesdays at 11am, 12pm, 2pm, and 3pm.

- **Tracy Aviary**
  Tracy Aviary offers **Book & Bird** on Wednesdays at 11am during the cold months and allows children to meet the bird highlighted in the books face to face. It is held in the Education Space in the Visitor's Center at the front of Tracy Aviary. This is a free program that is included in the price of admission.

- **Natural History Museum**
  The Chickadee Society is a pre-school story time held the fourth Thursday of every month from 11:00-11:30am. It includes science-themed stories and activities.

- **Treehouse Children's Museum**
  On Track to Reading is offered on Mondays, September through May (excluding major holidays). It is a reading readiness program specifically designed to help young children be ready to read and ready for kindergarden through interactive story activities and songs, art, and early learning activities. Alphabet Soup is offered on Friday nights from 6-8pm. It involves the whole family in literacy activities through stories, songs, theater, art, science, history, and more. Both are sponsored programs offered at a reduced admission price of $3 per child and $1 per adult.

- **Utah's Hogle Zoo**
  Zoo Story Time is offered occasionally at no additional cost for people with zoo memberships. This usually lasts 30 minutes and includes a children's story, and an animal encounter. See the website's events calendar to find the next story time.

Tours

Kids in the 1800s knew where milk and bacon came from and how it got to the table. They knew how long and tedious it was for their mom to make a new dress and for dad to plant, tend, and harvest crops. Nowadays, almost everything we use or consume is bought at a store. We see and enjoy the end product but are so disconnected to the process of how it got there. This chapter highlights many different behind-the-scenes tours that will give your child the chance to see the process behind a product. Whether it is how chocolates are made or what goes in to producing artwork or a play production, each of these tours is interesting and fun.

Courtesy of Sweet Candy Factory, Image by ADAIR – www.adairworks.com

BYU Broadcasting

Brigham Young University
Provo, 84602
1-866-662-9888
www.byub.org

Hours:
Tours are by appointment.

Admission:
FREE!

Parking:
There are limited visitor parking stalls in the north parking lot.

Food:
No food or drink is allowed.

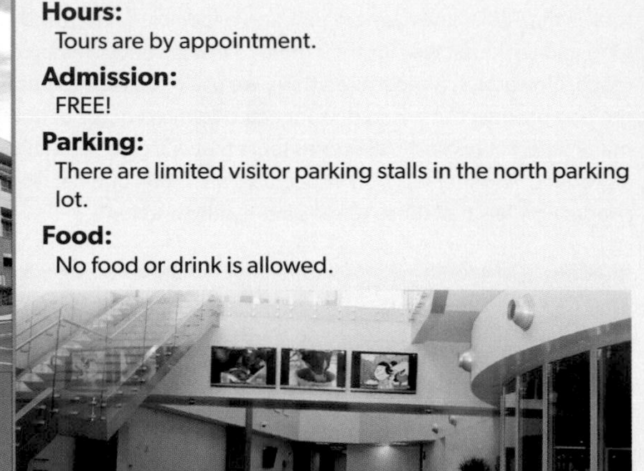

What to expect...

Did you know BYU is the only University in the United States with an HD production and broadcast building on campus? BYU Broadcasting provides 24-hour programming for five different channels (three national and two international).

A tour of BYU's state-of-the art Broadcasting Building offers an interesting look at what goes into producing radio, television, and internet programing. Tours are offered to the public by appointment only, and usually need to be scheduled by phone a few weeks in advance. The tour lasts about an hour, which is why I would recommend this tour for kids age eight and up.

The large and beautifully modern lobby of the Broadcasting Building is where a host will meet you to begin the tour. Many areas of the building have large glass panel walls that allow you to see into the different production and control rooms even though you cannot enter all of them. Stops on the tour include places like: the green rooms, hair and make-up room, and several control rooms with equipment and dozens of TV monitors used in the production of live television broadcasting. It was amazing to learn and see how many people it takes to create a seamless broadcast of a live basketball or football game. Our favorite stops were at the set of the True Blue sports show and Chef Brad's Fusion Grain Cooking Show.

The last part of the tour is the area where BYU radio is produced. You can see the recording studios of Classical 89 and other radio programs. My kids and I were impressed by the massive CD collection in the Classical 89 studio library. All forms of broadcasting require tremendous amounts of planning, creating, and editing.

Most jobs are done by students majoring in Film or Broadcast Journalism. No television production occurs during tour hours, but you may get to see students at work on other various projects.

Just Around the Corner...

- BYU Museum of Paleontology
- BYU Museum of Peoples and Cultures
- Children's Library at Provo City Library
- Creativity Art Studio
- Color Me Mine (Provo)
- Comedy Sportz
- FatCats (Provo)
- Hang Time Extreme Trampolines (Orem)
- Jake's Archery
- Krispy Kreme (Orem)
- Monte L. Bean Life Science Museum
- Nickel City
- Orem Owlz
- Provo Beach
- Provo Recreation Center
- Royden G. Derek Planetarium
- Scera Pool
- Seven Peaks (Provo)
- Seven Peaks Fun Center (Orem)
- Shops at Riverwoods
- University Mall Tree House Court
- Y Mountain Hike

Great Harvest Bread Co.

Hours:
Vary by location. Tours are by appointment.

Admission:
FREE!

Parking:
Free parking lot.

Food:
No food or drink is allowed on the tour.

Multiple locations
along the Wasatch
www.greatharvestutah.com

What to expect...

Great Harvest Bread Co. is an absolute local favorite. They sale many varieties of fresh baked breads, cookies, sweet rolls, and pastries.

Great Harvest reaches out to the community by offering free tours of their kitchen. The tours are specifically aimed for children ages 3-12. All tours require a reservation, but because each store is independently owned and operated, every store has their own way of giving tours and taking reservations.

We took a tour of the Great Harvest on 21st south in Salt Lake City because it was easier to schedule than some of the other locations. Our tour guide Sara was wonderful. After each child put on an apron, she started by reading a children's book about how bread is made, from the wheat growing in the fields, to the finished product. She then showed the kids the five ingredients used to make their bread. Next, we took a tour of the kitchen, with a look at all of the different bread making stations. We saw where the wheat is ground, the huge bowl and mixer where the dough is mixed, and where the yeast is stored. Guess how many loaves of bread can be cooked at a time in the enormous oven? (Hint: it's in the hundreds!)

After the kitchen tour, every child was given their own piece of dough to knead and form into a loaf (or something resembling a loaf). The bread takes 25-30 minutes to bake and another 10 to cool down. You can stay and eat lunch in the bakery or come back later to pick up the finished loaves.

Hale Centre Theatre Backstage Tour

3333 South Decker Lake Drive
West Valley City, 84119
(801)-984-9000
www.hct.org

Hours:
The second Wednesday after the opening of each production at 12pm

Admission:
FREE!

Parking:
Free parking lot.

Food:
No outside food or drink is allowed.

What to expect...

The Hale Centre Theatre, Utah's Premiere Family Theatre, is the nation's highest attended community theater, seating 610 people in a theater in the round. Started in 1985 by Ruth and Nathan Hale, it is a non-profit organization that relies on ticket sales and donations to meet yearly budget demands. The state of the art theater is the most attended arts venue in Utah, providing entertainment to over 250,000 patrons annually. Every production at Hale Centre Theatre is cast with local actors, many of whom have other full-time jobs and do acting on the side. If you have never seen a show here, I would highly recommend it. There are usually a couple of plays every year that would be very interesting for children.

The Hale Centre Theatre offers a free backstage tour to the public the second Wednesday after the opening of each production. Tour reservations are on a first come, first served basis and should be made in advance through the box office. You will see three large rehearsal rooms, the green room, dressing rooms, the costume shop, the set shop, and you may even get to walk on the actual theater stage! You will get a chance to ask questions to one of the set designers and go below into the pit to see the underside of the stage and all of its moving parts. Areas included in the tour are subject to change due to availability.

There is no official age requirement for the tour, but I would suggest ages 6 and older. The tour is not entirely stroller-accessible. It lasts about an hour.

Just Around the Corner...

- Hollywood Connection
- LDS Humanitarian Center
- Redwood Road Drive-In
- Taylorsville Community Swimming Pool
- Utah Grizzlies
- Valley Fair Mall

Holdman Studios

3001 North Thanksgiving Way
Lehi, 84043
(801) 766-4111
www.holdmanstudios.com

Hours:
Studio Hours Monday-Friday: 9am-5pm; *Saturday:* 10am-5pm

Glass Blowing Hours *Monday-Saturday:* 10am-4pm

Admission:
FREE!

Parking:
Free parking lot.

Food:
No food or drink allowed inside the studio.

What to expect...

Step into a vibrant world of art and color in the Holdman Glass Studios. This amazing artisan shop is extremely friendly and welcoming to the public. The studios produce both blown glass and stained glass creations. The first viewing area you see as you enter is the hot glass production area. Visitors are encouraged to take a seat in front of the large glass window and watch as skilled artists create beautiful and unique glass pieces. Glass blowing is a highly technical art form that is fascinating to watch. No two creations are the same. If by chance the glass blowers are not working when you visit, there is a television monitor running a film of the entire process. Artists are almost always working, but call ahead to make sure.

The back of the studio houses the stained glass production area. Feel free to walk through the double doors into the studio and watch the artists at work. You are invited to carefully wander through the work area and to observe and ask questions. You can also just wander and enjoy the many glass pieces on display and for sale throughout the studio. On our visit, we saw an enormous chandelier being put together and many stained glass windows headed for a Mormon temple.

For a fee of $30, the studios offer a special opportunity for a visitor to make a blown glass flower. Kids are able to enter the glass blowing work area and, with assistance, make their own glass flower. Art classes for kids are offered every Saturday in the studio's art classroom. See their website for hours and pricing.

Just Around the Corner...

- Cabela's
- Children's Discovery Garden at Thanksgiving Point
- Farm Country at Thanksgiving Point
- Hangtime Extreme Trampolines (Lehi)
- Highland Town Center Splash Pad
- Museum of Ancient Life
- Seven Peaks Fun Center (Lehi)
- Thanksgiving Point Gardens

Krispy Kreme

Multiple locations
www.krispykreme.com

Hours: Layton Location
Sunday-Thursday: 6am-10pm;
Friday-Saturday: 6am-11pm

Tours require a reservation.

Donuts are made from 6-11am and 6-11pm (or closing).

Admission:
FREE!

Parking:
Free parking lot.

Food:
No outside food or drink is allowed.

Social:

What to expect...

Location 1
968 North Main Street
Layton, 84041
(801) 497-9001

Location 2
417 West 1300 South
Orem, 84057
(801) 222-9995

Delicious Krispy Kreme donuts are made and distributed from two stores in Northern Utah. Although their donuts can be purchased in places like the grocery store or the gas station, the best way to experience a Krispy Kreme donut is in their store when the HOT DONUTS sign is lit up. Not only will you enjoy a fresh, melt-in-your-mouth donut, but you will get to see how they are made. A large glass window reveals the automatic production line at work. You can see where the dough balls rise, and then watch the donuts float along as they are fried and finally pass under the glazing waterfall. A long bench under the window allows children a great view. Anyone visiting the store during donut-making hours will get to see this fun production line make hundreds of donuts.

For a little more in-depth experience, tours are offered by reservation. Although you won't see anything more than what can be seen through the glass window, the tour makes the experience more official. The short 10 minute tour is given by an employee who will bring out some of the soft donut dough for kids to touch and will explain a little bit about the donut-making process and answer questions. Each person on the tour gets a Krispy Kreme hat and one free donut. My kids were thrilled about the hats and, of course, the donuts. I would recommend groups no larger than about 10. Tours are offered between 9am –noon, but if you want to watch the traditional donuts being made, plan to go between 9-11am when the "Hot Donuts" sign is on.

LDS Conference Center Tour

60 West North Temple
Salt Lake City, 84150
(801) 240-0075
www.visittemplesquare.com

Hours:
9am-9pm daily

Tours are offered continuously. The last tour begins at 8pm.

Admission:
FREE!

Parking:
Metered parking and surface parking are available on surrounding city streets. There is limited paid parking under the Conference Center. Do not park in residential areas north of the building.

Food:
No food or drink is allowed. There are restaurants on Temple Square or at City Creek Center.

What to expect...

The LDS Conference Center is a one-of-a-kind building that serves as the meeting place for the biannual General Conference of the Church of Jesus Christ of Latter-day Saints. These conferences are broadcast live across the world and translated on-site into many languages. The Mormon Tabernacle Choir also holds its live Sunday broadcast in this building throughout the summer and in December. The building is also used for artistic and cultural shows of all kinds and houses a 21,000-seat auditorium, a 7,667-pipe organ, and a 900-seat theater. There is plenty to see and explore in this four-story building with a waterfall flowing down the face and a garden growing on the roof!

The Conference Center offers free tours to visitors of all ages. The tour lasts about 30-45 minutes and is stroller-friendly. Enter the building at Door 15, located in the front of the building, and a volunteer will be assigned to you. On the tour, you will learn about the unique construction of the building, the organ, and other interesting facts about the facility. The tour also takes you through a number of lobbies and halls where you will see original LDS artwork, an indoor fountain, sculptures, and more.

When weather permits, visitors can request to walk along the garden roof at the end of their tour. This 4-acre roof is landscaped with trees, a grassy meadow, fountains, and a waterfall. Children love to wander the garden and to see the fountains, but are not allowed to play in the fountains. The garden roof is open for tours Monday through Friday from 10-2pm and Tuesday and Wednesday at 7pm. If you want to see the garden roof, be sure to plan your Conference Center tour during these hours.

Tours are free to the public and walk-ins are welcome. There is no waiting and no reservation required, though groups over 20 people should reserve a time in advance. The Conference Center is often host to special events, so consider calling ahead before visiting.

See Appendix 1 for Downtown Destinations close to this area

LDS Humanitarian Center

1665 Bennett Road
Salt Lake City, 84104
(801) 240-5954

Hours:
Monday-Friday: 10am-3pm

Admission:
FREE!

Parking:
Free parking lot.

Food:
There is no ideal place inside or outside for visitors to eat.

What to expect...

The LDS Humanitarian Center is a large facility used to process and prepare humanitarian supplies to be sent worldwide. Supplies include donated clothing, quilts, hygiene and school kits, and emergency medical modules. The facility also acts as a training program for refugees and others in need of gaining employable skills in the workforce. Taking a guided tour of the Center will teach your children the importance of helping those in need.

Guided tours are offered to the public free of charge on the hour, Monday through Friday, starting at 10am. Tours last about 45 minutes. The last tour of the day begins at 3pm. Tours begin in a large room where workers process and package clothing to be sent throughout the world to the needy. Many kids living in Utah give unwanted clothing to Deseret Industries; it is likely that some of their clothes have ended up at the Humanitarian Center.

Another portion of the tour leads you through displays. You will see exactly what goes into humanitarian kits prepared in the building, models of wheelchairs that the church donates to third world countries, homemade quilts and dresses, wooden toys, and many pictures of people receiving aid. There is also a map that marks each country to which the Church has sent humanitarian aid. Behind these displays are more workers creating kits and tying quilts. The final portion of the tour is a ten minute film depicting the role the Church has played in humanitarian service throughout the world.

Visitors age 12 and older may participate in making kits and tying quilts. Ages 16 and older may participate in separating clothing. Groups larger than 8 should call ahead and make a reserved time for tours and/or volunteering. You may also call and schedule an evening tour. The women's restroom has a changing table and a couch for nursing. The tour is stroller-friendly.

For more information you can visit their website at *www.lds.org/topics/humanitarian-service/center*.

Interesting Fact

The Humanitarian Center ships about 500,000 hygiene and school kits, 8 million pounds of shoes and clothing, and 20,000 quilts to help the needy in more than 50 countries per year.

Just Around the Corner...

- Hale Center Theatre
- Hollywood Connection
- International Peace Gardens
- Salt Lake Bees
- Seven Peaks (SLC)
- Sweet Candy Factory
- Utah Grizzlies
- Valley Fair Mall
- Welfare Square

Mrs. Cavanaugh's Chocolate Factory

835 Northpointe Drive
North Salt Lake, 84054
(801) 677-8888
www.mrscavanaughs.com

Hours:
Monday-Friday: 9am-5pm;
Saturday: 10am-4pm

Tours are by appointment.

Admission:
Cost is $1 per person, but you receive a $1 coupon to spend in the store. Major credit cards accepted. They do not accept checks.

Parking:
Free parking lot.

Food:
No outside food or drink is allowed.

Social:

What to expect...

Mrs. Cavanaugh's is a locally owned and operated chocolate company. There are eight stores throughout the state and a large factory where all of their chocolate is produced. The factory offers tours to the public by reservation Monday-Friday.

The tour begins with a ten-minute video about how chocolate is made. A second ten-minute video about the history of Mrs. Cavanaugh's chocolate company is played right after the first. I recommend asking the tour guide to skip the second video if you have children with you under the age of 8. Although I found it interesting and well-made, my kids lost interest and were restless through the second video.

Next you will look through big glass windows overlooking the factory down below. The factory works on supply and demand, so there is no exact schedule for production. There may or may not be a lot going on in the factory at the time of your tour. For this reason, there are two TVs located next to the windows that show a short clip of chocolate production. The best chance of seeing a lot of activity in the factory is between about 10-11am.

The next stop on the tour is a room with a beautiful little model village called "Cavanaugh Land" which features an electric train. From the windows in this room, you will get a closer look at the packaging areas on the factory floor. Before leaving, you will see another 10-minute video featuring scenes from the classic episode of "I love Lucy" where Ethel and Lucy get jobs at a chocolate factory and inevitably mess up. My kids loved this video.

If you are lucky, you may be there when hand-dipped chocolates are being made. One woman has been doing all the hand-dipped chocolates for 14 years. This was a definite highlight of the tour.

At the end of the tour, you will receive a sample chocolate and your $1 coupons which you can use in the factory store. Bathrooms do not have changing tables. The tour requires climbing stairs and there is no elevator.

Just Around the Corner...

- Kangaroo Zoo
- Legacy Park

Peery's Egyptian Theater

2415 Washington Blvd.
Ogden, 84401
(801) 689-8700
www.egyptiantheaterogden.com

Hours:
Tours are given by appointment.

Admission:
FREE!

Parking:
Free parking on the street after 6pm. There is a two-hour limit before 6pm.

Food:
No outside food or drink is allowed.

Social:

What to expect...

Peery's Egyptian Theater is unlike any other theater you have seen. The extravagant detail inside and out will definitely draw your kids' attention. Brothers Harman and Lewis Peery built the theater in 1924. It's hard to believe that this lavish theater was designed and constructed originally as a movie theater. It has been restored to reflect the opulence of the movie palace era.

The theater sets itself apart from all other buildings on the street. The intrigue of this building begins with the decorative exterior, which includes ornately painted columns and sphinx sculptures. The lobby is spectacular with a coiffured ceiling and beautiful lighting. Even more impressive is the actual auditorium itself. Above the stage, the proscenium arch is highly decorated with Egyptian images and hieroglyphs. The 800-seat theater now serves as a multi-use theatrical venue.

The tour starts in the lobby and continues into the theater, onto the stage, through the green room, dressing rooms, and even under the stage to the orchestra pit.

Because the theater was originally built during the days of silent movies, an organ was a part of the original building. In keeping with the history of the theater, an organ has been included in the restoration and is played during each tour. As we walked in, the kids got excited with the dramatic sounds of the organ playing music from *Mary Poppins*, which was the featured movie that week.

The theater occasionally shows free kid's movies. Get there early to enjoy the pipe organ prelude music. It's not like any church prelude music you might have heard.

For information on events or to request a tour, please visit the Theater website for an event calendar or to submit a request.

Just Around the Corner...

- Birdsong Trail
- Coleman's Motor-VU Drive-In
- Color Me Mine (Ogden)
- FastKart Speedway (Ogden)
- FatCats (Ogden)
- Fort Buenaventura
- Ogden Dinosaur Park and Museum
- Ogden Nature Center
- Ogden Raptors
- Ogden River Parkway
- Ogden's Union Station
- Ott Planetarium
- Riverdale Park
- Treehouse Children's Museum

Sweet Candy Factory

3780 West Directors Row (1100 South)
Salt Lake City, 84104
(801) 886-1444
www.sweetcandy.com

Hours:
Monday-Thursday: 8:40am-3:30pm

Tours last 40 minutes and are by appointment.

Tours are not offered from Labor Day through Halloween.

Admission:
FREE!

Parking:
Free parking lot.

Food:
No outside food, gum, or drink is allowed.

What to expect...

Sweet Candy has been making candy in Utah for over 100 years and you've probably seen their delicious bulk candy at many local grocery stores. The company gets its name from the founder Leon Sweet. Sweet produces 250 different candy items, which are distributed nationally and internationally. They have a wide range of products, and offer a behind-the-scenes look at the making of their candy.

Tours are made by reservation. Request a tour by email through their website and a receptionist will call you back to schedule a time. When I called, they were very prompt to call back the next morning. Most tour groups are restricted to adults. Family groups are allowed as long as there are adults accompanying the children.

Sweet is very stringent with their food safety and hygiene rules as they strive to stay compliant with many different types of food accreditations. Before starting the tour, visitors must remove all jewelry and check-in personal items including, cameras, keys, phones, and coats. Visitors are required to wear close-toed shoes and hairnets. If you have a child in a stroller, you will be asked to use a stroller they provide to keep outside contaminants from the factory floor.

The tour begins with an introductory movie that lasts about 2-3 minutes. A tour guide will then lead you through the enormous warehouse of packaged candy to the actual floor of the factory. There, you will have the opportunity to get a closer look at the candy making process. We were there when their Easter candy was in full production. We saw jellybeans being rolled in sugar barrels, taffy being pulled, and cinnamon bunnies in their molds. We also saw the production line of chocolate covered orange sticks. Small samples of different types of candy are offered throughout the tour. Guests must remain within the specified yellow lines that make a path throughout the factory. I would recommend young children, especially unpredictable toddlers be put in a stroller as they are very strict about staying within those yellow lines. At the end of the tour, you can stop by the factory store located in the lobby, which sells all of their products. Restrooms and a drinking fountain are available near the lobby.

Just Around the Corner...

- LDS Humanitarian Center
- Northwest Recreation Center
- Seven Peaks (SLC)
- Utah Truffles

Taffy Town

55 West 800 South
Salt Lake City 84101
(801) 355-4652
www.taffytown.com

Hours:
Monday-Friday: 10am-5pm
Tours are by appointment.

Admission:
FREE!

Parking:
Free parking lot on the east side of building.

Food:
No outside food or drink is allowed.

What to expect...

Formerly known as Glade Candy, Taffy Town has been making candy in Utah for over 100 years. The company adopted the new name of Taffy Town when they decided to produce salt-water taffy exclusively. The factory has been in the same building for 70 years, where the original hardwood floors add charm and history to this family-run business. Taffy Town produces 3,000,000 pounds of taffy each year!

As you enter the building, you walk into the factory retail store. The entire west wall is covered with taffy bins in dozens of flavors. A big screen TV in the corner plays a segment of the television show Unwrapped that features the entire process of taffy production at the Taffy Town factory.

Tours, by appointment only, begin on the main floor at the very end of the assembly process where the taffy is being bagged and boxed. Upstairs on the second floor, our favorite part of the tour was watching through enormous glass windows as the workers mix the taffy, and pour it out on to large cooling tables. The "cut and wrap and design room" lets you see how the large rolls of taffy are slowly stretched to become long and skinny so they can be cut into bite size pieces and then wrapped. If you have a child that is sensitive or afraid of loud noises, be aware that the machinery in this room is loud. At the end of the tour, each visitor gets a sample of taffy. The tour lasts about 20 minutes. Everyone is required to wear a hairnet. There is no elevator available for strollers. Restrooms are located in the lobby.

Utah Truffles

5060 West Amelia Earhart Drive
Salt Lake City, 84116
(801) 512-8183
www.dktruffles.com

Hours:
Just drop in during regular business hours and someone will give you a tour.

Admission:
FREE!

Parking:
Free parking lot.

Food:
No outside food or drink is allowed.

What to expect...

Utah Truffles is a family owned and operated business that has been creating delicious chocolate truffles for many years. Their smooth delicious truffles come in flavors like mint, orange, almond, raspberry, and toffee. Visitors are welcome to tour the factory at any time during business hours. Just drop in and ask for a tour; an employee will take you back for an up-close look at chocolate making.

This factory is smaller than some, which means you will get a closer look at the process. Through large glass windows, you will see chocolate being melted, poured, and carried along a conveyor belt to be bathed in a final coat of chocolate. The tour takes about 15-20 minutes. At the end of the tour, we were each given a truffle of our choice. Hair nets are required.

Just Around the Corner...

- Northwest Recreation Center
- Sweet Candy Factory

V Chocolates

850 South Main Street
Salt Lake City, 84101
(801) 269-8444
www.vchocolates.com

Hours:
Tours are by appointment March-September.

Admission:
FREE!

Parking:
There is free parking in front of the store. Additional parking is located in the lot south of building.

Food:
No outside food or drink is allowed.

What to expect...

V Chocolates is a locally-owned company that produces an assortment of delicious chocolate confections. It's hard to choose a favorite. They make caramels, toffee, truffles, and are well-known for their chocolate-dipped fruit. We sampled a chocolate-dipped strawberry and it was delicious.

As you can imagine, touring a chocolate factory is pretty much every kid's (and adult's) dream. Tours are offered by appointment and will not leave you disappointed. You will get a very close look at how and where V Chocolates are made.

A member of management gives each tour, which lasts about 20-30 minutes. The tour begins in the lobby of the factory store with a brief explanation of where the cacao bean comes from and how it is harvested. Next the tour moves to the kitchen where you will see equipment used to make their chocolates, like: large copper kettles where caramel is mixed and heated, cooling tables, special cutting devices, and the chocolate enrobing machine that bathes each confection with the final outer coating. The tour ends in the wrapping room where all V Chocolates are boxed or bagged in their signature, sophisticated packaging. And the best part, we all got to choose a few samples to taste.

All visitors must wear provided hairnets. Restrooms are available.

Welfare Square

780 West 800 South
Salt Lake City, 84104
(801) 240-4872
www.lds.org/locations

Hours:
Tours are offered Monday-Friday from 10am-3pm

Evening tours can be scheduled. Wednesday nights can be scheduled for youth service projects.

Admission:
FREE!

Parking:
Free parking lot.

Food:
No outside food or drink is allowed.

What to expect...

If you are looking for an activity with meaning that reaches beyond entertainment, a tour of Welfare Square is what you want. Welfare Square consists of several buildings dedicated to the production of food and goods to help the less fortunate. Although owned and operated by the Church of Jesus Christ of Latter-day Saints, everyone is welcome and encouraged to come experience a tour of the facilities.

The tour starts at the visitor center with a 15-minute movie that gives an overview of what Welfare Square is and who the beneficiaries are of the food produced there. There are several stops on the tour with large windows at each stop giving visitors a good look at the production process. Here is what you will see on your tour:

Bishops Storehouse: You will walk through the enormous warehouse of packaged food awaiting shipment and distribution.

Bakery: The bakery produces 3,000-5,000 loaves of bread a day, five days a week. You will be able to watch as the bread is made and packaged for shipment.

Cannery: At the Wet Pack Cannery we saw volunteers working along a processing line bottling spaghetti sauce. My kids liked watching the conveyor belt carry empty glass jars through an automated production line that filled and sealed the jars. The dry pack cannery is used to package dry foods like flour, sugar, oatmeal, and wheat.

Thrift Store: Deseret Industries distributes approximately 9 million pounds of clothes and shoes internationally every year. You will get to walk through the large Deseret Industries warehouse where workers sort and organize donated goods.

See Appendix 1 for Downtown Destinations close to this area

Dairy: The dairy on Welfare Square processes milk into whipping cream, cottage cheese, sour cream, chocolate milk, butter and cheddar cheese. You will see where they make the cheese and bottle the milk. At the end of the tour, there are samples of cheese, chocolate milk, bread, and jam. Restrooms are available along the tour.

Unique Adventures

There are some adventures so unique, they just didn't fit in a specific category. This chapter holds some of our all-time favorite activities, like a ropes course, a comedy club for families, zip lining, a train park, and a fun way to help kids in other countries. If you are looking for something out of the ordinary, these destinations fit the bill.

Courtesy of CLAS Ropes

Cabela's

2502 Cabela's Boulevard
Lehi 84043
(801) 766-2500
www.cabelas.com

Hours:
Monday- Friday: 9am-9pm;
Saturday: 8am-9pm; *Sunday:* 10am-6pm

Fish feeding hours *Monday-Thursday:* 6pm;
Friday-Saturday: noon and 6pm; *Sunday:* noon and 4pm

Admission:
FREE!

Parking:
Free parking lot.

Food:
No outside food or drink is allowed.

What to expect...

Cabela's is known by sportsmen as the mecca for everything hunting, fishing, and camping. It is more than a store. Just walk through the front doors and you become a part of the great outdoors with dozens of large game mounts on the walls and museum-quality animal displays re-creating game in their natural habitat. The large mountain display in the middle of the store features a waterfall with a small fish pond at the bottom. You can buy food to feed the fish for 25 cents.

The highlight of a visit to Cabela's is the huge fish aquarium. Just to the right of the front entrance is the opening to the aquarium where you will get an up-close look at dozens of varieties of trout, bass, walleye, and other fish native to Utah. Just seeing the fish is worth the trip but for an even bigger adventure, come at feeding time and watch the frenzy as fish scramble for the food dropped from above. I have to warn you that aside from regular fish pellet food, several goldfish are also dropped into the tank to be eaten. It might not be right for every family, but my kids, including my little girls were very excited and enthralled by it.

Another fun activity is the old-fashioned shooting gallery upstairs in the southeast corner of the store. See how many targets you can hit with your laser rifle. Most things move when you hit the target. You get four tokens for a dollar, and each token lets you shoot about 20 times. You can also ask for tokens at the front desk and they will give you a couple for free. There is a little café on the second floor that offers lunch and dinner or stop by the candy shop for a treat. Restrooms and drinking fountains are located in the northeast corner of the second floor.

Just Around the Corner...

- Farm Country at Thanksgiving Point
- Hangtime Extreme Trampolines (Lehi)
- Highland Town Center Splash Pad
- Holdman Studios
- Museum of Ancient Life
- Seven Peaks Fun Center (Lehi)
- Thanksgiving Point Gardens

&BAILEY
FISHING
and
HUNTING
STORE
GENERAL STORE
HARDWARE
and
PROVISIONS
BOAT
RENTALS & REPAIRS
Est. 1908
HUNTING
DRINK
Coca-Cola
IN BOTTLES
SOLD OUT
10
PROVISIONS
JACK DANIEL'S
WHISKEY
7

CLAS Ropes Course

3606 West Center Street
Provo, 84601
(801) 373- 8897
www.clasropes.com

Hours:
Office hours are Monday-Friday from 9am-5pm.

Groups can use the course anytime during daylight hours (8am-9pm) Monday –Saturday. Call ahead to schedule a time. They are open year-round.

Admission:
Very reasonably priced. Call for exact price.

Parking:
Free parking area at the entrance of the park.

Food:
Food and drinks are permitted.

Discounts:
Entertainment Book.

What to expect...

Located along the shady banks of the Provo River, CLAS Ropes Course was created in 1993, and is one of the few ropes courses open to the public. CLAS is an acronym for **C**hallenging **L**eadership **A**dventure **S**ystems. The course is designed as a team building challenge, to help bring groups closer and bring to light individual confidence. The activities on the course help participants understand concepts like problem solving, communication, conflict resolution, leadership, cooperation, trust, and self-confidence. It is a chance to step out of your everyday schedule and try something challenging, adventurous, and exciting. The course includes low activities and high activities.

The **low activities** include critical thinking games that involve physical movement and participation from the entire group. Usually the group must work together to complete a task. When we were there, our given task seemed impossible at first, but as we worked together, we were able to figure out a way to accomplish it.

High activities include activities where participants must wear a safety harness and attempt feats that have a perceived risk and may seem impossible. With encouragement from the group, individuals feel the triumph of overcoming fears to reach a level of personal achievement. One activity I enjoyed was a climb up to a high platform in a tree. The object was to climb up and then leap off the platform and grab a large iron ring hanging about 7 feet away from the platform. Of course the safety harness will suspend you after jumping, but it was hard to get the courage to do it. Even though I only touched the ring, I still felt the exhilaration of doing something that was daunting.

The course welcomes families, reunions, church groups, company retreats, school groups, birthday parties, or anyone else interested in building a positive group dynamic. One facilitator is assigned per group of 2-15 people. The facilitator will lead all of the activities and games, making sure everyone is comfortable and safe at all times. No one has to do anything they don't want to, but encouragement is given when confidence is waning. There are so many different types of activities that you could go multiple times and have a different experience each time. Activities can be tailored for your specific group needs or perhaps for the value you are trying to develop within the group. The facilitators' purpose is to make sure your group has the best experience possible. The shortest time available is 2 hours, but I would recommend no less than four. Time flies by quickly and the activities are so fun you will lose track of time.

Canoeing: Available as part of a package with the Ropes Course or individually, canoe rental is a fun way to experience the Provo River. Life jackets are provided. Groups can paddle up or down the river and enjoy the natural surroundings. We took our girls ages 3 and 5 and they got a little nervous in the canoe with the slight rocking motions. After about 10 minutes, they got used to the rocking and realized they weren't going to fall out and enjoyed the ride. I had never rowed a canoe, but between my husband and I, we found it very easy.

Restrooms are available on site. There are scattered picnic tables available for eating, and a small amphitheater that can be reserved for larger groups and larger food service needs.

Annual Events

Both the **Halloween Cruise** and **Christmas Cruise** take passengers on professional excursion boats down part of the Provo River at night to experience decorations, lights, and entertainment relevant to the holiday. These cruises are perfect for families.

Just Around the Corner...

- Children's Library at Provo City Library
- Comedy Sportz
- FatCats (Provo)
- Lowe's Xtreme Air Sports
- Provo Recreation Center

Coleman's Motor-VU Drive-In

5368 South 1050 West
Riverdale, 84405
(801) 394-1768
www.motorvu.com

Hours:
Movies start at dusk.

Box office
Friday & Saturday: 7pm;
Sunday-Thursday: 7:15pm (March-November)

Admission:
Age 12+: $7; *Ages 5-11:* $3; *Ages 4 and under:* FREE!

CASH ONLY.

Food:
Outside food and drink are permitted.

What to expect...

Don't let the summer pass by without taking the kids to the drive-in movies. Coleman's Motor-VU Drive-In offers a classic drive-in experience with four movie screens, each showing a double feature nightly. The first movie starts at dusk (around 9:30) and the second around 11:30. Admission pays for both movies. Kids' movies are usually slotted for the 9:30 hour so that you can leave if you don't want to stay for the second movie. The sound is transmitted over FM frequency, so make sure your car radio works.

For kids, the excitement of watching a movie outdoors is comparable to eating breakfast in bed. It's taking something we do regularly, and just changing the circumstances. Drive-ins are all about the experience of snuggling up under blankets, reclining in the back of a van or truck, and watching on the enormous screen with the backdrop of the night sky. You can bring in your own food or purchase some traditional movie snacks at the concessions building. Restrooms are also located there. Weekends are the busiest nights. Don't forget the mosquito repellent and jackets.

One small caution: as you leave the drive in, you will have a full view of all of the other screens. There was a somewhat gory movie being shown on one of the screens as we left, so we tried to divert our kids' attention.

Coleman's Motor VU also hosts a swap meet every Saturday and Sunday year-round. See website for details.

Just Around the Corner...

- Color Me Mine (Ogden)
- FastKart Speedway (Ogden)
- FatCats (Ogden)
- Fort Buenaventura
- Hill Aerospace Museum
- Ogden Raptors
- Ogden River Parkway
- Ogden's Union Station
- Peery's Egyptian Theater
- Riverdale Park
- Roy Aquatic Center
- Treehouse Children's Museum

Comedy Sportz

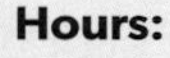

Hours:
Friday and Saturday: Shows at 8pm and 10:15pm.

Admission:
Students and adults: online before 7pm-$8; at the door-$10; *Kids 12 and under:* online before 7pm-$4; at the door-$5

Parking:
Free street parking.

Food:
No outside food or drink is allowed. Candy and drink concessions are available.

36 West Center Street
Provo, 84601
801-377-9700
www.comedysportzutah.com

What to expect...

It's rare to find a comedy club that has clean humor, but even more rare to find one that is appropriate for kids and families. Comedy Sportz is a national troupe of improvisational comedy clubs that offer family-friendly shows.

The show is played like a sport. Two teams of comedians compete for laughs and points to win the game. The referee is the host who makes up the scenarios with the help of audience suggestions. Nothing is rehearsed and every show is different. Be careful if you sit on the front row because you might be singled out to give an idea. One team is chosen by the audience or referee as the winner after each round and is then awarded points. The comedy team with the most points at the end wins the game. There is even a halftime where you can use the restroom or buy snacks.

The show is fast-paced, with little time for any comedian to bask in the limelight of a funny moment. There are just too many! I took my 10- year-old son and he laughed the entire time. There are so many songs, funny accents, and so much physical comedy that even when kids may not understand the joke, they are still entertained by the hilarity of the skit. I would recommend ages 7 and up for a kid to really enjoy the show. Younger children are certainly allowed, and would find the show funny, but may not understand many of the jokes or exactly what is going on. As far as being appropriate, there were a few innuendos, but they did a good job of staying clean, light hearted, and fun. If we lived closer, we would frequent the club. Even if you live far away, it's worth a trip down; just make a day of it.

Just Around the Corner...

- BYU Broadcasting
- BYU Museum of Art
- BYU Museum of Paleontology
- BYU Museum of Peoples and Cultures
- Children's Library at Provo City Library
- CLAS Ropes Course
- FatCats (Provo)
- Lowe's Xtreme Air Sports
- Monte L. Bean Life Science Museum
- Provo Recreation Center
- Provo Towne Centre Play Area
- Royden G. Derek Planetarium
- Seven Peaks (Provo)
- Y Mountain Hike

Dolly and Me Dress-Up Tea at Georgell Doll Shop

Gardner Village
1100 West 7800 South
West Jordan, 84088
(801) 561-1485
www.gardnervillage.com

Doll Shop Hours:
Monday-Saturday: 10am-8pm

Tea Party Hours:
Seasonal outdoor parties (by appointment only); *June - August*

Admission:
$12 per guest (Every mother sitting down for tea must pay too)

Parking:
Free parking lot at Gardner Village

Food:
Provided as part of the tea party.

What to expect...

Located in the heart of historic Gardner Village, the Georgell Doll Shop is a favorite destination for all doll-lovers. This specialty shop sells dolls of every shape and kind including old-fashioned, porcelain, and Madame Alexander dolls. Georgell Doll Shop also offers the largest variety of 18" doll accessories in Utah. These include things like: clothing, umbrellas, backpacks, and tiny toothbrushes.

Dolly and Me Dress Up Tea is held seasonally at the Doll Shop. Schedule your party ahead of time and then come on a special outing to the shop for your own dress-up tea. The tea parties are not formally hosted. The food and drink are served by an employee, but the actual tea party must be supervised by an adult.

The outdoor tea parties are held on the shop's charming back patio that overlooks a picturesque pond. Whimsical fairy-themed decorations set the mood for a magical experience and the shaded patio offers the perfect setting for a tea party the way a little girl would do tea. Girls bring their own doll to share the tea party experience.

Before sitting down at the table, guests are invited to the dress-up station where they can choose a hat for themselves and a miniature hat for their doll. Each guest may also choose an apron to wear. Place settings include teacups and saucers. Even the dolls have their own place settings with miniature utensils. Little desserts are served with a drink of "pink punch tea." The food is provided by the Naborhood Bakery, found in Gardner Village. For an additional cost, a small loaf of bread along with little packets of PB&J can be ordered. Each guest also receives a small porcelain fairy doll. Dolly and Me! Dress Up Tea is also available for Birthday Parties.

Just Around the Corner...

- Accessible Playground at Veteran's Memorial Park
- Classic Fun Center (SLC)
- Gale Center of History and Culture
- Gardner Village
- Gene Fullmer Recreation Center
- Jump 'N Bounce
- South Jordan Recreation Center
- Tiny Tim's Foundation for Kids
- (West Jordan) Conservation Garden Park
- Wild West Jordan Playground at Veteran's Memorial Park

MAX Zipline Canopy Tour

Provo Canyon
(801) 960-3113
www.maxzipline.com

Hours:
Open Monday-Saturday. Call to make a reservation.

Admission:
Prices range from $39 to $59 per person. Prices are based on the number in your group. The more people in your group, the lower the price.

Parking:
Free parking around the check-in area.

Food:
You may bring snacks, but there is no food available for purchase. Water is available on site.

What to expect...

MAX Zipline is the only Canopy zip line tour in Northern Utah. This family owned and operated business was started by Connie and Steve Ault who wanted to find a way to share the beautiful piece of property they own in Provo Canyon. After much thought and planning, they decided to build a canopy zip line which means that you will be whisked through and above the trees along a zip line trail. This is an exciting way to enjoy the beautiful nature and wildlife of the Provo Canyon.

The best way to get to the property is to follow the detailed instructions on their website. After turning down the steep road to the property, follow the dirt road and park near the check-in location, which is a long white trailer that serves as the office and equipment room. There, you will sign a waiver and get suited up with a harness, helmet, and gloves. Groups of about 12 or less are transported up the mountain to the start of the zip line. It's not uncommon to see wildlife on the ride up. At the top, it's just a short walk to the first platform that starts the first run.

The zip line is composed of five different runs that zig-zag their way down the mountainside. Every group is accompanied by two guides. Each run begins and ends on an elevated platform with one guide sending you off and the other waiting to help you at the arrival platform. At the first platform, simple and clear instructions are given about the ride and how to stop. State of the art equipment, including the newest and safest double cable engineering, lets you relax and enjoy the ride without being preoccupied with safety issues.

There is no age restriction on riders, just a weight restriction of at least 35 pounds and no more than 275 pounds. In our group we had my 8-year-old son, and a cute 6-year-old girl. They both loved it and had no problems riding on their own.

The tour lasts about 1½ - 2 hours depending on group size. Cameras can be brought along on the tour and secured in your pocket or a small mesh bag that attaches to your harness. Close-toed shoes are recommended. There are two portable toilets located near the trailer. Waivers can be printed out and signed ahead of time; simply call and request that a waiver be emailed to you. There are also moonlight canopy tours offered seasonally and a Halloween Zip (Fri & Sat) in October. See the website for details.

Just Around the Corner...

- Bridal Veil Falls
- Stewart Falls
- Sundance Mountain Resort
- Timpanogos Falls

Redwood Road Drive-In

3688 South Redwood Road
West Valley, 84119
(801) 973-7088
www.redwooddrive-in.com

Hours:
Ticket Office: Nightly 8:45pm- 1am

Movies start at dusk and around 11:30pm (March-November).

Admission:
Ages 10+: $7
Ages 5-9: $1;
Ages 5 and under: FREE! CASH ONLY.

What to expect...

Drive-in theaters are few and far between these days, so don't miss the chance to let your kids experience the Redwood Road Drive In. There are six screens, each playing a double feature nightly. The first movie starts at dusk (around 9:30) and the second at about 11:30. Kid's movies are almost always played in the 9:30 slot, so you can stay just for the first movie if you don't want your kids up until 1am. The best way to enjoy the drive-in is in the back of a pickup truck or van with sleeping bags and pillows. My kids thought it was exciting to snuggle up and watch out of the back of our van. I set up a camp chair next to the van and sat in that comfortably for the entire movie. The sound is transmitted over an FM frequency, so make sure your radio works. If it doesn't, you could still probably hear your neighbors' radio.

Unlike traditional theaters, you can bring your own food to the drive-in. If you have a craving for movie theater popcorn, there is a centrally-located concession building that offers all the typical movie food and snacks. Restrooms are located on the east and west sides of the concession building. Weekends are the busiest nights. Don't forget to bring mosquito repellent and jackets.

One small caution: as you leave the drive-in, you will have a full view of all of the other screens. You might need to divert your children's attention to prevent them from seeing something inappropriate.

The Drive-In also hosts a swap meet every Saturday and Sunday year round. See website for details.

Just Around the Corner...

- Hale Center Theatre
- Hollywood Connection
- Taylorsville Community Swimming Pool
- Utah Grizzlies
- Valley Fair Mall

S&S Shortline Train Park

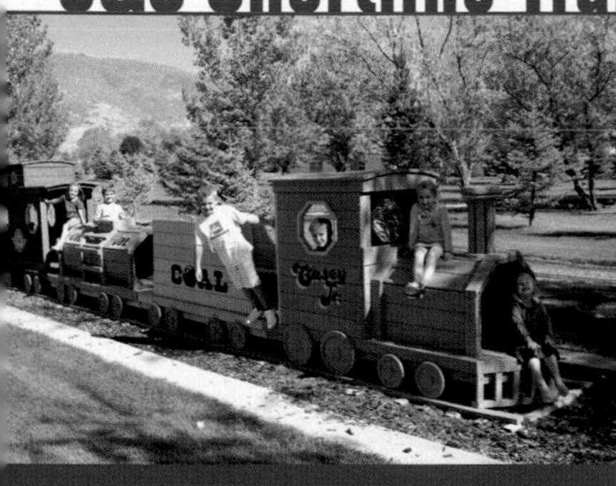

575 North 1525 West
Farmington, 84025
(801) 451-0222

Hours:
The first Saturday of every month from Memorial Day through Labor Day from 10am-4pm.

Admission:
Large Train Ride: $4.50; *Small Train Ride:* $5.50; *Handcart Ride:* $1.75.

Parking:
Free parking lot. If the parking lot is crowded, park along the street.

Food:
Concessions are available. Outside food is allowed. There is a large covered picnic pavilion with tables and a grassy area where you can spread out a blanket. The park is located in a residential/farm area so there aren't any food options nearby.

What to expect...

S&S Shortline Train Park is one of the best-kept secrets in Davis County—partly because it is only open a handful of days each year and partly because there is no website. If you are good at planning ahead, your family will really enjoy a visit to the park. The parking lot is small and can get crowded, but don't be deterred because the actual train park is large and sprawling.

The primary business of family owned S&S involves the sale and leasing of real life locomotives and train components. As a hobby, the family has created a train park that they enjoy sharing with the public a few times a year. The park is their way of sharing their love of trains with others and is not for revenue. In fact, the money made barely covers the extra insurance to have visitors come to the park!

A visit to the park begins in the large white building which is a replica of a 1920's Union Pacific Train Station. The S&S offices are upstairs and a small museum, gift shop, and concessions are on the main floor. Tickets are purchased inside. The main feature of the park includes miniature train rides that run along a 7½" gauge rail and larger trains that run on a 24" gauge rail. A ride on the larger train lasts about 8 minutes while a ride on the smaller train lasts about 15 minutes. The typical wait time is no more than 15-20 minutes. There is even a train station platform with benches, where passengers await the larger train. They also offer handcart rides, which are like pedal cars on a track for kids 12 and under.

You will be impressed with the planning and care that has gone into the design and landscape of the park. At one point, the landscaping of berms and hills create a small valley for the train tracks that wind through fir trees, over bridges, through a small train station, and even through a tunnel. You can wander through the grassy park and see all kinds of miniature buildings such as: a schoolhouse, a church, homes, water towers, and a coal tower. Towards the back of the park there is a large swing set and play train that kids can climb aboard. Back near the play area is a large engine house with a display of several 24" gauge rail cars.

There is also a small mini golf course that isn't in the best shape, but is still playable. Restrooms are available in the main building and in a centrally-located building out in the park. There are no changing tables.

Just Around the Corner...

- Boondocks (Kaysville)
- Cherry Hill
- Robert N. Hasenyager Great Salt Lake Nature Center
- Castle Heights Playground at Nicholls Park
- Lagoon
- Three Little Monkeys (Kaysville)

SCHEELS

11282 South State Street
Sandy, 84070
(801) 948-7080
www.scheels.com

Hours:
Monday-Saturday: 9am-9pm;
Sunday: 11am-5pm

Admission:
Entrance to the store is free. Ferris wheel $1, rollerball $3, shooting gallery $1.

Parking:
Free parking lot.

Food:
No outside food or drink is allowed. Grama Ginna's Restraunt and Fudge Shop sells gelato, ice cream, smoothies, sandwiches, fresh roasted nuts, and much more.

What to expect...

SCHEELS is a megastore that is said to offer the world's largest selection of sports equipment, sportswear, every-day fashionwear and footwear. Aside from the enormous inventory of everything sports, the store also offers some fun activities for kids and families.

The first thing you notice as you enter the store is the 65 ft. **Ferris wheel** rotating beneath an enormous skylight. Tokens to ride the Ferris wheel cost $1 and must be purchased at a register. This is a popular attraction, so the best time to avoid lines is in the morning.

Another major feature is the large double arched 16,000-gallon **saltwater aquarium** filled with colorful fish and sea life. At 6pm (M-W-F & Sat), the fish are fed by a diver who you can watch swim around the tank. If you are lucky, and it isn't too busy, the diver will come out and talk about the fish and answer questions.

A small play gym for kids is found on the first floor, right next to a large selection of BYU and Utah sports clothing. It is a climbing structure with slides, tunnels, and lookout points.

Rollerball is a miniature version of bowling with the pins on strings. For $3 you can play 10 frames on one of two lanes. Payment is made at the rollerball lanes.

A really fun activity is the **Laser Shooting Gallery**. One game costs $1, or 3 games for $2. Payment is made at the shooting gallery.

A large **Wildlife Mountain** on the second floor displays over 250 different museum quality animal mounts.

Scattered throughout the second floor you will find several booths that offer unique **photo opportunities.** You can take a picture with a monster jeep, a bear standing up on it's hind legs, and a skunk family. You just enter your email and the photos are sent to you for free.

The SCHEELS family is very patriotic. They have included two **animatronic presidents, Thomas Jefferson and Abraham Lincoln,** found at two separate locations on the second floor. Push a button and hear them speak about our individual rights and responsibility to uphold the constitution. Tours focusing on the presidents can be scheduled for small school groups.

SCHEELS offers a free **Kid's Klub** class every other Monday night. The classes are different each time and can last anywhere from 1 to 2 hours. Parents of younger children must stay and supervise. Classes might include things like: how to shoot a bow, how to build a bike, information about animals on the wildlife mountain, or even decorating cookies. Check with store for more details.

Just Around the Corner...

- Airborne
- Boondocks (Draper)
- Color Me Mine (Draper)
- Dimple Dell Recreation Center
- Gale Center of History and Culture
- Real Salt Lake
- South Jordan Recreation Center

Thanksgiving Point Special Events

3003 North Thanksgiving Way
Lehi, 84043
(801) 768-2300
www.thanksgivingpoint.org

What to expect...

Thanksgiving Point has been an exciting family destination for many years. It was founded in 1995 by Alan and Karen Ashton and was created as a place that provides unique learning experiences and family-friendly entertainment for the community. Funded by the Thanksgiving Point Institute, Thanksgiving Point is a non-profit organization.

Each destination at Thanksgiving Point warrants its own separate visit. These include: The Museum of Ancient Life, Farm Country, the Gardens and Children's Discovery Garden. Thanksgiving Point also houses a golf course, movie theaters, and the Water Tower Plaza. Thanksgiving Point hosts numerous special events throughout the year. Many of these events are held in areas outside of the major locations (gardens, museum, farm country). The following is a list of these special events.

Annual Events

Easter Eggstreme – Held in the Electric Park in April. Participate in an egg hunt, games, activities, and pony rides. Fees apply.

Princess Festival – June. Girls dress as princesses and participate in various princess-themed activities. Fees apply. Attendees must pre-register.

Scottish Festival – Held in the Electric Park in June. You can experience the culture and traditions of Scotland through food, activities, and entertainment. Children ages 11 and under enter for free! Entrance fees apply to all others.

Independence Day Celebration – Held in the Electric Park on July 4th. Enjoy a fireworks show. Concessions are available or bring your own picnic. FREE admission.

Cornbelly's Corn Maze & Pumpkin Fest – October. Walk through a corn maze, participate in activities, games, and rides related to the fall and Halloween. Fees apply.

East Like a Pilgrim – Held in the Show Barn in November. Experience a Thanksgiving feast like a pilgrim. Fees apply.

Breakfast with Santa – Held in the Show Barn in December. Meet Santa, play games, sing songs, eat breakfast, and decorate cookies. Fees apply.

Holiday Lights – Held in Electric Park in December. Drive your car through winding pathways full of Christmas lights and displays. Pay per car.

Other Unique Adventures in this book:

- Dairy Keen
- Homestead Cowboy Campfire
- Holdman Studios

Tiny Tim's Foundation for Kids

1423 West 8120 South
West Jordan, 84088
(801) 815-4602
www.tinytimstoys.org

Hours:
Tuesday, Wednesday, Thursday: 9am-5pm

Special appointments can be made to accommodate groups at night.

Call ahead to double-check hours.

Admission:
FREE! Donations welcome.

Parking:
Free parking lot in front of the garage where the toy factory is located.

Food:
No food or drink is allowed.

What to expect. . .

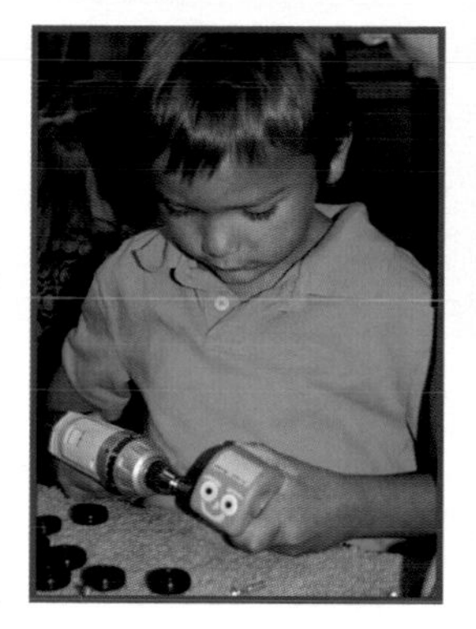

Tiny Tim's Foundation for Kids and Toy Factory was founded in 2000 by Alton and Cheryl Thacker in response to an experience they had while on a humanitarian trip to Mexico. Alton was touched by the joy shown on a young girl's face when given a little toy car. It took her a minute to examine it and figure out how to play with it, but once she did, her smile was contagious. An estimated 500 million children in the world have never had a toy (while an estimated 500 million toys occupy my basement). Basic toys can provide children the opportunity to explore and develop their imagination and creativity. Alton decided he wanted to do something to give more children the opportunity to have and play with a toy.

The foundation operates through donations of materials and time. With the help of volunteers, about 3,500 hardwood toy cars are sent to children around the world each month. Each car costs the foundation $1.50 to produce. Inmates in the prison do all the painting of the cars. Alton invites the public to come to the toy factory and help with specific parts of the production of the cars. Youth groups and Scouts may help with stenciling the car outline on to the wood and groups with young children will put the wheels on. My kids loved the time they spent assembling and screwing in wheels to the cars.

This activity is different from others in this book because it allows kids to think about others, not just their own needs and wants. There is no fee to participate. However, I would suggest allowing children to make the $1.50 donation to pay for a car. Even better, let them do jobs at home to earn the $1.50 so that they feel like they sacrificed a bit to help others less fortunate.

Call Alton to schedule a time to help. Kids five and older would be most suited for helping. Youth groups and boy scouts are frequent volunteers. Over 60 Eagle Scout awards have been earned through help given to the foundation.

Just Around the Corner...

- Accessible Playground at Veteran's Memorial Park
- Classic Fun Center (SLC)
- Gale Center of History and Culture
- Gardner Village
- Gene Fullmer Recreation Center
- Georgell Doll Shop
- Jump 'N Bounce
- South Jordan Recreation Center
- (West Jordan) Conservation Garden Park
- Wild West Jordan Playground at Veteran's Memorial Park

UTA TRAX & FrontRunner

Transportation Information Center
24 West 100 South
Salt Lake City, 84101
(801) 743-3882
www.rideuta.com

Hours:
See the website for a current schedule.

Fare:
It is free to ride TRAX in the Free Fare Zone in downtown Salt Lake City. Prices change based on the distance you travel. Up to two children age 5 and under may ride free with a paying adult. Buy tickets online or at vending machines at TRAX Stations. All accept cash. Some take credit/debit cards.

Parking:
Most FrontRunner and TRAX stations have free park and ride lots. Check the website to be sure your station has one. There are various downtown SLC parking options.

Food:
Food or drink is not allowed.

Discounts:
Seniors and persons with disabilities receive discounted rates. There are many options for passes. See the website.

What to expect...

Utah Transit Authority (UTA) offers two great options for a train excursion with children.

TRAX is a light rail system that runs from downtown Salt Lake City on various lines to South Jordan, Sandy, or West Valley. There are park-and-ride lots at many of the TRAX stations along the different lines. Downtown Salt Lake City offers a Free Fare Zone where you can ride for free if you enter and exit the train within that zone. See the website for a map of this area. It includes stations near Temple Square, City Creek, Abravanel Hall, The Gateway, The Galivan Center, and the Public Library.

FrontRunner is Utah's Commuter Rail line that runs from Ogden to Provo. All of the stations along the route have park-and-ride lots. FrontRunner is a great way to take your family on an outing into downtown Salt Lake, or any other destination along the route. You could park at your nearest FrontRunner station and take a day trip with your kids to a specific stop along the way or even just stay on the train for a round trip and enjoy the ride and scenery.

Before riding TRAX or FrontRunner, take a quick look at the map of stations on the website to be sure of your entry and exit points. Also, you might want to watch a short video on the website that teaches how to buy tickets using the vending machines. Always hold young children's hands when entering and exiting the train and watch them closely on the platforms when waiting at the station.

Go One Step Further

Kennecott Utah Copper Mine Did you know that Utah is home to the deepest open-pit copper mine in the world? Also called the Bingham Canyon Mine, this mine has been in production since 1906! In the past, the mine has been open to visitors for a small fee. Children love to see the large machinery at work from a safe overlook. There are also plans for a new Visitor's Center in the future. For the most updated information on how to visit this unique place, including updates on the new Visitor's Center go to *www.kennecott.com*.

Ski Areas & Resorts

Utah is one of America's snow capitals, having hosted the world for the 2002 Winter Olympics. The United States Ski and Snowboard Association (*ussa.org) is headquartered in Park City, Utah.* With over 500 inches of annual snowfall, Utah claims "The Greatest Snow on Earth ®." Eleven of Utah's fourteen ski resorts are within an hour's drive from the Salt Lake City International Airport.

Families across the globe flock to Utah's resorts, not only during winter months, but all throughout the year. The ski resorts provide relief from the summer heat, not to mention world-class hiking, fishing, picnicking, biking, and camping. Additionally, the drive to the ski resorts in the spring and autumn months are some of the most picturesque drives anywhere, with stunning color transformations from season to season.

This section provides an overview of winter and summer activities of interest to kids at seven resorts within an hour of Salt Lake City (find the three Park City resorts in the Park City & Heber Chapter). Each resort posts their seasonal (winter) and non-seasonal operational hours on their websites along with activity calendars, pricing information, resort and trail maps, driving directions, lodging and vacation packages, dining options, discount and holiday rates, and contact information. Resort websites also publish safety tips and current snow reports. Price information in this book will certainly change.

If you are interested in visiting more than one resort in a short period, we recommend inquiring with the resorts, or searching online for a multi-resort discounted pass (e.g. at the time of publishing, www.visitsaltlake.com is offering a Ski Salt Lake Super Pass that provides access to four resorts). Multi-day and advanced purchase tickets are always less expensive. Also watch for coupons to ski resorts in the Entertainment Book.

A note about driving to resorts in the winter: State law requires tire chains or snow tires in or on your vehicle between November 1 and May 1. Dialing 511 provides up-to-date information on Utah Road Conditions. When weather is severe, the Utah Department of Transportation (UDOT) may restrict travel on canyon roads. Driving times from Salt Lake City are approximations. Traffic and weather conditions vary by season and area. Many resorts offer free or paid shuttles from the Salt Lake airport, UTA Ski Bus Stops, TRAX lightrail, or parking lots near the base of the canyons. Plan ahead and drive safely!

Sundance Resort, photo by Willie Holdman

Alta Ski Area

Alta Ski Area
Little Cottonwood Canyon (Utah 210)
Alta, 84092
(801) 359-1078
www.alta.com

Distance from SLC:
30 miles

Drive Time:
45 minutes

Approx Lift Ticket Price:
Adult: $79;
12 & Under: $42.

What a Deal:
$10 after 3:00pm, both adult and child tickets

What to expect...

Alta is known as a "skier's mountain" because of its amazing snow, terrain, and views. In fact, it is one of three mountains in the United States reserved purely for skiing. A unique option is to buy a ticket that lets you ride an interconnected lift between Snowbird and Alta. This way, skiers have access to even more skiing terrain.

Winter: Alta Ski Area offers both group and private ski lessons for children as young as 4 years old. Parent/Tot classes are also available. Alta provides 115 trails with 25% of those specifically for beginners. Snowboarding is not allowed.

Summer: Alta does not offer summer activities.

Just Around the Corner...

- Cecret Lake Hike
- Lisa Falls
- Snowbird Ski and Summer Resort
- Temple Quarry Nature Trail

Brighton Ski Resort

Big Cottonwood Canyon
8302 South Brighton Loop Road
Brighton, 84121
(801) 532-4731
www.brightonresort.com

Distance from SLC:
33 miles

Drive Time:
47 minutes

Approx Lift Ticket Price:
Adult: $68;
Ages 8 - 12: $35.

What a Deal:
Two kids 7 and under can ski free with purchase of an adult ticket.

What to expect...

Brighton Ski Resort is located at the top of Big Cottonwood Canyon. *Utah Family Magazine* consistently rates this resort as #1 in terrain and affordability for families. Children age 7 and younger ski for free and ages 8-12 can ski for a lowered rate. An average of over 500 inches of snow falls per year at Brighton, making it a perfect ski destination.

Winter: Brighton offers both group and private ski lessons for kids as young as 3 years old. It is one of a handful of resorts that offers a half-pipe for snowboarding. Brighton also offers the largest amount of lighted night skiing in all of Utah. There are over 66 runs along the mountain, with 21% of those runs designated for beginners.

Summer: No regular summer activities are offered. See the website for occasional special events.

Just Around the Corner...

- Donut Falls
- Hidden Falls
- Silver Lake Trail
- Solitude Mountain Resort

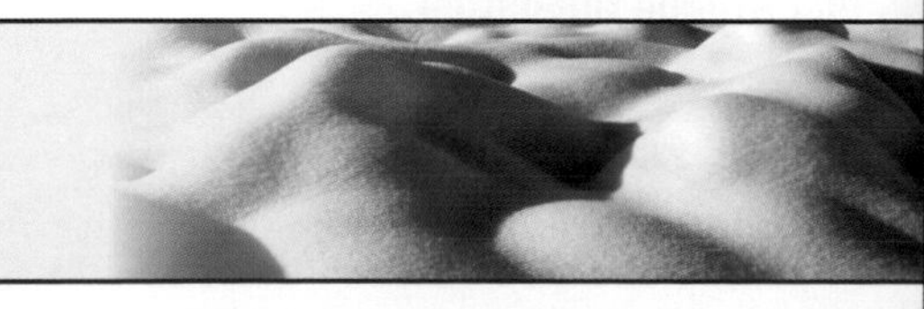

Powder Mountain

Accessed through Ogden Canyon
8000 North 100 East
Eden, 84310
(801) 745-3772
www.powdermountain.com

Distance from SLC:
54 miles

Drive Time:
1 hour, 20 minutes

Approx Lift Ticket Price:
Adult: $65;
12 & Under: $35.

What a Deal:
Kids 6 and under ski free with a paying adult. The website doesn't specify how many kids can be with one adult.

What to expect...

Powder Mountain is located 55 miles north of the Salt Lake International Airport and is best known for its uncrowded slopes. Here, visitors can discover new spots and untouched areas on their skiing adventures. The resort regularly receives top rankings for value and snow quality in *SKI magazine* every year.

Winter: Powder Mountain offers ski lessons for kids as young as 3½ years old. Snowboarding lessons are also offered for kids as young as 8. Powder Mountain has 154 ski runs with 25% of those runs designated for beginners. Lighted night skiing is offered daily, making for longer time available on the slopes. The Snowcat Sunset Expedition is a unique experience. This guided tour takes you in a large snowcat to high mountain peaks for beautiful views of the valley below. Tickets are pricey, but this sounds like a memorable adventure in the mountains and the snow.

Summer: During the summer months, you can take a unique Summer Safari Adventure Tour at Powder Mountain which is a three-hour guided tour of the resort's more than 10,000 acres in an oversized off-road vehicle. Children as young as 3 years old may participate. A boxed meal can also be paired with this adventure.

Just Around the Corner...

- Pineview Reservoir
- Snowbasin
- Wolf Mountain Resort

Snowbasin Resort

Ogden Canyon
3925 Snow Basin Rd.
Huntsville, 84317
(801) 620-1000
www.snowbasin.com

Distance from SLC:
42 miles

Drive Time:
40 minutes north of SLC

Approx Lift Ticket Price:
Adult: $82;
Child: $31.

What a Deal:
Children 6 and under ski for free.

What to expect...

Snowbasin is a ski resort located up Ogden Canyon. It was an official venue of the 2002 Winter Olympics, hosting the Downhill, Super G, and Combined Races. Visitors are greeted at the entry by an impressive display of flags from around the world. Snowbasin is known for its sweeping and picturesque terrain. The resort offers attractive activities for both summer and winter.

Winter: Snowbasin offers private and group skiing lessons for children as young as 3 years old. There are 104 trails along the mountain with 20% of those runs designated for beginners. Child lift passes are free for kids 6 and under. Kids 7-12 pay $44. Other activities of interest in the winter include: a lift-served tubing hill, adaptive skiing programs, snowboarding, and mountaintop dining. Needle's Lodge, located at the top of the mountain is a restaurant that offers meals and snacks. You can take a ride on the enclosed gondolas up to the restaurant year-round.

Summer: Snowbird offers guided and independent hiking, biking, gondola rides, mountaintop dining, disc golf, and Sunday Concerts throughout the summer months. Gondola rides can be especially fun in the summer/fall up to the Needle's Lodge for a snack or a full meal. You will notice that some gondolas honor Olympic or national champions with printed flags on the outside and stories within the cabin. During the summer, some families hike up and then ride the gondola down. And other families, like us, ride the gondola up and then take the easier hike down.

Just Around the Corner...

- Pineview Reservoir
- Powder Mountain
- Wolf Mountain Resort

Snowbird Ski and Summer Resort

Little Cottonwood Canyon
Utah Hwy 210, Little Cottonwood Canyon
Snowbird, 84092
(801) 742-2222
www.snowbird.com

Distance from SLC:
28 miles

Drive Time:
40 minutes

Approx Lift Ticket Price:
Adult: $92;
12 & Under: $42.

What a Deal:
Kids 6 and under ski free.

What to expect...

Snowbird Ski and Summer Resort is a large complex located up Little Cottonwood Canyon. It averages more than 500 inches of snow per year, making it the perfect location for winter sports. A pedestrian village with shopping and dining makes it very friendly for the entire family. This resort is not only known for excellent skiing, but also for its year-round activities.

Winter: Snowbird offers both group and private ski lessons for kids as young as 3 years old. The resort has 89 ski runs. Of those runs, 27% are designated for beginners. Lift passes are free for kids 6 and under. Kids ages 7-12 cost $42. Activities of interest include: skiing, snowboarding, snowshoeing, snowmobiling, aerial tram rides (tram rides are included in the Visit Salt Lake Connect Pass), an adaptive skiing program, and limited night skiing.

Summer: Snowbird offers a large variety of exciting summer activities. Choose from: Aerial Tram Rides, an Alpine Slides, a Bungee Trampoline, Kid's Inflatables (bounce houses), a Mountain Coaster, the Mountain Flyer (a comfortably seated zip line experience), the Peruvian Chair and Tunnel (an express chair lift, high in the mountains), a Ropes Course, Gold Panning, and a Climbing Wall. You can buy an all-day activity pass and enjoy any of the activities or try hiking, fishing, horseback riding tours, and mountain biking. Austin Pond at gives kids 12 and younger the opportunity to fish (Snowbird fishing license required). You can also take advantage of the Cool-Air Concert Series on Saturdays throughout the summer. Snowbird is home to one of the biggest festivals in Utah, Oktoberfest. It usually runs from the end of August through October. Admission is free.

Just Around the Corner...

- Alta Ski Area
- Cecret Lake Hike
- Lisa Falls
- Temple Quarry Nature Trail

Solitude Mountain Resort

Distance from SLC:
30 miles

Drive Time:
40 minutes

Approx Lift Ticket Price:
Adult: $74;
7-18: about $44

What a Deal:
Kids 6 & under ski free

12000 Big Cottonwood Canyon
Solitude, 84121
(801) 534-1400
www.skisolitude.com

What to expect...

Solitude Mountain Resort offers a variety of mountain experiences year-round. One of the unique features at Solitude is a European-style pedestrian village located at the base of the mountain which offers restaurant dining, shopping, lodging, and more.

Winter: Solitude provides both group and private ski lessons for kids as young as 2 years old. There are 65 trails at the resort and 20% of those trails are designated for beginners. Child lift passes are free for kids 6 and under; ages 7-13 cost $42. Other activities of interest include: snowboarding, outdoor ice skating, snowshoeing, and Nordic skiing. Solitude Nordic Center offers a clinic that teaches children ages 7-13 Nordic skiing.

Summer: There are a lot of choices for outdoor summer experiences at Solitude. You can enjoy mountain biking, hiking, fishing, mountain scooters (a cross between a street scooter and a mountain bike), disc golf, and lift rides. Mountain scooters are recommended for ages 10 and up. Kids 12 and younger can also fish in Solitude Pond without a license (only catch and release).

Just Around the Corner...

- Brighton Ski Resort
- Donut Falls
- Hidden Falls
- Silver Lake

Sundance Mountain Resort

Accessed through Provo Canyon
8841 Alpine Scenic Highway
Provo, 84604
(801) 225-4107
www.sundanceresort.com

Distance from SLC:
55 miles

Drive Time:
60 minutes

Approx Lift Ticket Price:
Adult: $55,
12 & Under $33.

What a Deal:
Kids 5 & under ski free

What to expect...

Sundance Mountain Resort is located at the base of one of Utah's most popular and photographed mountains, Mt. Timpanogos. Founded in 1969 by actor and filmmaker Robert Redford, the resort is one of four Utah sites that play host to the internationally acclaimed Sundance Film Festival, held every January *(www.sundance.org)*. Sell-out crowds also enjoy the Sundance Summer Theatre. The Resort offers diverse experiences with the arts as well as many mountain activities year-round.

Winter: The Resort offers group and private ski and snowboard lessons for children as young as 4 years old. There are 42 ski trails, 20% of which are designated for beginners. All-day lift passes cost $33 for kids age 6-12. Kids younger than 6 ski free. Other winter activities of interest include: cross-country skiing, snow shoeing, night skiing, and snowboarding.

Summer: The Resort also offers a large variety of summer activities. These include: scenic lift rides, hiking, mountain biking, year-round art classes (ask about classes for kids), a glassblowing (for observing), restaurants, fly fishing, horseback riding, river rafting down the Provo River, and an outdoor theater. The Summer Theatre usually shows a well-known musical for about three weeks in July and August.

Just Around the Corner...

- Bridal Veil Falls
- Max Zipline Canopy Tour
- Stewart Falls
- Timpanogos Falls

Wolf Mountain Resort

Accessed through Ogden Canyon
3567 Nordic Valley Way
Eden, 84310
(801) 745-3511
www.wolfmountainutah.com

Distance from SLC:
52 miles

Drive Time:
1 hour, 9 minutes

Approx Lift Ticket Price:
Prices vary. See website.

What a Deal:
Carpet only pass $11.

What to expect...

Wolf Mountain is known for being the most affordable place to ski in Utah and offers the state's lowest ticket prices and the longest hours. Although Wolf Mountain is the smallest of the ski areas in Utah, it is one of the best places for beginners.

Other Ski Resorts and Mountain Locations in this book:

- Canyons Resort
- Deer Valley Resort
- Park City Mountain Resort
- Silver Lake
- Utah Olympic Park
- Utah Olympic Park Museums

Winter: Wolf Mountain offers both private and group ski lessons for kids as young as 3 years old. Snowboard lessons are offered for kids as young as 8 years old. These lessons are all held in a large learning area where parents can watch nearby. Family ski and snowboard lessons are also available. Wolf Mountain has 26 ski runs with 20% of those runs designated for beginners. The entire mountain is regularly lit for night skiing which makes for longer hours and cheaper skiing (about $3 per hour for an adult).

Summer: During the summer months, Wolf Mountain hosts Music in the Mountains, a high-quality outdoor music concert series.

Just Around the Corner...

- Pineview Reservoir
- Powder Mountain
- Snowbasin

Sporting Events

There is nothing like the excitement and energy of the crowd at a live sports game and we are lucky to have seven professional sports teams playing right along the Wasatch Front. When attending a professional sports game with kids, remember it's less about the game and more about the experience. For them, half the fun of the game is the concessions, the prizes given out during time outs, the halftime show, the mascot doing tricks, and most of all, experiencing it with their parent. Kids won't be able to last through the entire game so plan on arriving late or leaving early.

Courtesy of Orem Owlz

Ogden Raptors

Ogden Raptors
2330 Lincoln Avenue
Ogden, 84401
(801) 393-2400
www.ogden-raptors.com

Schedule:
Season runs June through September. Games can be any day of the week. Most games are at 7pm and Sunday games are at 4pm About half of the games are home games.

Admission:
Tickets range in price from $5 to $12. Kids under 3 are free. Purchase tickets online at *www.smithstix.com*, by phone, or at the box office

Food:
No outside food or drink is allowed. Concessions sell hot dogs, drinks, and more.

Parking:
There is free street parking around the stadium.

Discounts:
Discounted group rates. Entertainment Book. Pass of All Passes.

Social:

What to expect...

The Ogden Raptors is a minor league baseball team established in 1977. The team is a rookie partner of the Los Angeles Dodgers. Proud fans attend home games in high numbers year after year. The Raptors have been playing in the heart of downtown Ogden at the Lindquist Field since 1997. This stadium offers beautiful views of the Wasatch Mountains as a backdrop to every ball game.

Ogden Raptors games are known for their affordability and offer a classic baseball experience. A basic ticket will give you access to just about any seat in the stadium. There is a small berm (grassy hill) where some spectators like to lay out a blanket to watch the game. A playground sits near this spot for restless kids to enjoy. Good seats are behind the home plate or along first base for close views.

Watch for Oggie the Raptors' official mascot. He is a cartoon Velociraptor who loves to meet fans and cheer on the Raptors.

Just Around the Corner...

- Birdsong Trail
- Coleman's Motor-VU Drive-In
- Color Me Mine (Ogden)
- FastKart Speedway (Ogden)
- FatCats (Ogden)
- Fort Buenaventura
- Ogden Dinosaur Park and Museum
- Ogden Nature Center
- Ogden River Parkway
- Ogden's Union Station
- Ott Planetarium
- Peery's Egyptian Theater
- Riverdale Park
- Treehouse Children's Museum

Orem Owlz

970 West University Parkway
Orem, 84058
(801) 377-2255
www.oremowlz.com

Schedule:
Season runs June through September. Most games are held at 4:05pm and can be on any day of the week. Some afternoon games are held on Sundays. There are about 38 home games. Visit the Owlz website to view the season's schedule.

Admission:
Tickets range from $5-$12. Berm seating (a grassy hill) is the most affordable way to watch a game. Purchase online at www.Smithtix.com, by phone, or at the box office.

Food:
No outside food or drink is allowed. The stadium offers many food options from snacks to full meals.

Parking:
Owlz game parking is in front of the UCCU Center off of 1200 West in Orem. Cost is $5 per vehicle (a $2 concessions voucher is given in exchange).

Discounts:
The Orem Owlz offer discounted group packages as well as Kidz Club memberships and other special packages. Pass of All Passes.

What to expect...

There is nothing like watching a live baseball game and the Orem Owlz offer a great baseball experience! The Owlz are a minor league baseball team established in 2005 and are a rookie affiliate of the Los Angeles Angels of Anaheim. All of their home games are played in the Brent Brown Ballpark on the Utah Valley University Campus.

The Berm – This is a great family-friendly area for enjoying games. This is a grassy hill where you can lay out a blanket, relax, and watch. Lawn chairs are not allowed.

Pacific States Play Area – This area consists of three playgrounds surrounded by a fence and covered by a net (for protection from stray balls) located alongside the berm. This is a great place for kids to burn energy and play during long games.

Hootz – Fans should watch for Hootz the official mascot for the Orem Owlz. He loves to dance, give high fives, sign autographs, and cheer on the Owlz. Also, keep an eye out for his girlfriend,Holly, and new co-mascot Rowly.

Honorary Bat Boy/Girl – At the beginning of each home game one youth (ages 10-14) is selected to sit in the dugout and help with bat boy duties. Contact the front office for more information.

The Owlz offer both group and birthday packages. These include tickets, food, and other special experiences. Gates open 30 minutes prior to the game. Family restrooms are located down the first and third base lines on the concourse.

Just Around the Corner...

- BYU Broadcasting
- BYU Museum of Art
- BYU Museum of Paleontology
- BYU Museum of Peoples and Cultures
- Creativity Art Studio
- Color Me Mine (Provo)
- FatCats (Provo)
- Hang Time Extreme Trampolines (Orem)
- Jake's Archery
- Krispy Kreme (Orem)
- Monte L. Bean Life Science Museum
- Nickel City Fun Center
- Provo Beach
- Royden G. Derek Planetarium
- Scera Pool
- Seven Peaks Fun Center (Orem)
- Shops at Riverwoods
- University Mall Tree House Court
- Y Mountain Hike

Real Salt Lake

9256 South State Street
Sandy, 84070
(801) 727-2700
www.realsaltlake.com

Schedule:
Season runs February through November. About half of the games are home games. Games start anytime between 4pm and 8pm and can take place any night of the week.

Tickets:
Single tickets range in price from $20 to $125. Purchase tickets through the Real Salt Lake website, or at www.riotintostadium.com. You may also purchase by phone or directly at the box office.

Food:
Concessions sell hot dogs, burritos, pizza, french fries, ice cream, drinks, and more.

Parking:
Go to www.riotintostadium.com to find a parking map. There are both paid and free public parking options near the stadium. TRAX will also drop you off about a 10-15 minute walk away.

Discounts:
Buy $16 tickets for the Maverick Mayhem corner at any Maverick.

Social:

What to expect...

Real Salt Lake is a Major League Soccer team created in 2004. All of their home games are held in the beautifully designed Rio Tinto Stadium located just 15 minutes away from downtown Salt Lake in Sandy City. Every seat in the stadium has a good view of the field. We are lucky to have one of the best soccer teams in the MLS right here in Utah. Real Salt Lake has previously won the MLS cup in 2009 and also reached the finals in 2010-2011 CONCACAF Champions League. They are an exciting team to watch!

The lights, music, loyal fans, and open-air feeling in Rio Tinto stadium can't be beat on a summer's night. The south end of the stadium is full of super fans that chant and play the drums the entire game. They add a fun element to the atmosphere, but that section may not be the best place for young children. Watch for Leonardo the Lion, the official mascot of the Real Salt Lake. He is a royal lion with some awesome soccer skills!

There are multiple entrance points to the stadium. Enter closest to your seats if possible. Section 24, located on the northwest corner, is called the "Family Section." There is no alcohol allowed in this section. Also, be aware that section 35 is a standing-only section.

Just Around the Corner...

- Airborne
- Classic Fun Center (SLC)
- Color Me Mine (Draper)
- Gale Center of History and Culture
- Dimple Dell Recreation Center
- Scheels
- South Jordan Recreation Center

Salt Lake Bees

77 West 1300 South
Salt Lake City, Utah 84115
(801) 325-2273
www.slbees.com

Schedule:
Season runs April through September. Games can happen any day of the week. Typical game times are 6:35pm or 7:05pm while Sunday games are usually at 1:05pm The Bees play 72 home games each season.

Admission:
Single tickets range in price from $5 to $26. Purchase tickets online at www.slbees.com, by phone, or in person at the box office.

Food:
Concessions sell everything from snacks to full meals.

Parking:
Parking is available in the lot just north of the ballpark; cost is $6. Or, take TRAX and get off at 1300 South and walk one block east.

Discounts:
Groups of 20 or more can receive discounts. Purchase a home game ticket for a Monday night on Smithstix.com and get a ticket and a hotdog for $5. Entertainment Book. Pass Of All Passes.

Social: 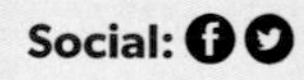

What to expect...

The Salt Lake Bees is a Minor League Baseball team that plays right in downtown Salt Lake City in the Spring Mobile Ballpark. This team is a Triple-A Affiliate of the Los Angeles Angels of Anaheim. Because the ballpark is downtown, there can be a lot of traffic on game days. TRAX is a good option for avoiding the traffic (and parking fees). The atmosphere at the ballpark is exciting, even for those not totally interested in the game. There are a lot of fun activities that require participation from the crowd.

Bumble – Watch for Bumble the official mascot of the Salt Lake Bees. He loves to take pictures, sign autographs and cheer on his team.

Berms – Two large grassy hills called berms are the most affordable seats in the ballpark. You can bring a blanket and sit on the grass. Be aware that during evening games, you may be looking into the sun from this side of the stadium.

Boondocks Fun Zone – This is a play area with a playground, a batting game and a bounce house along the outfield wall. It is the perfect place for kids to burn off energy during long games.

Bumble Express – This is a free train ride offered to kids during the games. It runs along the sidewalk behind the grassy berm.

Knothole Club – The official kid's club of the Salt Lake Bees for kids 12 and younger. Kids can join for just $12 and receive a ticket voucher, a t-shirt, discounted admission, and other special opportunities.

Zero Fatalities Kid's Run – After the game on Friday and Saturday nights kids have a chance to run the bases.

Larry H. Miller Honorary Bat Kid – You can stop by Larry H. Miller Chevrolet in Murray to enter your teen for a chance to be an Honorary Bat Kid with the opportunity to help with the equipment. Kids must be between the age of 14 and 18. If your teen is chosen you will get four tickets to a game and will be expected to arrive one hour early.

Utah Blaze

Schedule:
Season runs March through August. Games take place on Friday and Saturday evenings.

Admission:
Tickets range from $10-$100. Purchase tickets online through www.smithstix.com, by phone, or at the Energy Solutions Arena.

Food:
No outside food or drink is allowed. Concessions sell hot dogs, ice cream, snacks, candy, drinks, and more.

Parking:
Paid parking lots surround the building. Prices range from $3-$7. You may also take TRAX.

Discounts:
Discounted tickets are offered through package deals and season tickets on the website. Pass of All Passes.

301 West South Temple
Salt Lake City, 84101
(888) 992-5293
www.utblaze.com

What to expect...

The Utah Blaze is a professional arena football team that plays in the west division of the Arena Football League. Founded in 2006, this team offers an exciting option for football fans looking for a summer football fix. This indoor football team is known for drawing large crowds. You'll find the most avid fans in the end zones known as the "fire pits."

All home games are played in the Energy Solutions Arena in downtown Salt Lake. Arena football has a unique setup. The field is half the size of a football field and is made of an indoor padded surface. Because of the smaller indoor setting, games are fast-paced and high-scoring. To learn more about Arena Football and how it works, go to the website and click on "FANZONE," then click "Arena Football 101." Watch for the Official Mascot of Utah Blaze named Torch. He loves to entertain the crowd, do tricks, perform with the dancers, and cheer for the team.

Children can join the Kid's Club online for free. Members receive two free tickets, a t-shirt, and special discounts. Information screens throughout the building indicate the nearest concessions and bathrooms.

See Appendix 1 for Downtown Destinations close to this area

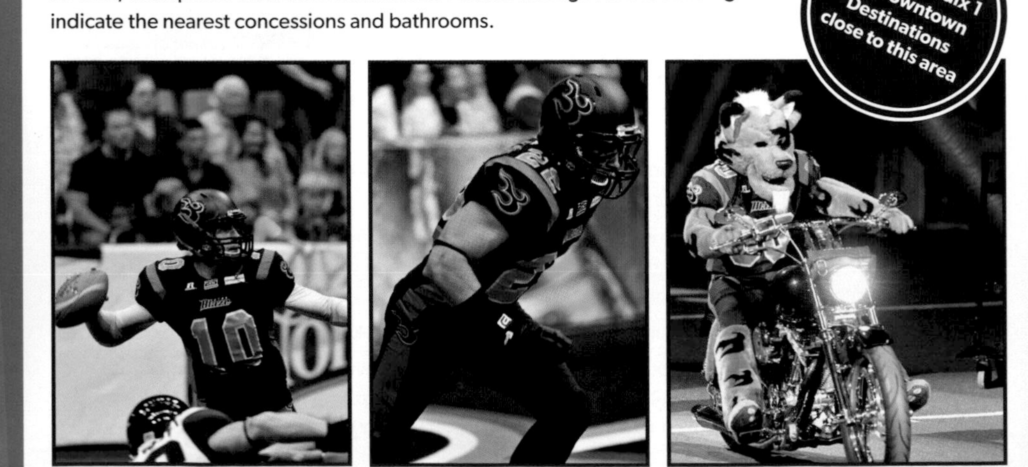

Utah Grizzlies

Maverik Center
3200 Decker Lake Drive
West Valley, Utah 84119
(801) 988-8000
www.utahgrizzlies.com

Schedule:
Season runs October through March. Games can happen any day of the week and typically start at 7 or 8pm, and sometimes as late as 9:15pm. There are a handful of afternoon games. About half the games each season are home games.

Admission:
Individual ticket prices range from $10 to $35. Buy tickets either online at www.ticketmaster.com, by phone, or at the Maverik Center box office.

Parking:
Cost is $5 per vehicle. There are two different parking lots available. Overflow parking is located at 3100 South Decker Lake Drive.

Food:
Outside food or drink is not permitted. Concessions sell ice cream, drinks, nachos, popcorn, hot dogs, and more.

Discounts:
Military and group discounts available. Season tickets and multi-game tickets are sold at a discounted rate. Entertainment Book. Pass of All Passes.

What to expect...

Hockey is an exciting, fast-paced, and very physical game. The Utah Grizzlies have been in Utah since 1995. They are part of a hockey league called the ECHL, which is one level before the professional American Hockey League. Over 200 players from the Utah Grizzlies have gone on to play in the AHL.

Home games are held in the Maverik Center located in West Valley. When buying tickets online, you may choose your seat location and even see what the view will be like from your chosen seat. Although the Maverik Center is an indoor arena, it can be chilly during games, so be sure to bring a jacket.

Watch out for the silly antics of Grizzbee, the Grizzlie's friendly mascot, during the game. The team offers special group packages as well as birthday packages. These can include tickets, food, and other special activities or treatment. See website for details.

Keep in mind that hockey is an extremely physical sport and fights break out regularly. This may be something you want to consider when deciding if this activity is right for your family.

Just Around the Corner...

- Hale Center Theatre
- Hollywood Connection
- LDS Humanitarian Center
- Redwood Road Drive-In
- Taylorsville Community Swimming Pool
- Valley Fair Mall

Utah Jazz

301 West South Temple
Salt Lake City, 84101
(801) 325-2000
www.utahjazz.com

Schedule:
Season runs October through April. Games can happen any night of the week and usually begin around 7pm or later.

Admission:
Single ticket prices can range from $16 to $200. Prices vary based on seat location and opposing team. Children ages 1 and older must have a ticket to attend. Buy tickets at *www.smithstix.com*, by phone, or at the box office.

Parking:
There are over 10,000 parking spaces available within two blocks of the Energy Solutions Arena. Prices range from $3-$7. TRAX will drop you off in front of the Arena. You can find parking lots and prices at *www.parkingslc.com*.

Food:
No outside food or drink is allowed. Concessions sell hot dogs, nachos, ice cream, burgers, drinks, and more.

Discounts:
There are a number of discounted ticket packages available, including a Family Night Package.

Social:

What to expect...

The Utah Jazz is Utah's very own professional NBA team. All home games are played in the large Energy Solutions Arena in downtown Salt Lake City. The Jazz is known for having a strong and enthusiastic fan base. In 2008, *Sports Illustrated* conducted an NBA players' poll, that showed Energy Solutions arena as "the most intimidating arena in the NBA" because of the loud fans. Games are always exciting and well-attended.

The Jazz Bear is the official mascot of the Utah Jazz. He wears the Utah Jazz jersey and loves to dance, do tricks, and interact with the crowd.

Games are fast-paced with short spots of entertainment and prize giveaways during timeouts. Even with the exciting atmosphere, it can be hard for kids to sit through an entire game. If your kids are restless, you can take them to the kid's play area called Bear's Backyard located on the 5th floor. It features play equipment like slides, a climbing structure, teeter-totters, and arcade-type basketball shooting games.

The main entrance is located at 300 West and South Temple. Gates open 1½ hours prior to tip off. Information screens throughout the building will direct you to the nearest concessions and bathrooms.

Park City

Park City is one of the most beautiful areas of Northern Utah. Millions of visitors come each year to enjoy what Park City has to offer. We are lucky to live a quick 45 minute drive away from all of the activities and entertainment available. Because it is a tourist town, activities can be expensive. We have highlighted activities that range in cost from free to expensive, so you can choose options that are within your budget. Most of the activities are outdoor-related. There are often overnight deals at many of the resorts during the off-season months (summer and fall).

Courtesy of Utah Olympic Park

Canyons Resort

4000 Canyons Resort Drive
Park City, 84098
(435) 649-5400
www.thecanyonsresort.com

What to expect...

Canyons Resort is known for its luxurious accommodations, offerings of a wide variety of activities, and 4000 acres of skiable terrain! One of the special features of this ski resort is a chair lift with enclosed cabins and heated seats called the Orange Bubble Express.

Winter: Canyons Resort offers both ski and snowboard lessons (group and private) to kids as young as 4 years old. The resort also provides a program that gives discounted lessons to local residents (Utah and Wyoming) as young as 4 years old. A separate program called Canyons Cubs is offered for kids ages 2-6. It is a full day of daycare with an hour of private ski lesson built in. There are 183 runs with 10% of those runs designated for beginners. Kids 4 and under ski for free. Unique winter adventures include: a zipline, horse-drawn sleigh rides, guided snowshoe tours, dog sledding, and snowmobile tours (5 years and up). The resort also offers a two hour ride in a snowcat called the Groomer Ride-Along. This is a pricey adventure, but very unique, and for kids 10 and older. You get an up-close look at how 4000 acres of ski slopes are groomed and maintained. A box lunch is included.

Summer: Canyons Resort offers a large variety of activities even in the warmer months. These include: Gondola rides, zip lining, mountain biking, hiking, mini-golf, disc golf, pedal boating, fishing, and hot air balloon rides.

Deer Valley Resort

2250 Deer Valley Drive
Park City, 84060
(435) 649-1000
www.deervalley.com

What to expect...

Deer Valley is a five star destination resort and has been ranked as one of the top three ski resorts in North America for the past 10 years by *SKI Magazine*. During the Olympics, Deer Valley hosted the freestyle moguls, aerials and alpine slalom competitions. With 6 mountains and over 2,000 skiable acres, there are endless possibilities year-round!

Winter: Deer Valley Resort offers private and group ski lessons for kids as young as 3 years old. No snowboarding is allowed on the mountain. There are 101 ski trails with 27% of those trails designated for beginners. A kid's ski lift pass costs $22 for ages 3 and under and $68 for ages 4-12. All Seasons Adventures (an on-site activity center) offers activities like snow shoeing, Nordic skiing, horse-drawn sleigh rides, dog sledding, hot air balloon rides, and more.

Summer: Visitors can enjoy scenic lift rides, hiking, mountain biking, horseback riding, fishing, and concerts at the Snow Park Outdoor Amphitheater. The Amphitheater also plays host every summer to the Utah Symphony/Utah Opera's Deer Valley Music Festival.

The Fieldhouse Splash Pad

1388 Center Drive
Park City, 84098
(435) 655-0999
www.basinrecreation.org/fieldhouse

Hours:
Memorial Day through Labor Day: 11am-7pm

Admission:
FREE!

Parking:
Free parking lot.

Picnic Areas:
There is plenty of grass as well as picnic tables and shade structures nearby.

What to expect...

The Fieldhouse is a large athletic center located just off Kimball Junction. Right in front of the Fieldhouse is a large splash pad. One of the unique features of this splash pad is that the water is heated. Other features include: leaf and cattail spraying structures, water cannons, and floor fountains. Touch the sensors on the ground to turn on the water. The splash pad is surrounded by large rocks and shade canopies. These completely block children from going onto the street and provide a perfect place for parents to rest and supervise children.

There are a number of rules posted near the splash pad. Food and pets are not allowed in the area. Kids under three or who are not potty-trained must wear a swim diaper with a plastic cover. Children may not climb the splash pad structures. There are no outdoor restrooms.

Monkey Mountain

1526 Ute Blvd.,
Silver Mountain Bldg., 2nd floor, Kimball Junction
Park City, 84098
(435) 214-7451
www.monkeymountain.com

Hours:
Sunday & Monday: 8:30am-5pm;
Tuesday-Saturday: 8:30am-7pm

Admission:
Age 2 and under, *Monday-Thursday:* $4.99: *Friday-Sunday*: $5.99; **Age 3 and up** *Monday-Thursday* : $9.99; *Friday-Sunday:* $11.99.

Food:
No outside food or drink is allowed. The front desk sells snacks and drinks.

Parking:
Park behind the Silver Mountain building. Monkey Mountain is located inside this building.

Discounts:
Monkey Mountain offers discounted group and family rates. Memberships are also available.

Social: f

What to expect...

Monkey Mountain is a fun indoor play center that offers a bright, clean, and safe place for children to play. Parents can sit back and relax in the Parent's Lounge while kids climb, slide, and actively play. Socks are required for both adults and kids.

Play Land – The entire play area is enclosed with a gated entry that only adults can open. A large four-tier tree house play structure sits in the middle of the room. The play structure has a climbing wall, monkey bars, spinners, hanging ropes, a log roll, and a fast twisty slide. The Toddler Soft-Play Zone includes soft animal sculptures for climbing, a soft bouncy floor, a soft toddler slide, and interactive play panels on the walls. Monkey Mountain is built for children ages 12 and younger. I would recommend it for ages 8 and younger, including babies and toddlers. Older kids can get bored quickly.

Parent's Lounge – Parents do not need to pay to enter the facility. A lounge is located in a corner of the play land for parents to relax and still keep a watchful eye on their children. The lounge provides comfortable seating, free WiFi, flatscreen TVs, and magazines.

Monkey Mountain is also a licensed hourly childcare facility. Parents may drop children off for supervised play. These children rotate between 30 minutes of play, then participate in a learning/craft activity upstairs in the activity room for 30 minutes. Monkey Mountain also offers seasonal events, camps, and birthday party packages. See the website for details. Bathrooms with a changing table are located just off the play area.

Park City Mountain Resort

1310 Lowell Ave
Park City, 84060
(435) 649-8111
www.parkcitymountain.com

What to expect...

Park City Mountain Resort is ranked as one of the top-five ski resorts in North America. It is the only resort with a lift that takes you directly to and from Park City Main Street. The resort itself is very large and offers plenty for families to do year-round.

Winter: Both group and private ski lessons for children as young as 3½ years old are available. There are 114 ski trails, 17% of which are designated for beginners. Other winter activities include: the Alpine Coaster (a roller-coaster-like experience down the mountainside), the Flying Eagle Zipline (suitable for kids), ice skating on the outdoor skate rink, and lighted night skiing. The resort also offers children's winter activities 7 miles away at Gorgoza Park. There is lift-served tubing, a winter kid's play area for children ages 8 and under, mini-snowmobiles, and a ski/snowboard lesson zone on a gentle slope.

Summer: Park City Mountain Resort offers a wide variety of exciting summer activities all in one location behind the resort. You can pay for the rides of your choice at the ticket window, and immediately get started. Activities include: four alpine slides, the Alpine Coaster (a roller-coaster-like experience down the mountainside), ziplines, miniature golf, an adventure zone for younger kids, Little Miner's Park (three amusement park rides for young kids), a climbing wall, the Legacy Launcher, and scenic lift rides. You can also buy a Combo Pass that allows you to ride everything all day.

Park City Museum

528 Main Street
Park City, 84060
(435) 649-7457
www.parkcityhistory.org

Hours:
Monday-Saturday: 10am-7pm; *Sunday:* Noon-6pm;
Closed: Thanksgiving and Christmas

Admission:
Under 7: Free; *Age 7-17:* $5; *Age 18-64:* $10;
Age 65+: $8; *Military, Students:* $8

Discounts:
Military and students get in for $8.

Parking:
Parking on Main Street is paid parking. Free parking is in the parking lots on the street behind the Museum (4 hour limit) or in the China Bridge Parking Structure (6 hour limit).

Food:
No food or drink is allowed in the museum.

What to expect...

The Park City Museum is housed in what used to be City Hall back in 1885. The building is on the National Register of Historic Places and still has the original brick facade from 1885 and the original jail cells in the basement! Recently renovated, this museum is of the highest quality in terms of displays and artifacts. All of the displays are visually appealing and interesting for kids. This was my favorite of all the museums I visited.

The entrance to the museum takes you into the gift shop which is filled with all kinds of novelty toys and Park City memorabilia. Entrance is paid at the register. Ask at the desk for a "Treasure Hunt" for kids to do while wandering the museum.

The museum has exhibits on all three levels which tell the story of what life was like for those who settled Park City. Artifacts include mining equipment and tools, a Kimball Stagecoach, early ski equipment, a small country store display, and telegraph and telephone equipment. One of my favorite exhibits is the two-story Mega Mine which cuts a slice from a mountain to reveal the inner tunnels, shafts, and support systems in a mine. Make sure to ask the front desk for a "Treasure Hunt" that kids can do while visiting the museum.

The basement features exhibits that give you a sense of what the dark, wet mining world is like. Be sure to explore the original territorial jail that has been in the basement of the City Hall building since its construction.

Swaner Preserve and EcoCenter

1258 Center Drive
Park City, 84098
(435) 649-1767
www.swanerecocenter.org

Hours:
Summer *Monday-Saturday:* 10am-6pm

Winter *Wednesday-Saturday:* 10am-4pm

Admission:
FREE! There is a $3 suggested donation for adults.

Parking:
Free parking lot.

Food:
No food or drink is allowed.

What to expect...

As a resource to the public, the EcoCenter offers a number of hands-on exhibits to help visitors understand the effect humans have on nature and educate them about the specific ecosystem that exists in the Preserve. Activities include: a simulated beaver habitat, a coyote den that kids can climb through, several displays that involve computerized activities, and a climbing wall. The climbing wall is open every Saturday and costs $5. Ask at the front desk for a treasure hunt activity that will help your kids explore the EcoCenter in a fun way.

An observation deck is located at the top of the building with sweeping views of the Preserve. It can be accessed by stairs or by elevator. On deck, there are tower binoculars for getting a closer look at the surrounding area.

Another fun activity would be to take the self-guided nature walk along the Wetland Discovery Trail. Ask for a brochure at the front desk and the combination code for the entry gate lock. The self-guided tour takes about an hour and features trail marker posts with information about the Preserve. Restrooms without changing tables are located on the main floor.

Did You Know?

The Swaner Preserve was established with the purpose of preserving the natural ecosystem of the wetlands and the uplands in the Park City area. The 350-acre preserve is owned and cared for by Utah State University. The beautiful EcoCenter building located on the preserve was built to serve as an educational facility to the public. The EcoCenter was built to meet the highest certification levels for design, construction, and operation of an energy-efficient, green building.

Trailside Park

5700 Trailside Drive
Park City, 84098
(435) 649-1564
www.basinrecreation.org

Hours:
Dawn to dusk

Admission:
FREE!

Parking:
Free parking lot at the bottom and top entrances.

Picnic Areas:
There is a large pavilion at the upper playground.

What to expect...

Exceptional planning went in to the design and construction of this 17-acre city park which starts at the base of the mountain and spreads out as it climbs uphill. You can access the park from the lower parking area and also from a higher parking area.

The lower area of the park has a playground with baby swings and a play structure geared for younger children. A short walk up a winding sidewalk takes you past sand volleyball courts, tennis courts, a dog park, and two huge soccer fields. Once at the top of the park, there are two more playground structures. One structure is definitely more appropriate for older children and is one of the most varied and entertaining ones I've seen. The other play structure would be most enjoyed by younger children. A large pavilion adjacent to the playground offers shade and picnic tables.

More of the park's developed recreation areas are located above the upper parking lot. These areas include: basketball courts, a skate park, biking trails, and a professionally designed bike park.

Restrooms are located at the top of the hill near the large playground area and also at the bottom near the smaller playground.

Olympic Park

3419 Olympic Parkway
Park City, 84098
(435) 658-4200
www.utaholympiclegacy.com

Hours:
Days and times vary. See the website for current activities. *Closed:* Thanksgiving, Christmas, New Years Day, and Easter Sunday.

See the website for a list of current activities. Summer activities tend to run through mid-October.

Admission:
It is free to enter the grounds and museums. Pay individually for each activity or buy an all-day pass.

Food:
Silver Bean Coffee Cafe, located on the 2nd floor of the Joe Quinney Winter Sports Center, sells coffee, sandwiches, burgers, and more.

Parking:
Free parking lot.

Discounts:
Deals have appeared on Groupon. Entertainment Book.

What to expect...

The Olympic Park was one of the premier sites for the 2002 Winter Olympics. The Park hosted bobsleigh, luge, skeleton, Nordic ski jumping and Nordic combined events. Today the park is an international tourist attraction, a beautiful location for high-adventure outdoor activities, a training ground for young athletes and an education center. The Park is open year-round to the public and offers many ways for visitors to experience Salt Lake City's Olympic legacy.

Museums – **Alf Engen Ski Museum** and **Eccles Salt Lake 2002 Olympic Winter Games Museum** are both housed in the Joe Quinney Winter Sports Center. Both warrant a visit!

Ziplines – **Extreme Zipline** ($20) requires a weight between 100-275 lbs. The **Freestyle Zipline** ($15) is shorter and less steep. It requires a weight between 50-275 lbs. There are no age requirements.

Adventure Courses – The Park offers three courses that increase in height and difficulty level. All are elevated courses that require a safe harness and helmet. Each person receives clear instruction and guidance at the beginning of the course. **Discovery Adventure Course** ($15) is for people ages 5 and older. The Park strongly recommends that an adult accompany children under age 7. There is a minimum weight of 35 lbs and a maximum weight of 215 lbs. **Canyon Adventure Course** ($15) is for ages 7 and older. The Park strongly recommends that an adult accompany children under age 9. Children under 7 may only attempt the course if they have received a pass card from completing the Nordic Course. Weight requirements range from 45-275 lbs. **Summit Adventure Course** ($20) is for ages 13 and older. Kids under age 13 must receive a pass from the Low Course to be approved. The Park strongly advises that an adult accompany anyone under age 13. All participants must wear close-toed shoes.

Drop Tower ($20) – This is a long zipline over the treetops to a high tower where you step off a platform for a 65-foot fall. Weight requirements are 45-260 lbs. Participants must be able to step off the tower without help. Close-toed shoes are required.

Alpine Slide – This is a long slide down the mountain on a rolling sled. Control the sled to go as fast or slow as you like. Drivers ($15) must be 8 years or older. Passengers ($7) must be 3-7 years old.

Chairlift Rides – $5 for youth and $10 for adults.

Guided Tours –This is a 1-hour tour of Olympic Park aboard a shuttle bus. Fees apply.

Flying Ace All Star Freestyle Show – Shows are on Saturdays at 5pm during the summer months. Watch professionals perform choreographed acrobatic tricks set to music, landing into the splash pool. Tickets are $10 for adults and $5 for kids and Seniors 65+. Kids under 3 are free.

Athlete Training at the Park – Many athletes train throughout the summer and you can watch them for free. When we were there, we observed ski jumpers in training as they flipped and splashed into a pool. You can call ahead for up-to-date schedules to be sure you get to see them: (435)658-4200.

Comet Bobsled Ride – Summer pricing is $75 per person. Winter Pricing is $200 per person. For ages 13 and older. Riders must be at least 100 lbs. Parents must sign a waiver.

Rocket Skeleton Ride – Offered in the Winter for ages 14 and up. Parents must be present to sign a waiver. Participants are instructed how to drive the skeleton sled down the fast track through 4 curves.

Utah Olympic Park Museums

3419 Olympic Parkway
Park City, Utah 84098
(435) 658-4200

Hours:
10am-6pm Open Daily;
Closed: Thanksgiving, Christmas, New Years Day, and Easter Sunday

Admission:
FREE!

Parking:
Free parking lot

Food:
Silver Bean Coffee Cafe, located on the 2nd floor, sells coffee, sandwiches, burgers, and more.

What to expect...

The Olympic Park was one of the premier sites for the 2002 Winter Olympics. The Park hosted bobsled, luge, skeleton, Nordic ski jumping, and Nordic combined events. Today, the park is an international tourist attraction, a beautiful location for high-adventure outdoor activities, a training ground for young athletes, and an education center. The Park is open year-round to the public and offers many ways for visitors to experience Salt Lake City's Olympic legacy. The two museums, housed in the Joe Quinney Winter Sports Center, both warrant a visit.

Alf Engen Ski Museum is located on the first floor. It features the proud heritage of skiing in Utah. You can explore things like the hall of fame, ski clothing displays, famous ski photos, and educational information. This museum has many interactive exhibits that are appealing to children. Some of my kids' favorites include: games that let you try the slalom or the ski jump with balls and levers; a large TV screen that simulates the skiing experience; and a topographical map of the Wasatch Front that lights up when you press buttons to see where each ski resort is located. On your way out, you can take advantage of a fun photo opportunity by putting your face in a cardboard cutout of a person skiing.

Eccles Salt Lake 2002 Olympic Winter Games Museum is located on the second floor. It displays many artifacts, pictures, and information from the games hosted in Salt Lake City in 2002. This museum is less interactive, but still captures children's interest. My kids enjoyed looking at the larger than life, hanging displays of animal puppets that were used in the opening ceremonies. They also loved seeing the encased Olympic medals. On a personal note, we took my daughter who has Spina Bifida to see the exhibit about the Paralympic games. We talked to her about her own unlimited potential and took a picture of her holding the Olympic Torch. It was a sweet and memorable experience.

Restrooms with changing tables are located on the first floor. There is also a small gift shop on the first floor that sells shirts, books, post cards, and other souvenirs.

For more information on the Alf Engen Ski Museum you can visit their website at www.utaholympiclegacy.com. For more information on the Eccles Salt Lake 2002 Olympic Winter Games Museum go to www.engenmuseum.org.

Willow Creek Park

Split Rail Lane
Kimball Junction, 84098
www.basinrecreation.org

Hours:
Dawn to dusk

Parking:
Free parking lot.

Food:
A large pavilion offers shaded picnicking and is surrounded by plenty of grassy area as well.

What to expect...

Willow Creek Park is a large park with 17.5 acres of developed land and 66 acres of undeveloped land. The park includes a 1-acre irrigation pond. You may feed ducks there in the summer or ice skate on the pond in the winter. Other features include three playing fields, two tennis courts, sand volleyball courts, and basketball courts.

The park has two farm-themed playgrounds. The larger play structure is for ages 5 to 12 and looks like a tall barn, including three slides. Next to the playground are a set of swings and a rock structure for climbing. The smaller playground looks like a tractor and is for ages 2 to 5. There are two baby swings nearby. Restrooms with changing tables are located between the two playgrounds.

Heber City

Heber City is located in the picturesque Heber Valley just a 10-minute drive from Park City. It is a beautiful farming area with a charming old town feel. Activities in Heber are mostly outdoor-related. One of the most popular attractions in Heber is the historic Heber Valley Railroad. There are major resorts in Midway (the city right next to Heber) that also offer off-season deals on overnight stays.

Courtesy of Heber Valley Railroad

Commemorative Air Force Utah Wing Museum

CAF Hangar-Russ McDonald Field
Heber City Airport, 84068
(435) 709-7269
www.cafutahwing.org

Hours:
May1-October 31: *Thursday-Sunday:* 10am-5pm.

Call ahead to make sure they are open.

Admission:
12+: $5; Under 12: Free; Family: $10

Parking:
Free parking in front of the museum.

Food:
No food or drink is allowed in the museum.

What to expect...

The Commemorative Air Force Museum is housed in an airplane hangar at the Heber Valley Airport. The goal of the CAF is to preserve WWII airplanes in flying-condition and is home to about a dozen restored planes. When they aren't on display in the museum, they are up in the sky at air shows throughout the state. There are a few airplanes in the hangar at all times. When we were there, the volunteer worker offered to let the kids get up into the cockpit of one of the planes.

Along with the planes, there are many displays and exhibits featuring WWII memorabilia. Things like uniforms, flight instruments, photos, an ejection seat and parachute pack, helmets and more. Some displays and donated artifacts highlight the story of local Utah pilots who served in WWII. This would be a great place to visit with a child who is studying WWII.

You'll notice a couch and TV situated in the corner of the hangar, surrounded by a large collection of WWII movies and books. If you have time, you are welcome to sit and read or watch one of the movies on your visit. Restrooms are available inside the hangar. The museum is a non-profit organization and is run entirely by volunteers. If you get to the museum and the doors are locked, just call the phone number posted on the door and a volunteer will come over to let you in.

Finding the museum can be a bit tricky. There are several different hangars and roads throughout the airport. Look for signs for the museum. You will drive pretty far into the airport, past a lot of buildings, and eventually end up on a gravel road that leads to the museum hangar.

Cowboy Campfires (Friday night, Homestead Resort)

700 North Homestead Drive
Midway, 84049
(800) 327-7220
www.homesteadresort.com

Hours:
Every Friday night at 8pm from Memorial Day through Labor Day.

Parking:
Free parking at The Homestead Resort main parking lot

What to expect. . .

The Homestead resort located in Midway invites the public to a night of cowboy storytelling every Friday during the summer. Sparky, the Cowboy and longtime Midway resident, entertains with tall tales and true cowboy stories about Butch Cassidy and others. His partner, Annie, is a cowgirl who plays the guitar and sings favorite cowboy tunes like *Home on the Range* in between stories. This isn't some guy and girl dressed up to put on a show. They are the real deal.

As Sparky tells stories, he warms up his branding irons of numbers 0-9 in the fire pit. In between stories, he takes a thin rectangular piece of wood and brands each child's birthdate into it as a keepsake. Being under the stars in the cool night air with the warm fire and listening to a truly entertaining storyteller was a very memorable experience. My kids really enjoyed the whole night. We all agree that it was one of our favorite activities.

Bench seating is limited, but there is plenty of room around the fire, so I would suggest bringing your own camp chairs. It gets cool, so bring a jacket. Restrooms are available nearby. There is a playground near the fire pit where kids can play before the storytelling starts. At the end of the campfire, guests are invited to have cookies and lemonade.

The Homestead Resort also offers an indoor and an outdoor swimming pool, an amazing geothermal hot springs called 'The Crater', two restaurants, a fudge shop, and other game-type activities that require a small fee. You could easily make a day of it by getting there early and going swimming, eating at family-friendly Fanny's Grill, and stopping for some fudge on your way over to the campfire. Or, make it a special adventure and stay over night in one of their quaint cottages.

Dairy Keen (Home of the Train)

199 South Main Street
Heber City, 84032
(435) 654-KEEN (5336)
www.dairykeen.com

Hours:
Monday-Thursday: 11am-10pm;
Friday-Saturday: 11am-10:30pm

Admission:
FREE!

Parking:
Free parking lot.

Food:
Outside food and drink is permitted.

What to expect...

Dairy Keen has been family owned and operated for over 60 years. Today, four generations work in the restaurant daily. The Dairy Keen serves delicious burgers and fries as well as their famous shakes. But aside from the great food, we chose to include it because of its train-themed dining area. If you have a train fan in your family, you can't miss this stop.

You will recognize the Dairy Keen by the colorful train cars located outside the restaurant. Kids can't resist hopping in a train car and parents can't resist taking a picture. But the real excitement is found inside the restaurant. One of the first things you notice upon entering is the model electric train that runs on a track overhead. The track circles around the dining area and even goes through a long tunnel. It runs past paintings depicting Heber Valley throughout its history, including old-time Heber Main Street, the Heber Valley train station, Provo Canyon, and the surrounding mountains. The artwork is wonderful. Look for small details in the train scenes like a train robber, a bird's nest, deer, a man fishing, little coke machines, and more.

While you wait for your food, the kids can play at the little train table with wooden tracks and train cars or build Legos at the small Lego table. Don't miss the beautiful model train display in the back dining room. Encased in glass sits a re-creation of Hogwarts from the Harry Potter book series. For a quarter you can make the train move back and forth between Hogwarts and the train station.

The prizes in the kid's meals are always something unique. During the Christmas season the train takes on a holiday look with Santa as the engineer.

Deer Creek Reservoir

Located 10 miles southwest of Heber City on Hwy 189
Heber City, 84032
(435) 654-0171

Hours:
Summer Daily 6am-10pm
Winter Daily 8am-5pm

Admission:
$10 day use per vehicle (fee is good all day at all entry points).

Parking:
The parking lots can be very crowded on the weekends.

Picnic Areas:
There are picnic tables and pavilions available on a first-come, first-served basis. The only exception is the large pavilion that must be reserved ahead of time.

What to expect. . .

You don't need to own a boat to enjoy Deer Creek Reservoir. The beaches offer play areas and an on-site boat rental facility makes it easy to rent a boat for the day. There are three main state park entry points into the reservoir. Island Beach, Rainbow Bay, and Deer Creek Main. The one I would suggest is Island Resort.

When the reservoir water is high in the spring and early summer, the sandy beach along the rock break is a nice place to set up an umbrella and relax. At the end of the summer when the water level is low, the shoreline falls back from the rock break, creating a longer beach. At this time of year, the long beach is great because you can set up a shade tent right next to the water, and relax while the kids play on the shoreline. It's not the white sand beaches of Hawaii, a little bit more on the gravelly sludge side, but still makes for a fun day of play.

The on-site rental shop named Deer Creek Island Resort makes it easy to rent a boat, wave runners, fishing boats, and any other water accessory. A lot of families with young children that want a boating experience but don't want to rent a large boat often rent an aluminum motorized fishing boat. This is a very affordable option at $25 per hour. If motorboating isn't your thing, you could rent single or double kayaks starting at the affordable rate of $15 an hour or even a stand-up paddleboard for $20 an hour. Life jackets are included with all rentals. Restrooms are available near the picnic pavilions. There are no showers. Because this is a popular area, it can be very busy and crowded on the weekends.

Please note that it is typical for afternoon winds to blow between about 1-4pm. So, for most boating activities, plan to get on the water before or after that window.

For more information visit their website at www.stateparks.utah.gov.

Heber Valley Artisan Cheese (Kohler Creamery)

920 North River Road
Midway, 84049
(435) 654-0291
www.hebervalleycheese.com

Hours:
Tours are offered every Thursday and require a reservation.

Admission:
Under 2: Free; *Ages 3 and up:* $5

Parking:
Free parking lot.

Food:
No food or drink is allowed on the tour.

What to expect...

Heber Valley Artisan Cheese is a family owned and operated business that takes pride in both their aged cheeses and their fresh handcrafted cheeses. The family's primary business has been dairy farming for over 80 years. They still bottle and sell raw milk, but now use a lot of it to make their cheese. It takes 10 pounds of milk to make one pound of cheese!

The creamery where the cheese is made offers tours to the public every Thursday. Tours require advance reservations made by phone. There are two parts to the tour: the cheese factory and a visit to the family dairy farm, located half a mile away. During the winter months, the ground is too wet and muddy for farm tours. I would strongly suggest planning your visit when you will be able to tour the farm too. That was the most interesting part for my children.

Farm Tour: This is a real working farm, so the conditions and smells are exactly what they should be. But for city folk, it can be quite a shock! The tour took us to where the cows are milked by machine and to where the milk is held and refrigerated. We got an up-close look (and smell!) of the cows in their pen, and heard their loud mooing, which delighted the kids. The walkways around the farm are dirt, so wear appropriate shoes. I think the $5 tour fee is especially worth it if you get to see the dairy farm.

Cheese Factory Tour: This part of the tour gives a look into the cheese production area, which is located in the creamery adjoining their store. Father and son work side by side to process the milk through just the right temperatures and steps to make the final cheese product. You may get to see them stirring milk in large vats, cutting cheese curds into small squares, or packing large cheese squares up to be aged.

Although the tour of the dairy farm is not stroller-friendly, the tour inside the creamery is. The creamery store sells all of their cheeses and freshly made ice cream.

Heber Valley Railroad

450 South 600 West
Heber, 84032
(435) 654-5601
www.hebervalleyrr.org

Hours:
Train rides are offered year-round. See the website for the current schedule.

Tickets:
Prices are based on the specific ride. See below. Purchase tickets online or over the phone.

Parking:
Free parking lot.

Food:
All train rides offer concessions onboard. Some offer a boxed meal option in addition to the ticket price. No outside food or drink is allowed on the train.

Discounts:
Group rates are available through the ticket office.

What to expect. . .

Heber Valley Railroad, dating back to 1899, offers train rides along a scenic 16 mile rail line between Heber and Provo. Today, Heber Valley Railroad is a non-profit organization that focuses on tourism, education and the restoration of historical railroad equipment. This old-fashioned train experience is perfect for all ages.

Daily Scenic Trains (see descriptions below) offer train rides with beautiful views and fun along the way. Watch out for a Black Jack Raven and the Soldier Hollow Gang (a band of old-fashioned train bandits) along your ride. There is a Snack Car on the train that sells drinks and snacks. Some offer an option to buy a ticket that includes a boxed lunch. Your meal must be purchased 24-hours before the train ride.

Provo Canyon Limited (ages 3-12: $15 or w/lunch $28; adults: $30 or w/lunch $43) – This is a 3 hour round-trip train ride. It takes you along scenic Deer Creek Reservoir all the way to Vivian Park in Provo Canyon. There, you take a 20 minute break. Vivian Park is located along the Provo River and provides restrooms, playgrounds and picnic areas. After the short stop, you will then board the train and return to the depot. One way tickets from the Heber Depot are also available.

Deer Creek Express (ages 3-12: $10; adults: $15) – This is a 90 minute round-trip train ride. It takes you from the Depot along the shores of Deer Creek Reservoir to Decker Bay, then returns.

Lakeside Limited (ages 3-12: $15 or w/lunch $28; adults: $25 or w/lunch $38) – This is a 2 hour train ride that runs in the Winter (January-April). Rides go along the shore of Deer Creek Reservoir.

Heber Valley Railroad offers many other unique train ride experiences, like Dinner Trains where a box dinner and music or a show are included. **Activity Trains** allow you to pair adventures like horseback riding, zip lining or river rafting along with your train ride. The Railroad also offers themed **Date Night Trains** and **Family Night Trains**. Check the website for current offerings and special events.

Trains leave from the Heber Valley Railroad Depot (unless otherwise noted). Arrive at least 45 minutes before your scheduled time of departure. Restrooms are available at the depot and on the train. Strollers and car seats are not allowed. Wheelchair access is limited; call ahead to make arrangements. No Dogs.

Annual Events

A Day Out with Thomas – Memorial Day Weekend. Meet Thomas the Train, take a short train ride and participate in other fun activities.

Pumpkin Festival – October. Enjoy a 40 minute train ride, entertainment, snacks, a haunted car and more.

North Pole Express – December. Enjoy entertainment, food, festivities, and Santa Clause.

Soldier Hollow Cross-Country Ski Resort

2002 Olympic Drive
Midway, 84049
(435) 654-2002
www.soldierhollow.com

What to expect...

Soldier Hollow is a cross-country ski resort located in Wasatch Mountain State Park, just outside of Midway. Created for the 2002 Winter Olympics, Soldier Hollow hosted the cross-country and biathlon events. Today, it is a great location for year-round mountain activities and special events.

Winter: Winter activities at Soldier Hollow are offered from mid-December through mid-March. Soldier Hollow is a perfect destination for lift-served tubing. It boasts the longest tubing lanes in Utah. The resort limits the sale of lift tickets so that your tubing experience will never be over-crowded. Tubing sessions run two hours at a time on the even hours. Music plays on the hill to add a fun atmosphere and the hill is lit at night. You may pre-purchase tickets by phone or in person. Kids under 3 cannot ride the lift, but they can use a tube for free on a small slope with parental supervision.

Soldier Hollow also offers beautifully groomed cross-country ski trails. Cross-country ski lessons are offered for kids as young as 3 years old. You can purchase day passes, various season passes, and 10-punch passes for access to all cross-country ski trails. Other winter activities offered at Soldier Hollow include: snow shoeing, a Biathlon Experience, and horseback riding (year-round).

Summer: During the summer you can enjoy scenic horseback rides (booked through Rocky Mountain Outfitters), mountain biking, and golfing. Soldier Hollow also hosts the Sheepdog Championships and the Heber Valley PowWow every summer.

Appendices: Great Resources

Downtown Destinations

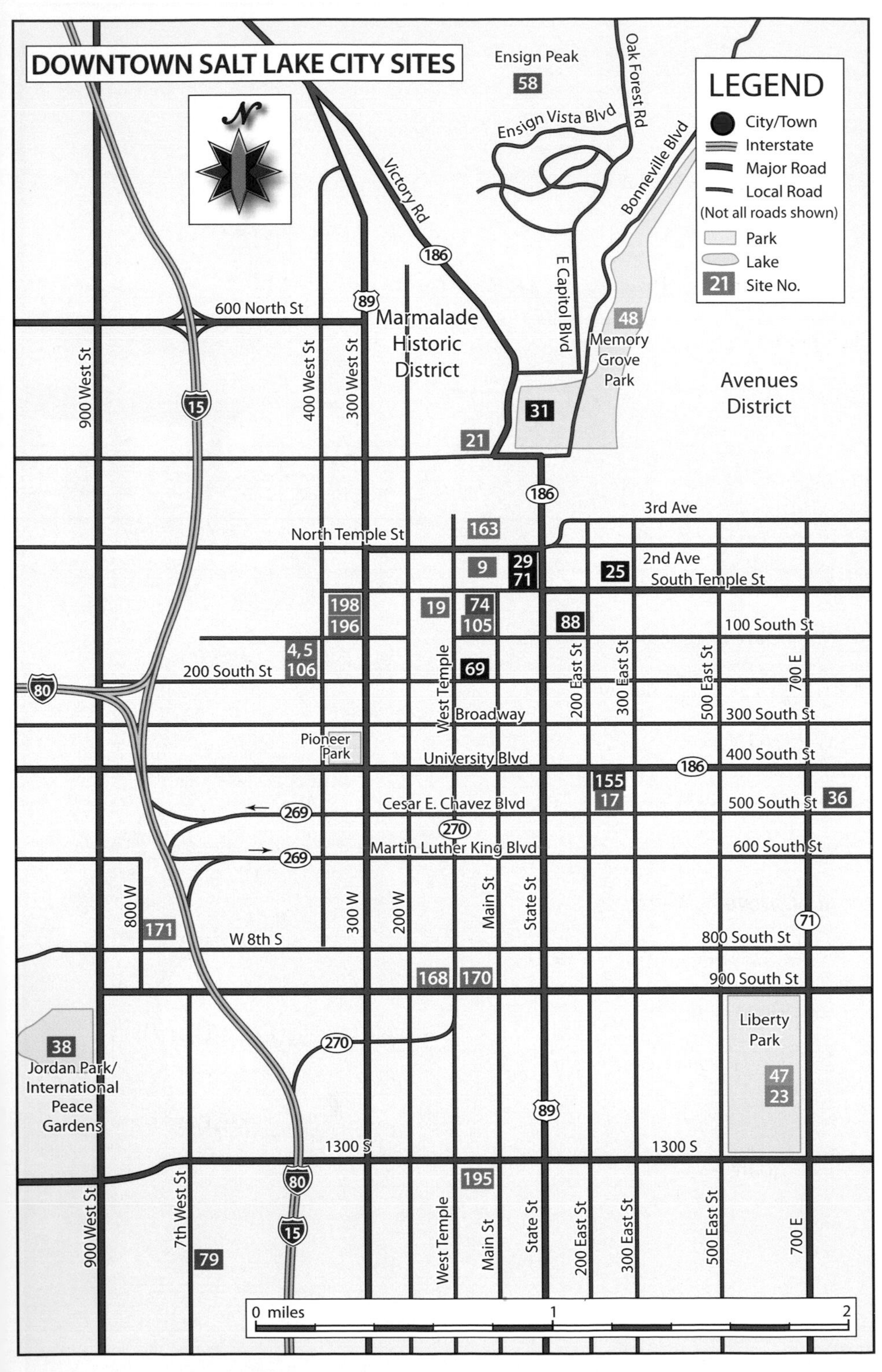

Downtown Site List

- Ballet West – site 69
- Cathedral of the Madeline – site 25
- City Creek Engage Fountain – site 105
- City Creek Dinosaur Play Area – site 74
- Clark Planetarium – site 4
- Discovery Gateway: The Children's Museum of Utah – site 5
- Ensign Peak Hike – site 58
- Gilgal Sculpture Garden – site 36
- Harmons Cooking School – site 88
- International Peace Gardens – site 38
- Jump Around Utah – site 79
- LDS Church History Museum – site 9
- LDS Conference Center – site 163
- Liberty Park – site 47
- Memory Grove Park – site 48
- Mormon Tabernacle Choir – site 71
- Salt Lake Bees – site 195
- Salt Lake City Public Library – site 155
- Taffy Town – site 168
- Temple Square – site 29
- The Gateway – site 106
- The Leonardo – site 17
- Tracy Aviary – site 23
- Utah Blaze – site 196
- Utah Jazz – site 198
- Utah Museum of Contemporary Art – site 19
- Utah Pioneer Museum – site 21
- Utah State Capitol – site 31
- Utah Symphony – Utah Opera – site 72
- V Chocolates – site 170
- Welfare Square – site 171

Site index

1. Museums & More 1-21
2. Animal Attractions 22-24
3. Historic Sites 25-32
4. Gardens & The Outdoors 33-43
5. Playgrounds & Parks 44-51
6. Hikes & Nature Walks 52-68
7. Performing Arts 69-72
8. Indoor Play Spaces 73-85
9. Hands-On Experiences 86-91
10. Amusement Parks 92-103
11. Splash Pads, Fountains 104-122
12. Indoor Swimming 123-135
13. Outdoor Swimming 136-151
14. Storytime & Libraries 152-157
15. Tours! 158-171
16. Unique Adventures 172-183
17. Ski Areas & Resorts 184-191
18. Sporting Events 192-198
19. Park City 199-209
20. Heber City 210-216

Instructions for Games at Legacy Park

Nova

Direction Correction – Speed and Coordination

- The computer is the red cluster and the player is the yellow dot.
- The computer will start to turn the red cluster in a random direction and speed.
- The player must match the speed of the red cluster with the yellow dot.
- When the yellow dot matches the red cluster, the red cluster turns green.
- Hold the yellow dot in the moving red cluster for 2 seconds to gain a point.

Speed Chaser – Speed and Performance

- The players have 30 seconds to turn the Nova wheel as fast as possible.
- Speed is shown on the game controller.
- The fastest speed held is the score.

Ping Pong – Speed and Teamwork

- A ball moves across the screen. Rotate the ring to move the paddle and keep the ball in play.
- A point is scored for each time the ball is struck with the paddle.
- The size of the paddle decreases as the game progresses.

Rocky

Rock the Boat – Strength and Memory

- The players navigate a rowboat along the river.
- Rock the structure back and forth in the direction of the river to activate the oars and gain speed.
- Tilt the structure side to side to steer the boat to both avoid obstacles and capture power stars, which extend your time.
- Gain points by traveling farther along the river.

Hold It – Strength and Endurance

- The game controller screen is divided into 4 areas/directions (one per player).
- Players must tug the Rocky in their direction to gain a point.
- The player with the most points wins.

Marble Drop – Strength and Agility

- The game controller screen will show a hole and a small cross (representing the marble).
- The player must get the marble to fall in the hole by tilting the Rocky.
- The hole will keep shrinking, increasing the level of difficulty.
- The game ends if the marble falls off the screen.
- A score is awarded based on how many times the marble falls into the hole.

Space

Capture – Agility and Strategy

- Two towers will light up, red and blue.
- The players, divided into two teams, must defend their tower's nodes and capture the other team's nodes by pressing them.
- Hitting the opponent's nodes converts them to a team's own color.
- Game stats can be seen on the game controller.
- The winner is the team with the most captured colors when time runs out.

Color Catch – Agility and Speed

- 1-7 players/teams. Each player/team chooses a color.
- Chase your color around the structure. Hit the node to capture the color.
- As you catch the nodes, new nodes will light up in your color.
- 10 catches lead to a victory.
- A score is awarded based on how quickly the players/teams achieve 10 catches.

Memory – Agility and Memory

- Eight different symbols (and their exact match) are hidden among the 16 nodes.
- Choose a node and press it; the node will display a unique color pattern and the game controller will reveal the node's symbol.
- Press another node to find the match.
- If a match is found, the player receives a point and continues play. If a match is not found, the other player takes a turn.
- Remember the symbols revealed throughout the game to assist in finding matches when your turn comes around again.

Pump It – Agility and Teamwork

- Rock back an forth on the game controller tilt board to charge the nodes.
- When the nodes turn green, players must run to hit them before they disappear.
- Each game consists of four charge cycles.
- The time allotted to press the nodes decreases with each cycle.

Duck Ponds

Did you know?

Bread can be a tasty treat for ducks, but should be eaten in moderation because it has very little nutritional value and can attract rodents and pests. Instead, consider bringing cracked corn, grape halves, or fresh peas. Also, be aware of signs at these parks to be sure they do not prohibit the feeding of ducks.

Beus Pond Park
4240 Country Hills Drive Ogden, 84403

Brigham Young University Botany Pond
441 East 800 North, Provo, 84606

Fairmont Park
1040 East Sugarmont Drive (2225 South), Salt Lake City, 84106

Gardner Village (site 55)
1100 West 7800 South, West Jordan, 84088

Highland Glenn Park
Located west of Lone Peak High School; (enter one street south) 4800 West, Highland, 84003

Layton Commons Park
437 North Wasatch Drive, Layton 84041

Liberty Park (site 47)
600 East 900 South, Salt Lake City, 84104

Paul Ream Wilderness Park
1600 West 500 North, Provo, 84604

Red Butte Garden (site 40)
300 Wakara Way, Salt Lake City, 84108

Silver Lake (site 185)
Brighton Ski Resort, Big Cottonwood Canyon

Sugar House Park
1400 East 2100 South, Salt Lake City, 84105

Weber State University Duck Pond
Dixon Dr. Ogden, 84403

Wheeler Historic Farm (site 32)
6351 South 900 East, Salt Lake City, 84121

Willow Pond Park (site 122)
6059 South Murray Parkway Avenue (1080 West), Murray, 84123

Fishing Locations

Did you know?

The following is a list of free community fisheries and other kid-friendly fishing locations along the Wasatch Front. For more detailed information on many of the community fishing ponds, download a free brochure provided by the Utah Division of Wildlife Resources at www.wildlife.utah.gov . Click "Fishing," then "Community fishing," then download the "Utah Community Fishing booklet." This resource gives basic information on each location including how many fish you are allowed to keep, which type of fish to release, if you can use a boat on the pond, and more.

Kids under age 12 can fish anywhere in Utah without a fishing license. For anyone 12 or older, fishing licenses can be purchased online at www.wildlife.utah.gov, at a retail store such as Walmart, Kmart, Sports Authority, Smith's, or at any Division of Wildlife Resources office.

Weber County

Fort Buenaventura
2450 A Avenue, Ogden, 84401

Glassman's Pond Park
1126 East 4600 South, Ogden, 84403

Meadow Creek Pond
4200 West 5075 South, Roy, 84067

Davis County

Andy Adams Reservoir
1725 East Gordon Street (across from Adam's Park), Layton, 84041

Bountiful Lake
West of Legacy Highway, take 500 South exit then head North 1.5 miles

Clinton Park Pond
3000 West 2415 North, Clinton, 84015

Farmington Pond
750 North 75 West, near the mouth of Farmington Canyon

Jensen Nature Park
3176 South Bluff Road, Syracuse, 84075

Mabey Pond
310 South 500 East, Clearfield, 84015

Steed Pond
300 North 1000 West, Clearfield, 84015

Utah Botanical Center
725 South 50 West, Kaysville, 84037

Salt Lake County

Austin Pond
Snowbird, Little Cottonwood Canyon

Kidney Pond
920 West 11200 South (south west side of River Front Park), South Jordan, 84095

Midas Pond
920 West 11200 South (south west side of River Front Park), South Jordan, 84095

Millrace Pond
1200 West 5400 South, Taylorsville, Utah 84123

Riverton City Pond
3200 West 13680 South (in old Farm Park), Riverton, 84065

Sandy Urban Fishery
1000 West 9800 South, Sandy, 84092

Silver Lake (Site 185)
Brighton Ski Resort, Big Cottonwood Canyon

Sunset Pond
898 East Riparian Drive (11815 South) Draper, 84020

The Cove at Herriman Springs Pond
7200 West 14200 South, Herriman, 84096

Willow Pond Park (Site 122)
6059 South Murray Parkway Avenue (1080 West), Murray, 84123

Utah County

Highland Glen Park
Located behind Lone Peak High School, enter from 4800 West via Knight Avenue

Manila Creek Pond (Site 145)
3300 North 900 West, Pleasant Grove, 84062

Vivian Park
Provo Canyon (about 9 miles up), on south side of Highway 189

Ice Rinks

Did you know?

There are plenty of options along the Wasatch Front for ice skating. Many rinks are indoors, although there are a handful of outdoor rinks that provide picturesque winter fun. Most ice rinks allow you to rent ice skates as small as child size 8. Be sure to wear warm clothes, including coats, gloves, and hats.

Year-round

Acord Ice Arena (West Valley)
www.slco.org

Cottonwood Heights Recreation Center (Cottonwood Heights)
www.cottonwoodheights.com

County Ice Center (Murray)
www.countyice.slco.org

Midway City Ice Rink (Midway)
www.midwaycityut.org

Park City Ice Arena (Park City)
www.parkcity.org

Peaks Ice Arena (Provo)
www.provo.org

SLC Sports Complex (Salt Lake City)
www.recreation.slco.org/slcsports

South Davis Recreation Center (Bountiful)
www.southdavisrecreation.com

The Ice Sheet (Ogden)
www.co.weber.ut.us

Utah Olympic Oval (Kearns)
www.utaholympiclegacy.com

Seasonal

Aside from the Gallivan Center, these outdoor ice rinks are small.

Gallivan Center (Salt Lake City)
www.thegallivancenter.com

Park City Mountain Resort (Park City)
www.parkcitymountain.org

Solitude Mountain Resort (Big Cottonwood Canyon, SLC)
www.skisolitude.com

Station Park (Farmington)
www.shopsatstationpark.com

The Plaza at South Jordan (South Jordan)
www.sjc.utah.gov

Outdoor Movies

Great idea!

The summer is a great time to throw down a blanket and watch a movie outdoors. This lists free outdoor venues that show family-friendly movies. Some cities change locations for each showing while others have a permanent showplace. Examine each website to be sure of the location and schedule.

Butterfield Park (Herriman)
www.herriman.org

Capitol Hill (Salt Lake City)
www.utahstatecapitol.utah.gov

Cottonwood Heights
www.cottonwoodheights.com

Draper City Amphitheater
www.draper.ut.us

Fort Buenaventura (Ogden)
www.co.weber.ut.us/parks/fortb/events

Founders Park (Centerville)
www.centervilleut.net

Kaysville City
www.kaysvillecity.com

Magna
www.magnautah.org

Municipal Gardens (Ogden)
www.ocae.org

North Salt Lake City
www.nslcity.org

Riverdale Park
www.moviesinthepark.wordpress.com

Riverton
www.recreation.rivertoncity.com

Rock Canyon Park (Provo)
www.provo.org

Salt Lake City
www.slcgov.com

Sandy City
www.sandy.utah.gov

Veteran's Memorial Park (West Jordan)
www.wjordan.com

Family Friendly Theaters

Did you know?

Utah is known for offering great family-friendly entertainment. The theaters listed below are known to present clean, quality plays and musicals. To be sure a play is right for your child, review the content before attending. Most websites offer a brief summary of the story. Some also recommend ages.

Capitol Theater (Salt Lake City)
www.arttix.org

Centerpoint Legacy Theater (Centerville)
www.centerpointtheatre.org

Desert Star Theatres (Murray)
www.desertstar.biz

Draper Historic Theatre (Draper)
www.drapertheatre.org

Empress Theater (Magna)
www.empresstheatre.com

Hale Center Theatre (Salt Lake City)
www.halecentertheatre.org

Hale Center Theater (Orem)
www.haletheater.org

Peery's Egyptian Theater (Ogden)
www.egyptiantheaterogden.com

Sundance Summer Theatre (Provo)
www.sundanceresort.com

Scera Center for the Arts (Orem)
www.scera.org

Scera Outdoor Shell (Orem)
www.scera.org

The Children's Theatre (Salt Lake City)
www.tctheatre.org

University of Utah Youth Theater (Salt Lake City)
www.youththeatre.utah.edu

Valley Center Playhouse (Lindon)
www.valleycenterplayhouse.com

Rodeos

Did you know?

Utah is host to many exciting annual rodeos. The following is a list of rodeos from Ogden to Provo, though there are many more rodeos that occur in small towns all throughout Utah including Spanish Fork, Delta, Tooele and more.

Davis County Fair & Rodeo (Farmington)
www.davisfair.org

Days of '47 Rodeo (West Valley)
www.daysof47rodeo.com

Herriman Days Rodeo (Herriman)
www.herriman.org

Highland Fling Play Day Rodeo (Highland)
www.highlandcity.org

Lehi Roundup Rodeo (Lehi)
www.lehirodeo.com

Mountain Valley Stampede (Heber)
www.mvstampede.com

Ogden Pioneer Days Rodeo (Ogden)
www.ogdenpioneerdays.com

Pony Express Days Rodeo (Eagle Mountain)
www.eaglemountaincity.org

Strawberry Days Rodeo (Pleasant Grove)
www.plgrove.org

Western Stampede Rodeo (West Jordan)
www.westernstampede.com

Utah State Fair Rodeo (Salt Lake City)
www.utahstatefair.com/rodeo

Online Activity Resources

The following is a list of blogs and websites that are great to check for updated activities and events in Utah.

Enjoy Utah!
www.enjoyutah.org

Fun Around Utah
www.funaroundutah.com/blog

I Heart Salt Lake
www.iheartsaltlake.com

Macaroni Kid (three local sites)
www.southvalley.macaronikid.com
www.cottonwood.macaronikid.com
www.layton.macaronikid.com

Things To Do, Utah
www.thingstodoinutah.blogspot.com

Today's Mama
www.todaysmama.com

Utah Deal Diva
www.utahdealdiva.com

Utah Kids Club
www.utahkidsclub.com

Utah Valley Family Adventures
www.utahvalleyfamilyadventures.blogspot.com

Calendar of Events & Festivals

In addition to the annual events listed under each location, a number of other fairs, festivals, and seasonal events occur each year. The following is a month-by-month calendar of the popular kid-friendly events. Summer months are an especially exciting time to be in Utah. There are many patriotic festivities, pioneer day events, and city day celebrations, as well as rodeos and parades!

May

Pony Express Days (Eagle Mountain)
www.eaglemountaincity.org

June

South Jordan City Country Fest (South Jordan)
www.sjc.utah.gov/recreation/countryfest.asp

Strawberry Days (Pleasant Grove)
www.sdaysrodeo.com

Herriman Days (Herriman)
www.herriman.org

Lehi Roundup (Lehi)
www.lehi-ut.gov/discover/roundup

Orem Summerfest (Orem)
www.summerfest.orem.org

Riverton Town Days Festival

July

American Fork Steel Days
www.afcity.org

Centerville Parade & Fireworks
www.centervilleut.net

Clearfield 4th of July Celebration
www.clearfieldcity.org

East MillCreek July 4th Community Celebration
www.emclions.org

Farmington Festival Days
www.farmington.utah.gov

Fruit Heights 4th of July Parade
www.fruitheightscity.com

Gallivan Plaza Fireworks
www.thegallivancenter.com

Holladay 4th of July Festivities
www.cityofholladay.com

Jordan Park Fireworks

Layton 4th of July Parade & Fireworks
www.laytoncity.org

Lehi Liberty Days Celebration

Magna 4th of July Festivities
www.magnautah.org

Midway 4th of July Festivities
www.midwaycityut.org

Murray 4th of July Parade &Fireworks
www.murray.utah.gov

North Salt Lake Eaglewood Fireworks
www.nslcity.org

Ogden's Cherry Days
www.northogdenrecreation.com/cherry-days.html

Park City Independence Day Celebration
www.visitparkcity.com

Pleasant Grove Fireworks
www.pgcity.org

Sandy Parade & Fireworks
www.sandy.utah.gov

South Salt Lake Freedom Festival
www.southsaltlakecity.com

Sugarhouse Park Fireworks
www.sugarhousefireworks.com

West Jordan Independence Day Festival
www.westernstampede.com

Stadium of Fire (Provo)
www.freedomfestival.org

America's Freedom Festival (Provo)
www.freedomfestival.org

America's Freedom Festival Balloon Fest (Provo)
www.freedomfestival.org

Handcart Days (Bountiful)
www.handcartdays.org

Days of '47 Parade (Salt Lake City)
www.daysof47.com

Days of '47 Float Preview Party (Salt Lake City)
www.daysof47.com

Days of '47 Union Pacific Youth Parade (Salt Lake City)
www.daysof47.com

Ogden Pioneer Days (Ogden)
www.ogdenpioneerdays.com

August

Davis County Fair (Farmington)
www.davisfair.org

Alpine Days
www.alpinecity.org

Lindon Days
www.lindondays.org

Utah County Fair (Spanish Fork)
www.utcountyfair.com

Weber County Fair (Ogden)
www.co.weber.ut.us/fair

September

Utah State Fair (Salt Lake City)
www.utahstatefair.com

Swiss Days (Midway)
www.midwayswissdays.com

October

Black Island Farms Harvest Festival (Syracuse)
www.blackislandfarms.com

Cornbelly's Corn Maze & Pumpkin Festival (Lehi)
www.cornbellys.com

Crazy Corn Maze (West Jordan)
www.utahmaze.com

Day Farms Pumpkin Patch (Layton)

Farnsworth Farms & Cider Mill (Sandy)

Hee Haw Farms Corn Maze, Halloween & fall Fun Activities (Pleasant Grove)
www.heehawfarms.com

Mabey's Pumpkin Patch (South Jordan)
10090 South 1000 West South Jordan,
Utah 84095

McCoard's Mystery Corn Maze
www.silvermaplemedia.com/sites/mccoards

Pack Farms Pumpkin Patch (Farmington)
www.packfarms.com/pumpkinpatch.htm

Petersen Family Farm Pumpkin Patch (Riverton)
www.petersenfamilyfarm.com

Pumpkin Point Farms (Riverton)
www.pumpkinpointfarms.com

Scarecrow Festival (West Jordan)
www.westridgeacademy.com/fundraising

November

Festival of Trees (Salt Lake City)
www.festivaloftreesutah.org

December

Electric Light Parade and Christmas Village (Ogden)
www.ogdencity.com

Provo Winter Fest
www.provo.org

Summer:

Timpanogos Storytelling Festival (Provo)
www.timpfest.org

Radio Disney Days at the Gallivan Center (Salt Lake City)
www.thegallivancenter.com

Photo Credits

All photos listed start from the top left corner of each page, then follow clockwise. All unlabeled photos are taken by Meilani Smith Kongaika or Emily Smith Robbins or are part of the Robbins/Kongaika collection.

18: By Emily Robbins; Photos Courtesy of BYU Museum of Art

19: Photos by Jenny Casper; By Emily Robbins

20: By Emily Robbins; Courtesy of BYU Museum of Peoples and Cultures

21: Courtesy of Clark Planetarium

22: By Neal Ernstrom; Courtesy of Discovery Gateway; By Rachel Clarke

23: Courtesy of Discovery Gateway; by Meilani Kongaika; By Rachel Clarke

27: Courtesy of the Church of Jesus Christ of Latter-Day Saints

28: Courtesy of Monte L. Bean Life Science Museum

29: Courtesy of Monte L. Bean Life Science Museum

30: Courtesy of Thanksgiving Point

31: Courtesy of Thanksgiving Point

32: Photos by Stuart Ruckman

33: Photos by Tom Smart

35: Courtesy of Ogden Dinosaur Park and Museum

36: Photos Courtesy of Ogden Union Station

37: Courtesy of Ott Planetarium; Courtesy of NASA Images

38: Photos Courtesy of NASA Images

39: Courtesy of The Leonardo

40-41: Photos Courtesy of Treehouse Children's Museum

42: Photos Courtesy of Utah Museum of Contemporary Art

43: Photos Courtesy of Utah Museum of Fine Arts

44: Photos Courtesy of Utah Pioneer Museum

46: Photos Courtesy of Thanksgiving Point

47: Photos Courtesy of Tracy Aviary

48: Courtesy of Utah's Hogle Zoo

49: By Brittany Bezanson; Photos Courtesy of Utah's Hogle Zoo

50: By Kyrie Collins; Use given by Stock.xchng.com; By Brittany Bezanson

52: Photos by Deacon Lynn R. Johnson

53: Photos Courtesy of Fort Buenaventura

55: Courtesy of Gardner Village

56-57: Photos Courtesy of The Church of Jesus Christ of Latter-Day Saints

58: Photos Courtesy of This is the Place Heritage Park

59: Photos Courtesy of This is the Place Heritage Park; By Emily Robbins

60: Photos by Sara Howard

61: By Joanna Oldham

62: By Mindy Quist; by Kristin Dirkmaat

66: Courtesy of Thanksgiving Point; Photos by Meilani Kongaika; Courtesy of Thanksgiving Point

67: By Emily Robbins; Courtesy of Cold Springs Trout Farm; Use given by Stock.xchng.com

69: By Stuart Ruckman

72: Photos Courtesy of Ogden Nature Center

73: Courtesy of Ogden Nature Center; by Meilani Kongaika; Courtesy of Ogden Nature Center

74-75: Photos Courtesy of Red Butte Garden

78-79: Photos Courtesy of Thanksgiving Point

80: Photos by Emily Robbins; Courtesy of Jordan Valley Conservancy District

83: By Meilani Kongaika; By Kristin Dirkmaat

84: By Emily Robbins; Courtesy of KOMPAN

85: By Meilani Kongaika; By Brittany Bezanson

101: Photos by Meilani Kongaika; Use given by Stock.xchng.com

113: Courtesy of The Children's Theater

114-115: Photos Courtesy of The Church of Jesus Christ of Latter-Day Saints

116: Photos Courtesy of Utah Symphony/Utah Opera

119: By Emily Robbins; Courtesy of City Creek Center

121: Courtesy of Get Air Sportsplex

122: Photos Courtesy of Hang

Time Extreme Trampolines

124: Photos Courtesy of Jump Around Utah

127: Courtesy of Kangaroo Zoo

129: Photos Courtesy of Provo Towne Centre

130: Photos Courtesy of University Mall

132: Photos Courtesy of Color Me Mine

133: Courtesy of Creativity Art Studio

134: Courtesy of Harmon's Cooking School

140: Courtesy of Boondocks Food and Fun

141: by Emily Robbins; Courtesy of Boondocks Food and Fun

146: Photos Courtesy of FatCats

149: Photos by Rachel Clarke

150: Courtesy of Lagoon

151: Courtesy of Lagoon; by Emily Robbins; Courtesy of Lagoon; By Rachel Clarke, Courtesy of Lagoon; By Rachel Clarke

152: Courtesy of Nickel City Fun Center

154-155: Photos Courtesy of Provo Resort

156: Courtesy of Seven Peaks Fun Center

157: Photos by Emily Robbins; Courtesy of Seven Peaks Fun Center

158: Use from stock.xchng.com

161: By Meilani Kongaika; Courtesy of City Creek Center

162: By Rachel Clarke; By Katie Smith; By Rachel Clarke

165: Photos Courtesy of Water Design Inc.

166: Courtesy of iHeartSaltLake.com; by Corie Balls

171: By Meilani Kongaika; By Michael Winget

180: Courtesy of Clearfield Aquatic Center

182: Photos by Meilani Kongaika; Courtesy of Salt Lake County Parks and Recreation

185: Courtesy of Salt Lake County Parks and Recreation

186-187: Photos Courtesy of Lehi City

188: Photos Courtesy of Salt Lake County Parks and Recreation

189: Photos Courtesy of Murray City

192: Courtesy of South Davis Recreation Center

193: Photos Courtesy of Water Design Inc.

194: Courtesy of West Valley Family Fitness Center

196: Courtesy of American Fork Fitness Center

197: Photos by Katie Smith

198: By Meilani Kongaika; Photos Courtesy of Salt Lake County Parks and Recreation

199: Photos Courtesy of Cherry Hill; By Rachel Clarke

200: Courtesy of Cottonwood Heights Recreation Center

201: Courtesy of Water Design Inc.; Courtesy of Kearns Oquirrh Park Fitness Center

202: Courtesy of Salt Lake County Parks and Recreation

203: Photos Courtesy of Layton Surf 'N Swim

204: Courtesy of Lindon Aquatic Center

206: Photos Courtesy of Water Design Inc.; Use given by Stock.xchng.com

209: By Kelly Nordfelt

210-211: Photos Courtesy of Seven Peaks

212: Courtesy of Salt Lake County Parks and Recreation

214: The King's English, By Emily Robbins

215: Use from stock.xchng.com

216: By Emily Robbins; By Sonia Knapp

217: Courtesy of Provo Public Library

218: By Emily Robbins; Use given by Stock.xchng.com

221: Photos by Amanda Robbins

222: By Sonia Knapp

226: By Emily Robbins; Courtesy of Hale Center Theater

227: Courtesy of Holdman Studios

229: Photos Courtesy of The Church of Jesus Christ of Latter-Day Saints

231: Photos Courtesy of Mrs. Cavanaugh's Chocolate

232-233: Photos Courtesy of Peery's Egyptian Theater

Photo Credits

234: Images by ADAIR – www.adairworks.com

235: Photos Courtesy of Taffy Town

237: Courtesy of V Chocolates

238: Photos Courtesy of The Church of Jesus Christ of Latter-Day Saints

240: Courtesy of Cabela's

242: Photos Courtesy of CLAS Ropes

245: Photos Courtesy of Comedy Sportz Provo

246: By Emily Robbins; Courtesy of Georgell Doll Shop

248: Photos by Jacob Kongaika

252: Courtesy of Thanksgiving Point

254: By Rachel Clarke

256: Photos Courtesy of Alta Ski Area

257: Photos by Richard Cheski

258: Photos Courtesy of Powder Mountain

259: Photos Courtesy of Snowbasin Resort

260-261: Photos Courtesy of Snowbird Ski and Summer Resort

262: By Todd Spector; Photos by Michael Brown

263: Photos by Willie Holdman; Use given by Stock.xchng.com

264: Photos by Bill Singleton

266: Photos Courtesy of Ogden Raptors

267: Courtesy of Orem Owlz

268: Photo by George Frey, Getty Images; Courtesy of Real Salt Lake Communications

269: By Rachel Clarke

270: Photos by Al Walters

271: Photos Courtesy of Utah Grizzlies

274: Photos Courtesy of Canyons Resort

275: Photos Courtesy of Deer Valley Resort

277: By Meilani Kongaika; Courtesy of Monkey Mountain

278: Photos Courtesy of Park City Mountain Resort

282: Photos Courtesy of Utah Olympic Park

283: Courtesy of Utah Olympic Park; by Meilani Kongaika; Courtesy of Utah Olympic Park

284: Courtesy of Utah Olympic Park

289: Courtesy of Homestead Resort

290: Courtesy of Dairy Keen; by Emily Robbins; Courtesy of Dairy Keen

292: Photos Courtesy of Heber Valley Artisan Cheese

293: Courtesy of Heber Valley Railroad

294: Courtesy of Soldier Hollow Cross-Country Ski Resort

295: Neptune Park, by Meilani Kongaika

300: Use given by Stock.xchng.com

302: Photos Courtesy of Utah Olympic Park

304: Courtesy of Hale Center Theater

307: By Kristin Dirkmaat

Resources

Breastfeeding Support

Bosom Buddies
www.bosombuddies.com

International Lactation Consultant Association
www.ilca.org

La Leche League of Utah
www.lllusa.org/UT/Utah.html

Utah Breastfeeding Coalition
www.utahbreastfeeding.org

Childcare Resources

Care About Childcare
www.careaboutchildcare.utah.gov

ChildcareCenter.us
www.childcarecenter.us

Daycare.com Utah State Requirements
www.daycare.com/utah

Utah Department of Health
www.health.utah.gov/licensing/FindProvider.htm

Discount Websites

www.citydeals.com

www.dealpickle.com

www.eversave.com

www.groupon.com/salt-lake-city

www.hubzub.com

www.ksl.com/deals

www.livingsocial.com

www.plumdistrict.com

www.slcdailydeal.com

www.travelzoo.com

www.utahsweetsavings.com

Grandparent Resources and Support

Children's Service Society
www.cssutah.org

Grandparents online magazine
www.granparents.com

Grandparents raising grandchildren
www.gransplace.org

Grandparents raising grandchildren
www.raisingyourgrandchildren.com

Living Frugally

America's Cheapest Family
www.americascheapestfamily.com

Coupons 4 Utah
www.coupons4utah.com

Miserly Moms
www.miserlymoms.com

Mom Advice
www.momadvice.com

Mommy Savers
www.mommysavers.com

Pinching Your Pennies
www.pinchingyourpennies.com

Savvy Shopper Deals
www.savvyshopperdeals.com/utah

The Dollar Stretcher
www.stretcher.com

Utah Deal Diva
www.utahdealdiva.com

The Fun, Cheap or Free Queen
www.funcheaporfree.com

Moms Groups

Meet-up Groups
www.moms.meetup.com

Moms Club
www.momsclub.org

Mom's Time Out
www.momstimeout.org

Mothers of Preschoolers
www.mops.org

Salt Lake City Mommies
www.saltlakecitymommies.com

Multiples Groups

National Organization of Mothers of Twins Club
www.nomotc.org

Northwest Association Mothers of Twins Clubs
www.nwamotc.org

Salt Lake Mothers of Twins
www.slmot.com

Utah Valley Mothers of Multiples
www.uvmom.com

Parent Magazines

American Baby
www.parents.com/american-baby-magazine

Brain, Child
www.brainchildmag.com

Exceptional Parent
www.eparent.com

Fathering Magazine
www.fathermag.com

Mothering Magazine
www.mothering.com

Resources

Parent Magazines (cont'd)

Parenting
www.parenting.com

Parents
www.parents.com

Working Mother Magazine
www.workingmother.com

Utah Family Magazine
www.utahfamily.com

Parenting Education

The Center for Parenting Education
www.centerforparentingeducation.org

Uplift Utah Families
www.upliftutahfamilies.org

Utah Parent Center
www.utahparentcenter.org

Values Parenting
www.valuesparenting.com

Postpartum Depression Support

Postpartum Progress
www.postpartumprogress.com

Postpartum Support
www.postpartum.net

The Online PPMD Support Group
www.ppdsupportpage.com

Single Parents

Family Support Network of Utah
www.fsnutah.com/singles_resources.htm

Parents without Partners
www.parentswithoutpartners.org

Special Needs Resources and Support

Adaptive Recreation through Salt Lake County
www.recreation.slco.org/adaptive

Angel's Hands
www.angelshands.org

Camp Kostopulos
www.campk.org

Children and Adults with Attention-Deficit/Hyperactivity Disorder
www.chaddofutah.com

Courage Reins
www.couragereins.org

Foundations for Independence – Cerebral Palsy of Utah
www.ffiutah.org

HopeKids
www.hopekids.org

Intermountain Spina Bifida Support Group
www.utahspinabifida.org

Make-A-Wish Utah
www.utah.wish.org

Miracle League Adaptive Baseball
www.recreation.slco.org/genefullmer/youthsports/Miracleleague.html

National Ability Center
www.discovernac.org

National Association for Child Development
www.nacd.org

U-FIT (Physical activities for kids with special needs)
www.health.utah.edu/ess/ufit/index.html

Utah Association for the Deaf
www.uad.org

Utah Department of Health – Children with Special Health Care Needs
www.health.utah.gov/cshcn

Utah Down Syndrome Foundation
www.udsf.org

Utah FEAT – Autism Support
www.utahfeat.org

Utah Special Needs Assistance Program Fund
www.utahspecialneeds.org

Utah Special Needs Registry
www.specialneedsutah.org

Utah Parent Center
www.utahparentcenter.org

Utah Registry of Autism and Developmental Disorders
www.utahautismregistry.com

Wasatch Adaptive Sports
www.wasatchadaptivesports.org

National Federation of the Blind of Utah
www.nfbutah.org

Visitor Centers

The Salt Lake Tourist & Visitor Center
www.saltlakecityutah.org

Visit Salt Lake
www.visitsaltlake.com

Utah Travel Council
www.utah.com

Utah Travel Office
www.travel.utah.gov

Utah Valley
www.utahvalley.com

Working Mothers

Blue Suit Mom
www.bluesuitmom.com

Working Moms Agains Guilt
www.workingmomsagainst-guilt.com

Working Moms Refuge
www.momsrefuge.com

Working Mother Magazine
www.workingmother.com

Sites Listed by County

Weber County

Birdsong Trail - Site 53

Cold Springs Trout Farm - Site 35

Color Me Mine - Site 86

Fastkart Speedway - Site 94

FatCats - Site 95

Fort Buenaventura - Site 26

Great Harvest Bread Co. - Site 159

Harmons Cooking School - Site 88

Harrisville City Park - Site 107

The Home Depot Kids Workshops - Site 91

Lowes Build and Grow Clinics - Site 90

Nature Park (South Ogden Nature Park) - Site 112

Ogden Dinosaur Park and Museum - Site 13

Ogden Nature Center - Site 39

Ogden Raptors - Site 192

Ogden River Parkway - Site 61

Ogden Union Station - Site 14

Ott Planetarium - Site 15

Peery's Egyptian Theater - Site 166

Pineview Reservoir - Site 147

Powder Mountain - Site 186

Riverdale Park - Site 116

Roy City Aquatic Center - Site 148

Snowbasin Resort - Site 187

Toad's Fun Zone - Site 103

Treehouse Children's Museum - Site 18

UTA TRAX & FrontRunner - Site 183

Wolf Mountain Resort - Site 191

Davis County

Antelope Island - Site 33

Barnes & Noble Story Time - Site 153

Boondocks Food & Fun - Site 92

Castle Heights Playground at Nicholls Park - Site 45

Cherry Hill - Site 139

Clearfield Aquatic Center - Site 123

Coleman's Motor-VU Drive-In - Site 174

Get Air Sportsplex - Site 76

Great Harvest Bread Co. - Site 159

The Great Salt Lake Shorelands Preserve - Site 37

Harmons Cooking School - Site 88

Heritage Park - Site 108

Hill Aerospace Museum - Site 7

The Home Depot Kids Workshops - Site 91

Kangaroo Zoo - Site 82

Krispy Kreme - Site 162

Lagoon - Site 99

Layton Surf 'N Swim - Site 143

Legacy Electric Park - Site 46

Legacy Park - Site 110

Lowes Build and Grow Clinics - Site 90

Robert N. Hasenyager Great Salt Lake Nature Center - Site 41

S&S Shortline Train Park - Site 179

South Davis Recreation Center - Site 133

Three Little Monkeys - Site 157

UTA TRAX & FrontRunner - Site 183

Salt Lake County

Accessible Playground at Veteran's Memorial Park - Site 44

Airborne - Site 73

Alta Ski Area - Site 184

Barnes & Noble Story Time - Site 153

Ballet West - Site 69

Blackridge Reservoir - Site137

Brighton Ski Resort - Site 185

Cathedral of the Madeleine - Site 25

Cecret Lake Hike - Site 56

Centennial Pool - Site 138

City Creek Dinosaur Play Area - Site 74

Clark Planetarium - Site 4

Classic Fun Center - Site 93

Color Me Mine - Site 86

Cottonwood Heights Recreation Center - Site 140

Dimple Dell Recreation Center Pool - Site 124

Discovery Gateway: The Children's Museum of Utah - Site 5

Donut Falls - Site 57

Edutainment Play Center - Site 75
Engage Fountain at City Creek - Site 105
Ensign Peak Hike - Site 58
Fairmont Aquatic Center - Site 125
Fort Douglas Military Museum - Site 27
The Gale Center of History and Culture - Site 6
Gardner Village - Site 28
Gene Fullmer Recreation Center - Site 126
Dolly and Me Dress up Tea at Georgell Doll Shop - Site 176
Gilgal Sculpture Garden - Site 36
Great Harvest Bread Co. - Site 159
Hale Centre Theatre Backstage Tour - Site 160
Harmons Cooking School - Site 88
Hidden Falls - Site 59
Holladay Lions Fitness and Recreation Center - Site 127
Hollywood Connection - Site 96
The Home Depot Kids Workshops - Site 91
International Peace Gardens - Site 38
J.L. Sorenson Recreation Center - Site 128
Jump Around Utah - Site 79
Jump 'N Bounce - Site 80
Jungle Jim's Playland - Site 98
Kearns Oquirrh Park Fitness Center - Site 141
Kennecott-Magna Aquatics Complex - Site 142
Lakeshore Learning - Site 89
LDS Church History Museum- Site 9
LDS Conference Center Tour - Site 163
Later-day Saint Humanitarian Center - Site 164
Liberty Park - Site 47
Lisa Falls - Site 60
Lowes Build and Grow Clinics - Site 90
Memory Grove Park - Site 48
Mormon Tabernacle Choir - Site 71
Mountview Park - Site 111
Mrs. Cavanaugh's Chocolate Factory - Site 165
Murray Aquatics Center - Site 146
Natural History Museum of Utah - Site 12
Northwest Recreation Center - Site 130
Old Farm Splash Park - Site 114
Red Butte Garden - Site 40
Redwood Road Drive-In - Site 178
Rosecrest Park - Site 117
Salt Lake Bees - Site 195
Salt Lake City Public Library - Site 155
Real Salt Lake - Site 194
Seven Peaks - Site 150
Silver Lake Trail - Site 63
Snowbird Ski and Summer Resort - Site 188
Solitude Mountain Resort - Site 189
South Jordan Recreation Center - Site 134
Sweet Candy Factory - Site 167
Taffy Town - Site 168
Taylorsville Community Swimming Pool - Site 151
Temple Quarry Nature Trail - Site 65
Temple Square - Site 29
The Children's Theatre - Site 70
The Gateway - Site 106
The King's English Story Time - Site 156
The Leonardo - Site 17
The Park Center - Site 131
This is the Place Heritage Park - Site 30
Tiny Tim's Foundation for Kids - Site 182
Tracy Aviary - Site 23
Umbria Splash Park - Site 119
Urban Park Interactive Fountain
UTA TRAX & FrontRunner - Site 183
Utah Blaze - Site 196
Utah Grizzlies - Site 197
Utah Jazz - Site 198
Utah Museum of Contemporary Art - Site 19
Utah Museum of Fine Arts - Site 20
Utah Pioneer Museum - Site 21
Utah State Capitol - Site 31
Utah Symphony/Utah Opera Family Concerts - Site 72
Utah Truffles - Site 169
Utah's Hogle Zoo - Site 24
V Chocolates - Site 170
Valley Fair Mall - Site 120
Welfare Square - Site 171
(West Jordan) Conservation Garden Park - Site 43
West Valley Family Fitness Center - Site 135

Sites Listed by County

Western Springs Park - Site 121

Wheeler Historic Farm - Site 32

Wild West Jordan Playground at Veteran's Memorial Park - Site 51

Willow Pond Park - Site 122

Utah County

American Fork Fitness Center Leisure Pool - Site 136

Barnes & Noble Story Time - Site 153

Battle Creek Falls Hike - Site 52

Bridal Veil Falls - Site 54

BYU Broadcasting - Site 158

BYU Museum of Art - Site 1

BYU Museum of Paleontology - Site 2

BYU Museum of Peoples and Cultures - Site 3

Cabela's - Site 172

Cascade Springs Nature Trail - Site 55

Children's Discovery Garden at Thanksgiving Point - Site 34

Children's Library at the Provo City Library - Site 154

CLAS Ropes Course - Site 173

Color Me Mine - Site 86

Comedy Sportz - Site 175

Creativity Art Studio - Site 87

Creekside Park - Site 104

Farm Country at Thanksgiving Point - Site 22

FatCats - Site 95

Great Harvest Bread Co. - Site 159

Hang Time Extreme Trampolines - Site 77

Harmons Cooking School - Site 88

Highland Town Center Splash Pad - Site 109

Holdman Studios - Site 161

The Home Depot Kids Workshops - Site 91

Jack and Jill Lanes - Site 97

Jake's Archery - Site 78

John Hutchings Museum of Natural History - Site 8

Jump On It! - Site 81

Krispy Kreme - Site 162

Lehi Legacy Recreation Center - Site 129

Lindon Aquatic Center - Site 144

Lowes Build and Grow Clinics - Site 90

Lowes Xtreme Air Sports - Site 83

MAX Zipline Canopy Tour - Site 177

Manila Creek Pond - Site 145

Monte L. Bean Life Science Museum - Site 10

Museum of Ancient Life at Thanksgiving Point - Site 11

Neptune Park - Site 49

Nickel City Fun Center - Site 100

Nolan Park - Site 113

Novell Children's Discovery Park - Site 50

Orem Owlz - Site 193

Pioneer Park - Site 115

Provo Beach - Site 101

Provo Recreation Center - Site 132

Provo River Parkway - Site 62

Provo Towne Centre Play Area - Site 84

Royden G. Derek Planetarium

Scera Pool - Site 149

SCHEELS - Site 180

Seven Peaks - Site 150

Seven Peaks Fun Center - Site 102

Shops at Riverwoods - Site 118

Stewart Falls - Site 64

Sundance Mountain Resort - Site 190

Thanksgiving Point Gardens - Site 42

Thanksgiving Point Special Events - Site 181

Timpanogos Caves - Site 66

Timpanogos Falls - Site 67

Tree House Court - Site 85

UTA TRAX & FrontRunner - Site 183

Y Mountain Hike - Site 68

Alphabetical Index of Sites

A

Accessible Playground at Veteran's Memorial Park 82
Airborne 118
Alta Ski Area 256
American Fork Fitness Center Leisure Pool 196
Antelope Island 64

B

Ballet West 112
Barnes and Noble Story Time 216
Battle Creek Falls Hike 92
Birdsong Trail 93
Blackridge Reservoir 197
Boondocks 140
Bridal Veil Falls 94
Brighton Ski Resort 257
BYU Broadcasting 224
BYU Museum of Art 18
BYU Museum of Paleontology 19
BYU Museum of Peoples and Cultures 20

C

Cabela's 240
Canyons Resort 274
Cascade Springs Nature Trail 95
Castle Heights Playground at Nicholls Park 83
Cathedral of the Madeleine 52
Cecret Lake Hike 96
Centennial Pool 198
Cherry Hill 199
Children's Discovery Garden at Thanksgiving Point 66
Children's Library at the Provo City Library 217
The Children's Theatre 113
City Creek Dinosaur Play Area 119
Clark Planetarium 21
CLAS Ropes Course 242
Classic Fun Center 142
Clearfield Aquatic Center (also outdoor) 180
Cold Springs Trout Farm 67
Coleman's Motor-VU Drive-In 244
Color Me Mine 132
Comedy Sportz 245
Commemorative Air Force Utah Wing Museum 288
West Jordan Conservation Garden Park 80
Cottonwood Heights Rec Center (also indoor) 200
Cowboy Campfires (Friday night, Homestead Resort) 289
Creativity Art Studio 133
Creekside Park 160

D

Dairy Keen (Home of the Train) 290
Deer Creek Reservoir 291
Deer Valley Resort 275
Dimple Dell Recreation Center Pool 181
Discovery Gateway Children's Museum 22
Dolly and Me Dress-Up Tea at Georgell Doll Shop 246
Donut Falls 97

E

Edutainment Play Center 120
Engage Fountain at City Creek 161
Ensign Peak Hike 98

F

Fairmont Aquatic Center 182
Farm Country at Thanksgiving Point 46
Fastkart Speedway 144
The Fieldhouse Splash Pad 276
Fort Buenaventura 53
Fort Douglas Military Museum 54

G

The Gale Center of History and Culture 24
Gardner Village 55
The Gateway 162
Gene Fullmer Recreation Center 183
Get Air Sportsplex 121
Gilgal Sculpture Garden 68
Great Harvest Bread Co 225
The Great Salt Lake Shorelands Preserve 69

H

Hale Centre Theatre Backstage Tour 226
Hang Time Extreme Trampolines 122
Harmon's Cooking School 134
Harrisville City Park 163
Heber Valley Artisan Cheese (Kohler Creamery) 292
Heber Valley Railroad 293
Heritage Park 164
Hidden Falls 99
Highland Town Center Splash Pad 165
Hill Aerospace Museum 25

Alphabetical Index of Sites

Holdman Studios 227
Holladay Lions Fitness and Recreation Center 184
Hollywood Connection 147

I

International Peace Gardens 70

J

Jack and Jill Lanes 148
Jake's Archery 123
J.L. Sorenson Recreation Center 185
John Hutchings Museum of Natural History 26
Jump Around Utah 124
Jump 'N Bounce 125
Jump On It! 126
Jungle Jim's Playland 149

K

Kangaroo Zoo 127
Kearns Oquirrh Park Fitness Center (also indoor) 201
Kennecott-Magna Aquatics Complex 202
The King's English Story Time 220
Krispy Kreme 228

L

Lagoon 150
Lakeshore Learning 136
Later-day Saint Humanitarian Center 230
Layton Surf 'N Swim (also indoor) 203
LDS Church History Museum 27
LDS Conference Center Tour 229
Legacy Electric Park 84
Legacy Park 166
Lehi Legacy Recreation Center (also outdoor) 186
The Leonardo 39
Liberty Park 85
Lindon Aquatic Center 204
Lisa Falls 100
Local Pet Stores 50
The Loveland Living Planet Aquarium 50
Lowes Build and Grow Clinics 137
Lowes Xtreme Air Sports 128

M

Manila Creek Pond 205
MAX Zipline Canopy Tour 247
Memory Grove Park 86
Monkey Mountain 277
Monte L. Bean Life Science Museum 28
Mormon Tabernacle Choir 114
Mountview Park 167
Mrs. Cavanaugh's Chocolate Factory 231
Murray Aquatics Center 206
Museum of Ancient Life at Thanksgiving Point 30

N

Natural History Museum of Utah 32
Nature Park 168
Neptune Park 88
Nickel City Fun Center 152
Nolan Park 169
Northwest Recreation Center 188
Novell Children's Discovery Park 89

O

Ogden Dinosaur Park and Museum 34
Ogden Nature Center 72
Ogden Raptors 266
Ogden River Parkway 101
Old Farm Splash Park 170
Olympic Park 282
Orem Owlz 267
Ott Planetarium 37

P

The Park Center 189
Park City Mountain Resort 278
Park City Museum 279
Peery's Egyptian Theater 232
Pineview Reservoir 207
Pioneer Park 171
Powder Mountain 258
Provo Beach 154
Provo Recreation Center (also outdoor) 190
Provo River Parkway 102
Provo Town Center Play Area 129
Public Libraries 214

R

Real Salt Lake 268
Red Butte Garden 74
Redwood Road Drive-In 248
Riverdale Park 172
Robert N. Hasenyager Great Salt Lake Nature Center 76
Rosecrest Park 173

Roy City Aquatic Center 208
Royden G. Derrek Planetarium 38

S

Salt Lake Bees 269
Salt Lake City Library 218
Scera Pool 209
Scheels 250
Seven Peaks 210
Seven Peaks Fun Center 156
Shops at Riverwoods 174
Silver Lake Trail 104
Snowbasin Resort 259
Snowbird Ski and Summer Resort 260
Soldier Hollow Cross-Country Ski Resort 294
Solitude Mountain Resort 262
South Davis Recreation Center (also outdoor) 192
South Jordan Recreation Center 193
S&S Shortline Train Park 249
Stewart Falls 105
Sundance Mountain Resort 263
Swaner Preserve and EcoCenter 280
Sweet Candy Factory 234

T

Taffy Town 235
Taylorsville Community Swimming Pool 212
Temple Quarry Nature Trail 106
Temple Square 56
Thanksgiving Point Gardens 78
Thanksgiving Point Special Events 252
The Home Depot Kids Workshops 138
This is the Place Heritage Park 58
Three Little Monkeys 221
Timpanogos Caves 107
Timpanogos Falls 108
Tiny Tim's Foundation 253
Tracy Aviary 47
Trailside Park 281
Treehouse Children's Museum 40
Tree House Court 130

U

Umbria Splash Park 175
Union Station 36
Utah Blaze 270
Utah Grizzlies 271
Utah Jazz 272
Utah Museum of Contemporary Art 42
Utah Museum of Fine Arts 43
Utah Olympic Park Museums 284
Utah Pioneer Museum 44
Utah's Hogle Zoo 48
Utah State Capitol 60
Utah Symphony Family & Lollipops Concerts 116
Utah Truffles 236
UTA TRAX & FrontRunner 254

V

Valley Fair Mall 176
V Chocolates 237

W

Welfare Square 238
Western Springs Park 177
West Valley Family Fitness Center 194
Wheeler Historic Farm 62
Wild West Jordan Playground at Veteran's
Memorial Park 90
Willow Creek Park 286
Willow Pond Park 178
Wolf Mountain Resort 264

Y

Y Mountain Hike 110

About the Authors

Emily Smith Robbins loves being a stay-at-home mom to her four children. She enjoys gardening, reading, and doing projects around the house with her husband, Andy. She says that writing this book and balancing family life has been the most challenging thing she has ever done but, as she always tells her children, "Doing hard things feels good. Easy is nothing special."

Submit any recommendations or corrections directly to the authors at www.playdateslc.com.

Meilani Smith Kongaika is a stay-at-home mom and this is her first published book! She has four children, including a daughter with spina bifida. She loved the opportunity this project gave her to prove to herself and others that there is so much you can do, despite being in a wheelchair. Meilani loves singing (especially with her husband and her dad), reading, serving in her church, and taking care of her family. She is an active volunteer in the Intermountain Spina Bifida Support Group and takes great joy in working together with her husband in serving their special needs community. While working on this book, she gained a newfound love for the mountains of Utah!

Playdate Publishing
An imprint of Sharp End Publishing

www.PlaydatePublishing.com